WOMEN, PHILOSOPHY, AND SPORT:

A Collection of New Essays

edited by
BETSY C. POSTOW

The Scarecrow Press, Inc.
Metuchen, N.J., & London
1983

The author gratefully acknowledges permission to use the following:

Excerpt on pages 85-87 from Equality in Sport for Women edited by Patricia Gaedelmann, et al. (Washington, D.C.: AAHPER, 1977). Reprinted by permission of the American Alliance for Health, Physical Education, Recreation and Dance, 1900 Association Drive, Reston, VA 22091.

Some material in Chapter 7 from Raymond A. Belliotti's "Women, Sex, and Sports," in Journal of the Philosophy of Sport, VI (Fall 1979), 67-72. Used by permission of the Philosophic Society for the Study of Sport and the Journal of the Philosophy of Sport.

Some material in Chapter 10 from Drew A. Hyland's "Competition and Friendship," in Journal of the Philosophy of Sport, V (Fall 1978), 27-37. Used by permission of the Philosophic Society for the Study of Sport and the Journal of the Philosophy of Sport.

Excerpt on pages 256-257 from Memoirs of an Ex-Prom Queen by Alix Kates Shulman. Copyright © 1969, 1971, 1972 by Alix Kates Shulman. Reprinted by permission of Alfred A. Knopf, Inc. and Granada Publishing, Limited.

Library of Congress Cataloging in Publication Data
Main entry under title:

Women, philosophy, and sport.

Includes index.
1. Sports for women--United States--Addresses, essays, lectures. 2. School sports--United States--Addresses, essays, lectures. 3. Sex discrimination in sports--United States--Addresses, essays, lectures.
I. Postow, Betsy C., 1945-   .
GV709.W575 1983   796'.01'94   83-10146
ISBN 0-8108-1638-5

This book is dedicated to

MARY VETTERLING-BRAGGIN

CONTENTS

ACKNOWLEDGMENTS

My greatest debt is to Mary Vetterling-Braggin for the original idea of this book, and for her very generous encouragement and able advice throughout its germination and growth.

I am indebted to Madge Phillips, William Morgan, and Ralph Jones for their gracious and unfailing willingness to answer my requests for help and advice in areas relevant to the philosophy of sport and physical education.

Much appreciation goes to Dianne Meagher for her helpful comments from a pedagogical perspective on the editor's introductions and questions.

I would also like to thank Dolores Scates and Barbara Moser, the capable secretaries of the Department of Philosophy at The University of Tennessee, for typing large portions of the manuscript.

Of course, by helping me, these kind people did not incur any responsibility for the faults of this book.

GENERAL INTRODUCTION

This book will lead the reader through an exploration of some of the important issues that lie at the intersection of a thoughtful interest in sports and the concerns of feminists. Although most of the authors do endorse some feminist position or other, there is no attempt to impose a "party line." The authors evaluate the merit of various positions in an open-minded manner, and the reader is encouraged to do likewise.

The first issue that is taken up is fairness to women in sports. A strong presumptive case that unfairness currently exists is established by such factors as school budgets that lopsidedly favor men's sport programs over women's and programs that provide no opportunity for women to try out for certain sports. However, it is surprisingly difficult to give a reasoned account of what is fair to women athletes in sports and what is unfair. Physiological differences between the sexes allow men as a group to achieve higher levels of athletic performance than women in many sports. This fact makes it impossible simply to transfer our beliefs about fairness to women in an intellectual area, such as admission to professional schools, to the physical area of sports. The essays in Section A of Part I of this volume examine the question of fairness to female athletes in school sports, taking into consideration the special features of sports that make this issue especially problematic. The other essays in Part I deal with two other aspects of equity for women in sports: fairness to women in athletic employment and fair media coverage of women's athletics. The first of these essays surveys the philosophical literature on preferential hiring for women and applies it to the case of employment in athletics. The second applies the notions of desert and entitlement to media coverage of athletic activities.

The second broad topic of the book is competition. The authors in Part II consider the questions of what kinds of competition are possible, what kinds are desirable, and why. Since competition is at the heart of sports, these questions are at the heart of the philosophy of sport. They are also of special interest to feminists. At one time it was believed that a competitive model of sport was appropriate for men but not for women; the accepted model for women's sports was typified by field days, which emphasized participation, comradeship, and cooperation rather than competition. This "feminine" model has been criticized as a means of keeping women out of serious sport, and it has been largely abandoned. Recently, however, some feminists have argued that women should reject the competitive, traditionally masculine model of sport and return to something like the old feminine model. The essays in Part II provide a basis for an intelligent decision.

The essays in Part III distill (from general theories of education and feminist insights) conclusions about the ways in which physical education can promote or hinder women's interests. These considerations lead to recommendations for the improvement of physical education programs.

So far we have seen why the words "women" and "sport" appear in the title of this book, but it may not be very clear why the word "philosophy" is included. It appears there because the heart of philosophy is the activity of philosophical thinking, and the authors in their essays are engaged in philosophical thinking. One example of this is to distinguish the different senses of a key word, such as "competition," whose different senses had previously been recognized dimly or not at all. To uncover, formulate, and clarify a nonempirical question which had not previously been recognized as a question with alternative possible answers is to think philosophically. An example question of this type is "What constitutes fair treatment of women athletes in a school sports program?" Other demonstrations of philosophical thinking are the consideration of the various possible alternative answers to a nonempirical question, and the formulation and evaluation of the reasons for and against the various answers. It is also philosophical thinking to offer a reasoned defense of a goal (such as a model of sport or of physical education) as morally desirable. All these examples of philosophical thinking are embodied in one or more of the essays in this volume. The authors draw on the relevant philosophical literature in a way accessible to the lay reader, and they also make their own contributions to the advancement of thought on their topics.

It is clear, then, that this book is an introduction to

philosophical thinking via some selected issues of contemporary interest. But the introduction aimed at is not a mere familiarity with philosophical thinking, or a merely passive appreciation of it. The main aim of the book is to stimulate and guide the reader through an independent philosophical exploration of the issues. The questions for reflection and discussion included at the end of every essay are meant to help the reader to think critically about the positions endorsed by the authors and to explore the issues independently in a methodical way. Independent thinking is also encouraged by the inclusion of conflicting opinions, which of course guarantees that at least some of the opinions included must be at least somewhat mistaken. The authors often provide suggestions for further reading to supplement the references in their notes.

The philosophical term "argument" is one which the reader should become familiar with before launching seriously into the rest of the book. A background on arguments is provided in the next section of this Introduction. It should be read now and also referred to again as often as necessary when the readings deal with arguments. Incomplete understanding of this section now is certainly no cause for despair, for it is often much easier to grasp new concepts when they can be applied directly to material in which one is actively involved. The short third section, "Formulating Our Own Arguments," should also be read now even if the second section is not completely understood.

Background on Arguments

An ARGUMENT is a group of two or more assertions that express a piece of reasoning. These assertions need not be expressed in complete English sentences. Here is an example of an argument which contains two assertions in one sentence:

> It must have rained last night because the ground was very wet this morning.

In this argument the assertion that the ground was very wet this morning is offered as evidence supporting the assertion that it rained last night. In every argument one or more of the assertions are offered as evidence for another of the assertions. The assertions that are offered as evidence are called PREMISES, and the one that is supposed to be supported by this evidence is called the CONCLUSION. In the example above, the premise is the assertion that the ground was very wet this morning, and the conclusion is the assertion that it rained last night.

In evaluating an argument, we ask two questions: 1) Is it reasonable to accept all the premises? 2) Assuming that all the premises are acceptable, how strong is the evidence which they provide for the conclusion? If the answers to both these questions are satisfactory, then the argument succeeds in establishing that it is reasonable to accept the conclusion. If the answer to either one of the questions is unsatisfactory, then the argument fails to establish that it is reasonable to accept the conclusion. This does not mean, however, that it is reasonable to reject the conclusion, for there may be other reasons to accept it. In order to establish that it is reasonable to reject a given conclusion, we need a successful argument whose conclusion is the negation of the original conclusion. So, for example, if a particular argument fails to establish that it is reasonable to believe that God exists, this does not by itself establish that it is reasonable to believe that God does not exist. To establish that, we would need a successful argument with the conclusion that God does not exist.

The first question asked in evaluating an argument (viz., "Is it reasonable to accept all the premises?") must be answered with a "yes" for the argument to be satisfactory. If it is reasonable to accept all the premises, then the argument passes the first test, and if it is unreasonable to accept one or more of the premises, then the argument fails the first test. Of course it may be controversial whether it is reasonable to accept a given premise, and further arguments may be needed to establish that it is or is not reasonable.

The second question asked in evaluating an argument (viz., "Assuming that all the premises are acceptable, how strong is the evidence which they provide for the conclusion?") has many possible answers, for there are various degrees of strength of evidence which the premises of an argument may provide for the conclusion. So for the second test which we use in evaluating arguments, there is no clearcut line of demarcation between satisfactory answers and unsatisfactory answers. The amount of confidence that is reasonable to have in the conclusion of an argument on the basis of its premises (assuming that the premises are themselves acceptable) is proportional to the degree of strength of the evidence which the premises provide for the conclusion.

At one extreme are arguments in which the premises have no strength at all as evidence for the conclusion. An example of such an argument is this:

> I will win the Irish Sweepstakes because I want to win very, very much.

The premise that I want to win very, very much provides no reason to believe the conclusion that I will win.

At the other extreme are arguments in which the premises provide watertight evidence for the conclusion. When this is the case, we say that the argument is DEDUCTIVELY VALID. Here is an example of a deductively valid argument:

> If philosophy class meets today, then today is either Tuesday or Thursday. Philosophy class does meet today. Therefore, today is either Tuesday or Thursday.

Even a miracle could not bring it about that the conclusion of a deductively valid argument is false <u>if the premises remain</u> true. In the argument above, as long as it remains true that philosophy class meets today and that the if-then connection asserted by the first premise holds, the conclusion <u>must</u> be true.

Often the premises of an argument will not provide determinative evidence for the conclusion, but they will provide considerable evidence which makes it probable that the conclusion is true. In this case we say that the argument is INDUCTIVELY STRONG. There are degrees of inductive strength. Here are two inductively strong arguments, the first of which has a much higher degree of inductive strength than the second. The strength of the first argument is so great that it may appear to be deductively valid, but it is not, for a miracle could bring it about that its conclusion was false while its premise remained true.

> Every time anything has fallen to earth in the past, it has fallen with an acceleration of 32 ft. /sec^2. Therefore, the next object which falls to earth will fall with an acceleration of 32 ft. /sec^2.

> The University of Tennessee has roughly equal numbers of men and women students. Therefore, most classes at the University of Tennessee have some men and some women students.

The opening argument, about the ground being wet, is also inductively strong. Unfortunately, we have no way to measure precisely the degree of inductive strength of an argument, but we can make rough comparisons of inductive strength readily enough so that some real guidance is offered by the rule that our degree of confidence in a conclusion should be proportional to the strength of evidence for it.

If we think an argument fails one of the two tests used for evaluating arguments, we should frame an objection to the argument. An OBJECTION to an argument is itself an argument, and it tries to show that the original argument fails one of the two evaluative tests. An objection, then, tries to show either that a premise of the original argument is unacceptable, or that the premises, even if they are all true, do not provide enough support for the conclusion. Here is an argument followed by two objections to it--one objection of each type.

> All members of Sigma Sorority wear blue slacks and Sue is wearing blue slacks. Therefore, Sue is a member of Sigma Sorority.
>
> Objection #1:
> Anne, Beth, and Cindy are all members of Sigma, and they always wear white slacks. Therefore it is not true that all members of Sigma wear blue slacks.
>
> Objection #2:
> Most students on campus are wearing blue slacks these days, not just members of Sigma Sorority. Therefore even if it is true both that all members of Sigma wear blue slacks and that Sue wears blue slacks, this is not significant evidence that Sue is a member of Sigma.

Objections to arguments may themselves be objected to, for the objections may have false premises or be inductively weak. The replies to the objections may in turn be objected to, and so on. This process does not always go on very long, however, for everyone may agree that the original argument is not vulnerable to any objections, or that an objection cannot be replied to.

Formulating clear arguments and objections in discussion may be the most important tool available to us for determining which positions on issues of interest to us are supported

by the best reasons. If we are unclear about our arguments
and objections and their relations to each other, then our discussions are in danger of degenerating into bull sessions.

For additional reading about arguments and how to
evaluate them, see Brian Skyrms, Choice and Chance: An
Introduction to Inductive Logic, 2nd ed. (Encino, CA: Dickenson Publishing Co., 1975). See also Irving M. Copi,
Introduction to Logic (New York: Macmillan Publishing Company, 1982 or any other edition.)

Formulating Arguments on Our Own

Sometimes it will not be quite clear just which argument an author means to be presenting. What should we do
in this case? This depends on our aim. If our primary aim
is exegesis or if we are concerned about determining which
author deserved some honor, then we have to devote most of
our energies to textual analysis in order to determine exactly
how the author should be understood. But we are independent
investigators in our own right. Our main concern should not
be to determine the exact intentions of an author where there
are alternative plausible interpretations of the author's words.
Nor should we confine ourselves to examining only those arguments that we can plausibly interpret the author as endorsing.
On the contrary, we should always aim to formulate the most
plausible arguments we can for each position that we consider
--from whatever source these arguments come. Our goal is
to determine which position is supported by the best arguments, not which author has come down on the winning side.
If the most plausible arguments we can find are definitely
presented by a given author, we should, of course, credit
that author definitely. If the most plausible arguments seem
to be endorsed by a given author but this is a matter of interpretation, then we should acknowledge this. And if the
most plausible arguments are obtained by revising or rejecting
what an author has said, then we should make this clear, too.
The authors are our fellow inquirers, and we are all trying
to arrive at the clearest possible understanding of the issues
and the most reasonable positions on them.

PART I:

WHAT CONSTITUTES FAIRNESS
TO WOMEN IN SPORTS?

About Section A

The general topic of this section is "What constitutes fairness to female students in school sports programs?"[1] The reader may wonder why this section is written by philosophers and not by lawyers, for it may appear that questions about fairness to females in school sports can be answered only by a careful study of the applicable laws. But this is not so. Even if the law clearly prescribed the legal rights of female and male students and the legal duties of school officials with respect to sports programs, this would not necessarily tell us what was fair, for legislators sometimes make unfair laws. We can recognize any unfair laws that bear on school sports programs only if we have an independent account of what constitutes fairness in school sports programs. The authors in this section offer us their suggestions for formulating such an account of fairness. Since they do not appeal to the law or to any other authority to back up their positions, we must judge what they say on its own merits. If we are to judge these merits soundly, we must undertake our own exploration of the issues and our own careful evaluation of the cases that can be made in support of the various views. The questions which follow each article are meant to lead the individual reader into this investigation and also to provide structure for discussions among readers so that the investigation can be a cooperative venture.

The Anti-Equal Opportunity Position

Some people accept the traditional doctrine that the two sexes should have separate spheres of activity and separate roles. These people often hold that there is nothing unfair about failing to provide equal opportunity for female students to participate in sports, for sports are a traditionally

3

masculine activity. On this view, it is morally permissible (or even downright desirable), for school sports programs to have rules prohibiting or limiting participation by females. With this view, it is also permissible to have sex-segregated teams with far greater resources allotted to the male teams than to the female teams. Although the authors in this section all reject the view that unequal opportunity for females is morally permissible in school sports, Mary Anne Warren, the first author in the section, does examine and criticize the major arguments that have been made in support of this view. These include, among others, an argument based on the premise that sports participation builds manly character, an argument based on the premise that males need sports to learn how to master their own bodies, and an argument based on the premise that sports are hazardous to females. [2]

Warren's Position

Mary Anne Warren's account of why it is unfair to deprive females of equal opportunity to participate in school sports programs can, in skeleton, be construed as follows: 1) Participation in athletic programs is one of the basic benefits which schools are designed to provide to students. 2) The methods by which schools are funded--student fees and tax support--create a presumption that both males and females should have an equal opportunity to receive the basic benefits which the school is designed to provide. 3) No factor that has been mentioned by opponents of equal opportunity succeeds in rebutting this presumption. 4) Therefore, it is unjust to deprive females (and, by a similar argument, unjust to deprive the athletically disadvantaged or any other group) of equal opportunity to participate in school sports.

As she elaborates in her "Reply to Moulton and Lemos," Warren also holds that an opportunity to compete for a place on a team is not equivalent to an opportunity actually to participate in school sports. Thus, a school sports program could be said to provide equal opportunity for all students, according to Warren, only if all students can actually participate on teams. These teams must themselves be treated fairly, with no teams systematically receiving inferior training, equipment, schedules, etc. Many sports programs, of course, fall short of this ideal; they provide places on teams only for selected students. Warren therefore discusses various strategies of sex-integration and sex-segregation of teams to minimize inequality of opportunity between male and female students in such programs. [3]

Moulton's Position

Janice Moulton agrees with Warren's basic position, but she does not think that Warren offers a satisfactory explanation of why public funds should be committed to insure that every student can participate in school sports. Moulton supplements Warren's analysis by offering her own explanation of this. Here, in skeleton, is Moulton's explanation: 1) Sports are an important aspect of civilization on which our culture spends immense time and energy. 2) People who do not participate in school sports "are unlikely to develop the interest or knowledge" that would enable them to participate in this important aspect of our civilization. 3) Therefore, if school sports participation is not available to a person, that person is excluded from an important part of our civilization. 4) It is unjust to exclude a member of any society from an important aspect of that society's civilization. 5) Therefore, justice requires that school sports participation be made available to every student in our society.

Before presenting this argument of her own, Moulton considers various other arguments, including one by Warren, which favor extending sports opportunities to more students. Although she thinks that some of these arguments have merit, she points out that not one of them establishes that school sports programs should be available to everyone. It is to establish this sweeping conclusion that she offers her argument which presents sport as an important aspect of civilization.

Lemos's Position

Ramon M. Lemos regards the principle that everyone has an absolute moral right to equality of treatment as an adequate basis for the position that every student has a right to an equal opportunity to participate in school sports. But he means something different from what Warren and Moulton mean by the expression "equal opportunity to participate." According to Lemos, all students who are allowed to compete for a place on a team and are not wrongly discouraged from doing so have an equal opportunity to participate. Thus, he says that females have an equal opportunity with males to participate on a varsity team if competition for a place on the team is open equally to females and males. If no females make the team, they still had an equal opportunity to participate on it. (Warren, in contrast, holds that opportunity to compete for a chance to participate is not equivalent to oppor-

tunity to participate.) Much of Lemos's paper is devoted to
noting and clarifying what he takes to be confusions in Warren's paper.

Postow's Afterword

Betsy Postow reviews several rival answers to the
question "What makes a school sports program fair or unfair
to potential participants?" She lists considerations that should
be taken into account in evaluating the rival answers. Finally,
she suggests a procedure for deciding for oneself what an
equal-opportunity sports program would look like.

About Section B

In this section Ruth B. Heizer presents a conceptual map
which allows us to explore the issue of fairness to women
in employment generally, and in athletics-related employment
in particular. She classifies and summarizes the arguments
that various philosophers have given in support of or in opposition to preferential treatment of women in hiring. She also
points out what she sees as weaknesses in the arguments that
support preferential treatment, and she finally rejects preferential treatment as unjust. Affirmative action, as opposed to
preferential treatment, can provide fair treatment of women
in employment according to Heizer. She closes by citing
specific affirmative action measures that can promote fair
treatment of women in athletics-related employment.

About Section C

This third segment of Part I concerns fairness to women
athletes in the allocation of media coverage of sports. Unlike the previous section's topic, the topic of this section is
not the subject of a developed philosophical literature. Raymond A. Belliotti does pioneering work in exploring the issue
of fairness to athletes in media sports coverage.

Belliotti argues that media coverage of competitive,
non-professional athletic activities, such as high school sports,
should be proportional to the effort and participation of the
players, and that media coverage of professional and quasi-
professional activities should be proportional to the proficiency
of the players. (He sometimes speaks as if effort-proportionate
media coverage will always result in equal coverage of male

and female athletes. As he points out in note # 11, however, effort-proportionate coverage can be expected to result in equal coverage of the sexes only when there are equal numbers of male and female participants in a given sport.)

On one reading, Belliotti offers the following three arguments in support of the conclusion that media coverage of competitive, non-professional sports should be proportional to the effort of the players.

A. 1. The primary rewards for participation in competitive (non-professional) athletic activities are rewards that can and should be enjoyed by all--e. g., stimulation and improved health--not scarce rewards such as fame and money.

   2. Therefore, it is appropriate that in <u>promoting</u> competitive athletic activities, our principal concern should be to cultivate effort and participation, not to cultivate a competition for fame and money.

   3. When we promote competitive athletic activities via media coverage, we can cultivate effort and participation better if we proportion the coverage to the athletes' effort than if we proportion the coverage to the athletes' proficiency.

   4. Therefore, media coverage of non-professional competitive athletic activities should be proportional to the effort of the players rather than to their proficiency.

B. 1. The basic rewards of participation in competitive sports should be available to all without reference to sex.

   2. Effort-proportionate media coverage of competitive sports is more likely than is proficiency-proportionate media coverage to promote everyone's participation in these sports without reference to sex.

   3. Therefore, media coverage of competitive sports should be proportional to effort rather than to proficiency.

C. 1. Any departure from equal allocation of anything that is desired (including media coverage of sports) must be justified by reference to some relevant differences between those treated unequally--such as differences in desert or differences in entitlement.

   2. Entitlement is a contractual or quasi-contractual notion.

3. Therefore, just distribution of media coverage of competitive athletic activities should be based on differences in entitlement only if there is a contractual or quasi-contractual basis for awarding media coverage of these activities.
4. To accept the notion of a contract or quasi-contract for media coverage in competitive athletic activities would be to detract from the primary goals of these activities, such as stimulation and improved health.
5. We should not detract from the primary goals of competitive activities.
6. Therefore, we should not use the notion of entitlement to determine what distribution of media coverage of competitive athletic activities is just to the athletes.
7. Differences in desert are based on differences in prior actions, including the amount of effort expended.
8. It is harmonious with the primary goals of competitive athletic activities that we accept desert based on effort as the principle which determines a just distribution of media coverage of competitive athletic activities.
9. Therefore, given (1), (6), and (8) above, we should accept desert based on effort as the principle that determines what distribution of media coverage of competitive athletic activities is just to the athletes.
10. The goals that people other than the participating athletes hope to achieve through media coverage of competitive activities (e.g., fostering community spirit) can all be achieved by using effort rather than proficiency as a criterion for allocating media coverage.
11. Therefore, all things considered, the most appropriate criterion by which justly to allocate media coverage of competitive athletic activities is the criterion of desert based on effort.

NOTES

1. Following Janice Moulton, we shall use the term "sports program" or "athletic program" to refer to a program with team and league or tournament organization which also includes coaching, refereeing, and record-keeping for games. The program may be intramural and/or intermural. Physical education classes alone do not

normally constitute a sports program, and a student who does not play on a team will not be said to participate in a sports program, on this usage.

2. The separate spheres position is discussed in a broader context by Kathryn Pyne Addelson in her essay, "Equality and Competition: Can Sports Make a Woman of a Girl?," which appears in Part II of this volume. The position that there are separate manly virtues and womanly virtues is discussed by Margaret Atherton in her essay, "Education for Equality," which appears in Part III of this volume.

3. Arguments for and against sex-integrated physical education are reviewed by Ann Diller and Barbara Houston in their essay, "Women's Physical Education: A Gender-Sensitive Perspective," which appears in Part III of this volume.

Fairness to Female Students in
School Sports Programs

1. JUSTICE AND GENDER IN SCHOOL SPORTS

Mary Anne Warren

In 1973, Sports Illustrated aptly described the situation facing females interested in athletic competition:

> There may be worse (more socially serious) forms of prejudice in the United States, but there is no sharper example of discrimination today than that which operates against girls and women who take part in competitive sports. [1]

At the time this statement was made, it was not unusual for co-educational high schools and colleges to spend less than one percent of their athletic budgets on sports for women. [2] Interscholastic and even intramural competition in most sports was generally reserved for males only. Where teams for females existed they were typically underfunded, less well coached and equipped, denied equal access to facilities, and largely ignored by school and public media. The vast majority of athletic scholarships were available only to males. Women who retained an interest in competitive team sports (e. g., basketball, football, or baseball) were often subjected to invidious doubts about their "femininity" or sexual orientation. True, there were other athletic activities that were not considered inappropriate for females--particularly those (such as diving, figure skating, or gymnastics) that emphasized aesthetic display and/or precise skill in movement, rather than direct struggle between competitors. But these sports were less often offered, and virtually never given anything like the support lavished on the sports from which females were excluded.

Today, after a decade of legal activism, the situation is somewhat improved; yet equal opportunity for women in

school sports has yet to be achieved. Since 1975, the HEW
regulations implementing Title IX of the 1972 Educational
Amendments have required all schools receiving federal aid
to provide, or move towards providing, [3] "equal opportunity
for both sexes to participate in interscholastic, intercollegiate,
intramural, and club athletic programs."[4] Schools may provide separate teams for females and males, but may not discriminate on the basis of sex in the provision of supplies and
equipment, access to facilities, coaching and academic tutoring opportunities, medical services, housing and dining, travel
allowances, publicity, or the like. [5] Where only one team
exists, which has previously been limited to males, females
must be permitted to compete for positions on the team--
except in the case of the so-called "contact" sports, such as
wrestling, football, basketball, and baseball.

As modest as these legal requirements are, they have
proved extremely difficult to enforce. Many male coaches
and athletic directors continue to resist reforms, apparently
because they think that women's athletic programs do not deserve parity with programs for men. And now further efforts
to enforce the equal opportunity provisions of Title IX are
threatened by the present administration's campaign to eliminate "unnecessary" federal regulations, as well as by recent
court rulings that the Title IX regulations do not apply to
school sports programs which receive no direct federal aid. [6]

In the present climate of fiscal and political conserva-
tism, while budgets for education and social programs are
being slashed and individual rights are increasingly threatened
on many fronts, there is danger that the issue of sex equality
in school sports may be overshadowed by seemingly more
vital issues. So it is especially important now that we consider such basic moral questions as Why should all students,
female and male, have an equal opportunity to participate in
school sports programs? and What exactly does such equality
of opportunity require? Is it possible in the context of a
(wholly or partially) sex segregated program? Does it, for
that matter, require sex segregation in some cases? If so,
when is segregation necessary? Should exceptions be made
for exceptional female (or male) athletes?

Part I of this paper presents the moral case for equal
athletic opportunity and answers the most common arguments
for considering it to be morally optional or even undesirable.
Part II addresses the more difficult issue of sex segregation.
I shall argue that sex integration is an important goal, but

that in many sports, particularly those in which males tend
to have a significant but not overwhelming physiological advantage over females, justice is served by neither strict sex
segregation nor a policy of strict sex-blindness, i.e., open
competition for team membership, regardless of sex. For
such sports, we need to explore various compromise strategies, which permit at least some degree of sex integration
without reducing females' opportunities to participate. More
importantly in the long run, however, we need 1) to provide
equal support for sports that do not inherently favor male
physiological traits; and 2) to expand and/or democratize
sports programs to enable all interested students to take part.

I.   The Case for Equal Opportunity

Justice requires that all students have an equal opportunity to
participate in the school's sports program. We will presently
consider the reasons why this is so; but first we must ask
just what it means. Equality of opportunity is a difficult notion to define, since it is compatible with some inequalities
of outcome--provided that those inequalities are not the result
of injustice. Thus, for example, if male and female students
have the same apparent opportunity to participate in a certain
sport, but males choose to do so more often than females,
equality of opportunity is not necessarily violated. It is violated, however, if the rules, regulations, or prevailing practices or attitudes are such that no, or fewer, females are
permitted to take part; or if females are in some way wrongly
discouraged from taking part, or wanting to. It is also violated if equal numbers of females participate, but they receive inferior training, equipment, game or practice schedules,
etc. Furthermore, it can be violated simply because of the
kinds of sports offered, e.g., if all or most are of a sort
generally more appealing to males, or more suited to male
physiques--e.g. boxing, wrestling, or football.

    Without attempting to present any general analysis of
what equality of opportunity entails, I would suggest that in
this context it requires that school athletic programs be designed to provide as equally and as well as possible for the
athletic needs and interests of each and every student. This
does not mean treating all students identically, or ignoring
their individual characteristics. Students' size, level of skill,
or physical or medical condition may sometimes be used to
place them in different teams or competition classes, or even
(in rare cases) to exclude them from certain sports entirely.

But there should be a sufficient variety of sports offered that
virtually any student who wants to take part in a sport can
find one suited to her interests and abilities. In the absence
of extreme medical or physical danger, everyone should be
permitted to take part in the sport of his or her choice.
And, finally, there must be a fair distribution of resources
among the different sports offered, and the different teams
and individuals within a given sport.

We have not yet considered the argument for providing
equal sports opportunities to all students. Before we do, we
should note that the case for equal sports opportunities for
females is also applicable to other athletically discriminated
against groups, such as the physically handicapped, or males
who are relatively small, overweight, or the like. Although
we are primarily concerned here with sex equality in school
sports, it should be remembered that it is not only females
who have often had less than an equal chance to take part.

There is a very simple reason why all students should
have an equal opportunity to participate in athletic programs;
namely, that this is one of the basic benefits which schools
are designed to provide for students. Although physical education is probably somewhat less important for most students
than academic education, this is no argument for unequal access. Some academic courses are probably less important
than others, but that does not justify providing such courses
(for example, auto mechanics or home economics) only or
primarily for members of one sex. If female students pay
the same fees as males, and/or if the school is aided by tax
money collected from women and men alike, then it is unjust
to deprive female students of any significant class of benefits
that male students enjoy. Even if sports participation is construed as a privilege rather than a right, all students should
have the same opportunity to earn that privilege. But I do
not think that sports participation should be treated as a
privilege, as something which only some students deserve.
Sports participation is too important a part of a person's
education to be treated as a bonus which can be granted to
some students and withheld from others who could also have
benefited from it.

Those who reject this simple argument for equality
generally maintain that females do not benefit from sports
participation as much, or in the same way, as males do.
It is appropriate to provide certain opportunities primarily
for those who will benefit most from them, e.g., remedial

reading classes only for those who read poorly. But there is absolutely no evidence that males derive greater benefits from sports than do females, when both participate. The presumption that males do gain more from athletics is nevertheless very deeply engrained in American culture. This presumption is illustrated by the rather astonishing statement made by a Connecticut judge in a 1971 case, in which girls were denied the right to participate in a high school cross-country team. "Athletic competition, " the judge said, "builds character in our boys. We do not need that kind of character in our girls, the women of tomorrow. "[7]

What sort of "character" is this, which is thought to be 1) developed by sports participation, and 2) more desirable for boys than girls? The answer, presumably, is to be found in the usual list of stereotypically "masculine" virtues, such as self-confidence, pride in achievement, perseverance, aggressiveness (in some non-pejorative sense), and the ability to function as part of a team. For well over two thousand years, patriarchal tradition has held that these virtues are important in males and unimportant or positively undesirable in females, primarily because the former are destined to play a dominant role in society and the family, while the latter are destined to enact a subordinate, nurturant role. Since the so-called "feminine" virtues (such as empathy, patience, and compassion) have not been thought to be the sort that can be developed through participation in competitive sports, sports have been viewed as essentially a kind of sex-role training for males.

This argument from the standpoint of male character development fails on at least four counts. First, the sharply differentiated sex roles that it presupposes are both morally objectionable in themselves and clearly outmoded in our economy, which requires most adults of both sexes to sell their labor to support themselves and their families. Second, even if it were appropriate for schools to seek to reinforce traditional sex roles, it would not follow that they ought to encourage the development of the traditionally "masculine" virtues only or primarily in male students. For, as Plato pointed out, the management of a household requires the same basic strengths of character as the management of a state[8]--or, he might have added, a career, or a commercial enterprise. Modern supporters of the ideal of androgyny maintain that to the extent that self-confidence, initiative, and so forth are valuable to men, they are equally valuable in women.[9] Sandra Bem's experimental research demonstrates that androgynous women and men (i.e., those who have both stereotypically "feminine" and "masculine" virtues) perform well in a wider range of circumstances than do individuals whose character is predominantly "feminine" or "masculine."[10] This highly predictable finding confirms the feminist insight that, to the extent that these are virtues at all, they are human virtues, not traits which are naturally or properly linked to sex.[11]

A third objection to the judge's argument is that it is by no means clear that the current practice of allotting disproportionate amounts of money, resources, and attention to a few all-male teams does improve the character of male students--either those who participate or those who do not. There are two conflicting theories about the effect of competitive sports on human character, neither of which is supported by much more than intuition and guess work. The first is that participation in sports tends to make people more aggressive, self-confident, etc. On this theory we should be skeptical of the value of a system which provides "aggressiveness-training" only for those male students who are already aggressive enough to enjoy and excel in competitive sports. Might this not be too much of an (allegedly) good thing? The males who may actually need such training are probably much less apt to make the football team, or to want to; and females, who probably need it most, are excluded altogether.

The second theory is that participation in competitive sports tends to make people less aggressive by providing a socially-sanctioned outlet for aggressive impulses that might otherwise be expressed in more antisocial ways. This theory is supported by certain ethologists and sociobiologists, who also believe that human males are naturally and inevitably more aggressive than human females, and therefore more in need of the sort of outlet that sports can provide.[12]

This debate over the effects of sports on character development is reminiscent of the debate over the effects of pornography, especially sadistic and violent pornography. Does exposure to such material make males more apt to rape or otherwise abuse women (or children, or other males)? Or does it make them less apt to do so, by providing a relatively harmless expression for whatever hostile impulses they may already have? Since the existing evidence--what little there is--seems to provide about equal support for both hypotheses, it seems reasonable to conclude that pornography may <u>sometimes</u> have effects of either sort. Probably its effects (if any) on the character development of the user are a highly individual matter, and influenced by so many other factors as to render all such simple generalizations useless. The effects of participation in competitive sports are probably equally varied and complex.

But suppose that it were possible to prove that, for one reason or another, participation in sports is especially important for the character development of males, more so than in the case of females. This would at most show that it would be unwise or unfair to deprive <u>male</u> students of sports opportunities. The further conclusion, that it is fair and reasonable to deprive <u>female</u> students of equal sports opportunities, would in no way follow. The last, but not least important fallacy in the judge's argument is that it ignores all of the potential benefits of sports participation apart from its (highly speculative) contribution to male character development. It ignores, indeed, all of those benefits that are most easily observable, least speculative, and almost certainly similar for both sexes. These include, for instance:

> 1) The intrinsic pleasures of participation, of camaraderie, of the perfecting of skills, and of the physical activity itself;

> 2) physical conditioning, i.e., the development of strength, endurance, speed, agility, etc.; and

> 3) the establishment of beneficial habits of exercise and recreation.

To ignore these other benefits is both irrational and unjust. It is irrational because these benefits are not only less speculative than the supposed improvement of male character in which so much faith is placed, but more difficult to bring about in other ways. Regardless of whether or not males might derive some <u>extra</u> benefits from sports participation, it is unjust to deprive females of <u>these</u> benefits.

This being the case, we could safely ignore all of the other arguments that purport to show that males derive greater benefits from sports than do females. No such argument can undermine the moral case for equal opportunity. Yet, I cannot resist mentioning one other argument of this sort, if only to illustrate the lengths to which some people will go to "prove" this inherently implausible hypothesis. I refer to

philosopher Paul Weiss's claim that males have greater difficulty "mastering" their bodies, and thus a greater need for
athletic training. Weiss says that

> [m]en are able to live in their bodies only if they
> are taught and trained ... (whereas) a woman's bi-
> ological growth is part of a larger process in which,
> without training or deliberation, she progressively
> becomes one with her body ... she masters her
> body more effortlessly and surely than he does.[13]

The implausibility of this claim is shown not only by
the absence of any actual evidence in its favor, but also by
the ease with which one can construct parallel arguments that
point to the opposite conclusion, i.e., that females have the
greater need for athletic training. One might, for instance,
follow Simone de Beauvoir, who argues that women's reproductive biology and the alienating meanings placed upon it in
our society make it considerably more difficult for women to
feel at home in their own bodies.[14] Or, one might argue
that since males in our society unquestionably tend to behave
more aggressively than females (whether because of their
hormones or because of social learning, or both), and since
less aggressive persons are apt to be at a disadvantage in
the struggle for self-preservation and advancement, if sports
participation increases aggressiveness then we should encourage females to participate to a greater degree than males by
giving them superior facilities, training, publicity, etc.

I am not suggesting that either of these arguments for
the greater importance of sports for females is valid. What
I am suggesting is that they are just as plausible as the arguments on the other side, and that a rational person must reject both sets of arguments. By contrast, we need no scien-
tifically dubious presumptions to know that human beings of
both sexes are capable of enjoying sports and deriving physical, and probably also psychological, benefits from participation. If these benefits are made available to some students,
then they should be available to all.

We must also consider the potential harms of sports
participation. In the past, females have been categorically
excluded from many athletic activities (e.g., Little League
baseball; the Boston, New York, and Olympic marathons, and
other long distance races) on the grounds that participation
would be harmful to them. Many people still believe that
vigorous physical activities like these are apt to "masculin-

ize" women's appearance, or damage their reproductive organs. Wherever such beliefs have been tested in practice
they have proven false. There is some evidence that women
may actually have somewhat superior powers of physical endurance; ultramarathons may prove an area in which they excel, as they have excelled in long distance swimming.

Whether or not this proves true, there is certainly no
evidence that women are less able to perform feats of physical endurance or exertion without sustaining serious or permanent injury. Damage to reproductive organs is a potential
problem for both sexes, but not usually a serious one for
either. Prolapsed uteruses sometimes occur, but usually in
association with childbearing; appropriate care can prevent
this. Breasts, like male genitals, can be adequately shielded
from accidental blows, and/or declared off-limits to intentional ones, as in boxing.

The belief that sports participation makes women look
like men is likewise false. Many sports tend to promote
strength and muscular development; but these are not masculine prerogatives. Women have as much right to develop
their strength as men do. Besides, even women body builders, who specialize in developing impressive muscles, do not
look even remotely like men. They are as different from
male body builders as female ballet dancers are from male
ones. Physical exercise alone cannot eliminate natural sexual differences.

There is, in short, no sound reason for supposing that
sports are more beneficial to male participants, or more
harmful to female participants. But what about the effects
on nonparticipants? Defenders of the old-fashioned system,
in which most of the schools' athletic budgets go to support
a few male-only or male-dominated sports, often argue that
these are what spectators want to see, that they contribute
to school spirit and prestige, and (sometimes) make money
as well. But integrated or female-only sports or teams can
also prove popular; certainly it is unjust to assume that they
won't as an excuse for not giving them a chance. Besides,
it can be argued that female student athletes deserve equal
support, even should they sometimes prove less popular with
spectators.

I suspect that the predominance of male-only or mostly-
male sports in most school athletics programs has a wider
cultural significance than is generally recognized. It func-

tions as a symbol of male domination elsewhere--in politics, business, and the more lucrative professions. It helps to make it seem natural and appropriate, or at least pragmatically inevitable. If there were other school-sponsored activities in which only females took part, and which brought equal status and recognition to an equal number of female students, then all-male sports would not have the social and symbolic significance that they have now. Offering inferior sports opportunities to women would still be unjust, but it would not convey the same implicit message that the most prestigious social roles may be justly reserved for males. The point here is not just that the male hegemony in school sports reduces the self-respect of individual women students, or of women in general, as Jane English suggests.[15] Most women probably base their self-respect on things more personal to themselves than the proportion of females involved in school sports. The point is, rather, that male hegemony in school sports requires students of both sexes to accept sexual inequality, to accede to a social system in which maleness of males must "be underwritten by preventing women from entering some field or performing some feat."[16]

For all of these reasons, simple justice requires that schools and colleges cease to discriminate against female students--or any other group of students--in the provision of athletic opportunities. As we have already noted, equal opportunity does not necessarily imply identical outcomes. It does not necessarily require that equal numbers of males and females participate in every sport, at every level. Nor does it preclude offering some sports in which only or primarily students of one sex or the other will choose to take part--so long as these choices are genuinely informed, voluntary, and not the result of false sexual stereotypes which the school has done nothing, or too little, to counteract. It does preclude the official or de facto exclusion of women from participation in any sports offered, or the unequal treatment of female participants. Thus, the full implementation of the Title IX regulations would be a step in the right direction. But this will not be sufficient to bring about genuine equality of opportunity, so long as the culture itself discriminates against female athletes, and so long as the sports offered retain a masculine flavor which discourages female participation. Furthermore, Title IX does not deal adequately with the issue of sex segregated versus integrated play; and this issue must also be fairly resolved if sports opportunities are to be equal.

II. The Segregation Issue

The issue of sex segregation in school sports is considerably more controversial than that of equal opportunity. Physical educators who agree about the importance of equality are nevertheless sharply divided on this issue. Some argue that to maintain separate teams or competition classes is inherently denigrating to females,[17] while others hold that in some cases it is the only feasible way to ensure equal opportunity for females.[18] This issue arises, or _should_ arise, primarily with respect to sports in which one sex, for strictly physiological reasons, has a significant and inevitable advantage. The vast majority of the sports offered by American high schools and universities favor traits in which the average male of high school age or older has an advantage over the average female--e.g., height, weight, upper body strength, running speed, etc. Betsy Postow refers to such sports as "masculine$_d$" to distinguish them from those which might be thought of as masculine for some other reason, such as that only males participate.[19] English and Postow have both pointed out that it is important that more sports be developed and offered that favor traits in which females are advantaged, such as small size, balance, and agility; for the current situation perpetuates the false assumption that women are generally inferior to men in _all_ athletic dimensions.[20] Consequently, Postow concludes, women have a moral reason "for withdrawing support from the [masculine$_d$] activities and promoting activities in which women have a natural advantage over men."[21] But this in no way implies that female students should not take part in masculine$_d$ sports, when this is their preference, or when the alternative is no sports participation at all. Nor does it imply that we can tolerate policies which deny female students an equal opportunity to participate in whatever sports are offered, masculine$_d$ or otherwise.

The key question, then, is whether equal opportunity for females who participate in masculine$_d$ sports, at the high school level and above, is best served by a policy of sex segregation. For there are no plausible objections to sex integration in sports that give no significant advantage to either sex.[22] Furthermore, since there are no significant differences between the athletic capacities of prepubescent girls and boys, there is no legitimate basis for sex segregation at the elementary school level.

One often hears it said that sex integration--in any

sport and at any age level--is unfair to males, because they do not enjoy competing with females, and are terribly humiliated by losing to them. For instance, in arguing against a 1973 suit which sought the admission of girls to Little League baseball, the directors of the Avonworth Baseball Conference said that the presence of girls would

> ... inhibit the play, complicate the task of getting fathers to volunteer for coaching and managing duties, and greatly embarrass the boys who had to sit on the bench while a girl was on the playing field.[23]

A common variation of this argument is that the "masculine identity" of males is damaged by participation in integrated sports, presumably because males can become sure of their own maleness only through taking part in groups or activities from which females are barred. A. Craig Fisher, for example, claims that, "The clear male identity is beclouded by feminine participation in traditional male activities," and that for this reason some sports should be not only sex segregated but "reserved for males."[24]

Arguments of this sort are not only invalid, but morally offensive. Continued discrimination can never be justified on the grounds that members of the favored group might be disturbed by a nondiscriminatory policy, when that attitude is based on nothing more than the prejudice born of past discrimination. We would not, I trust, condone the segregation of blacks, or homosexuals, or members of a minority religion, on the grounds that heterosexual WASP's might prefer to compete only with others of their own kind, or that they might become unsure of their own identities were they to interact with persons different from themselves. Discrimination of this sort perpetuates the very biases which are alleged to justify it. If males fear embarrassment or identity problems in coeducational sports, then these fears should be confronted directly, not used as an excuse for continued segregation.

Furthermore, the fear that males will be psychologically damaged or disturbed by participating in integrated sports appears to be entirely unfounded. A systematic study of the effects of sex integration in noncontact sports was conducted in New York public schools in 1969-1970, after a legal challenge was brought against state regulations that prevented girls from playing on boys' teams. The study found no evidence of either physical or psychological damage to students of either sex, and no evidence that males enjoyed themselves less or put forth less effort when competing with females.[25]

Given that there are no plausible objections to sex integration in sports where neither sex has a distinct physical advantage, mixed competition is clearly preferable in these sports. This is in part because "separate but equal" teams for females and males have the same sort of pejorative implications for females that racially segregated schools have for nonwhites. Separation of the sexes is inevitably perceived as implying the inferiority of females and for this reason, it has been argued, the "prestige factor" will always accrue to the male team.[26] The further harmful or unjust results of segregation include the following:

1) The perpetuation of social barriers between the sexes, e.g., the lack of communication, and the reluctance of males to accept females as "team members."

2) Injustice to exceptional female or male athletes, e.g., females who could make the males' team if allowed to do so, and males who can't make the males' team but might be able to make the females' team. Both are unfairly judged, not on the basis of their individual skill level, but on their sex membership, which ought to be irrelevant.

3) The perpetuation of de facto inequalities between the opportunities offered females and males, e.g., when the females' team is less well equipped and funded, coached by a lower-paid instructor, or not given equal media attention.

4) The concealment of the important fact that, even in the most masculine sports, there are many women who are better than many men; sharp sex segregation preserves the illusion that there is no overlap of this sort.[27]

5) The legitimation of sex as a social category which may be used to limit the opportunities of individual persons, regardless of their individual interests or abilities.

Insofar as these harmful results of segregation are

both real and severely unjust, they constitute a strong prima facie case for integration even in the masculine$_d$ sports, and a thoroughly compelling case for integrating all other sports. It is not excessively idealistic to hope that joint sports participation "can prepare girls and boys to play, live, and work together in mutual respect in ways that sex-segregated sports and culture never have."[28]

Why, then, do most physical educators, women as well as men, continue to oppose the integration of masculine$_d$ sports? One reason is the fear that women will be more apt to sustain serious injuries when competing with men, particularly in the contact sports. It is difficult to say to what extent this might prove true, since these sports are rarely sex integrated at the high school level or above, and thus there are few data about relative injury rates in integrated competition. But it is clearly most apt to prove true with respect to what might be called the "combat" sports, i.e., sports such as football, boxing, and wrestling, which involve the direct and deliberate use of severe force against one's opponent(s). This is a rather powerful argument against sex integrated combat sports, at least above the elementary school level.

Another argument against mixed-sex combat sports in schools is that they might tend to encourage or further erode the social taboo against the use of force by males against females. That they would have such an effect is probably unprovable. That they might is a realistic concern in a society which already suffers from a high and apparently increasing incidence of male-against-female violence. At any rate there seems to be little demand on the part of female students for integrated combat sports, so the question of whether they should be offered is not a particularly pressing one.

But what about sex integration in masculine$_d$ sports other than the more extreme or combat ones (e.g., basketball, baseball, tennis, golf, running, or speed swimming)? Here there is much less reason to suppose that women's smaller size and lesser upper body strength would make them more vulnerable to injury. For all we know, women who run, or play basketball with men may be no more apt to be seriously injured than the men are; or even less so. Besides, there are many more females who want to participate in these kinds of sports, in competition (and cooperation) with males. So it will not do to assume that they should be excluded or segregated for their own physical safety.

Another reason for the continuing opposition to the integration of masculine$_d$ sports is that it seems unfair to women to expect them to compete against men in activities wherein they are inherently disadvantaged by their physiology.

> If athletic competition is to be controlled so that at the onset competitors have relatively equal opportunities to win, then it seems quite evident that women should not compete against men ... [in masculine$_d$ sports] for any extrinsic reward, be it team membership, trophies, or athletic scholarships.[29]

This objection to integrating masculine$_d$ sports is persuasive only as long as one thinks in terms of just two alternative models: either 1) strict sex segregation is retained; or 2) students compete on a sex-blind basis for a very limited number of opportunities to participate in school sports, most of which continue to be of the masculine$_d$ variety. Given only these alternatives, it is reasonable to prefer the first, since the obvious result of the second would be that relatively few women would have a chance to participate: separate and less than equal is certainly better than integrated and de facto excluded.

But this dilemma is a false one. It is not necessary to choose between strict sex segregation and the type of sex-blind competition that would result in greatly inferior opportunities for female athletes. A partial solution would be to have sex-blind competition for places on teams, etc., while at the same time offering and providing fully equal support to an equal number of sports in which females have a significant physiological advantage, as well as other sports in which neither sex has an advantage. This solution is only partial, because although women would have the same overall number and quality of athletic opportunities, they would still have less opportunity to participate in masculine$_d$ sports; and this would be unfair to women who happen to prefer these sports to any of the others.

In the ideal school sports program, this problem would be solved by establishing as many teams or competition classes in each sport as necessary to permit all students who wish to participate to do so, whatever their relative ability level. Such a system would provide all students an equal opportunity to enjoy the basic benefits of sports participation--not only the best athletes of each sex, but also those who are athletically average or below-average, for whatever reasons. The exclusion of these students is as great an injustice as the exclusion of women, and for the same reason: they have the same right to obtain the basic benefits of sports participation as those who may be larger, stronger, or swifter.

The problem of how to eliminate sex segregation without sacrificing equal opportunity for women would be optimally solved by combining the two strategies outlined above--i.e., by offering an equal number of male- and female-favoring sports, with sex-blind competition for places on the most skilled teams (etc.), but opportunities for even the least athletically able students to participate in the sport of their choice. In such a system, women would no doubt still be scarce on the highest ranked teams in some masculine$_d$ sports, but men would be equally underrepresented in the various "feminine$_d$" sports. Since the feminine$_d$ sports would receive equal status and resources, the generally inferior performance of women in masculine$_d$ sports would lend no support to the myth of general female inferiority, athletic or otherwise. Competitions would be decided on the basis of individual skill only, not sex or any other irrelevant factor; yet the athletic strengths of men would not be valued more highly than those of women, and no one would be deprived of the benefits of sports participation.

This optimal solution is obviously not one which can be implemented immediately. A suitable range of feminine$_d$ sports has yet to be developed; and even if it were available there would remain serious economic, social, and political obstacles to their acceptance on an equal basis with the established masculine$_d$ sports. Must we therefore be content, for the time being, with the separate but equal approach to all or most masculine$_d$ sports? I think not, for there are a number of strategies available that can be used to achieve some degree of integration without sacrificing equal opportunity. The options that have been discussed, and sometimes implemented, in recent years include the following:

1) The one-way crossover approach, in which separate teams are provided for females and males, but females are permitted to try out for the males' team, although males are not permitted to try out for the females' team.

2) The quota approach, in which each team consists of 50 percent males and 50 percent females (or possibly some other set ratio). Women would thus

compete for positions on the team only with other
women, and men only with other men, but practice
and play would be fully integrated.

3) The components approach, in which each school
fields a composite team composed of a male and
a female subteam. The subteams play separate
games, but the outcome of the match is determined
by their combined scores.

4) The separate-and-mixed approach, in which there
are three teams in each sport; the first team consists of the best players, chosen without regard for
sex, and there is a segregated second-level team
for each sex.

Each of these approaches represents a distinct improvement over a separate and de facto unequal system; yet each
has its own disadvantages, and none can be viewed as more
than an interim solution. Each avoids some, but not all, of
the problems of strict segregation.

The one-way crossover approach permits exceptional
female athletes to compete with males, but it does not allow
males below the first team level to compete with females.
This is patently unfair; yet to allow unlimited cross-overs
in both directions would be apt to result in a preponderance
of males on both teams. This system might also result in
the best players on the females' team being continually si-
phoned away, which might be quite demoralizing to those who
remained. Thus, it has the advantage of being relatively easy
and inexpensive to implement, but it is probably the least
satisfactory of the compromise approaches.

The quota approach--common in volleyball and bowling
leagues--is considerably more promising. It has not been
given the attention it deserves, perhaps because racial and
sexual quotas have so often been used, in other contexts, in
ways that are clearly unjust. 30 The tide of opinion has turned
against the use of affirmative action quotas in hiring, for reasons which, as I have argued elsewhere, are largely invalid. 31 There is nothing inherently invidious about quotas, so
long as they are used to promote equal opportunity rather than
to undermine it. The quota system results in a greater degree of sex integration than any of the alternatives. More
than any of the other compromise approaches, it would require women and men to learn cooperative strategies which
make best use of the relative strengths of each sex.

There are three major objections to quota-integrated teams, none of which is conclusive. The first is that

> [t]he quota system would provide half as many teams and half as many positions in each sport as would the "separate-but-equal" alternative. Thus, although quotas permit the sexes to compete in equal numbers, they have great potential for excluding the most deserving individuals and limiting the total number of inter-scholastic participants. [32]

This objection is irrelevant to the use of sex quotas per se. A school can just as well support two <u>integrated</u> teams as two <u>segregated</u> teams, and there is no reason why integration should be accepted as an excuse for halving the total number of participants.

A more serious objection is that a quota system would be inconsistent with the "straight merit" principle for determining team membership, i.e., "that each individual should be judged by his athletic qualities (alone) and that the team should represent the best available talent."[33] Thus, it might tend to cause resentment among those males who might have made the top team, were it not for the quota-dictated inclusion of some females whose performance is inferior to theirs. Such resentment would be unjustified, however, insofar as it is not always appropriate to measure and reward athletic merit on the basis of a single unisex standard. The best female players may be inferior to the best male players in certain absolute measurements, yet just as excellent <u>relative to the relevant standard of comparison,</u> and thus equally deserving of reward or recognition. Still, so long as absolute standards continue to be considered important, quota systems are apt to be resented. Unless that resentment is defused, e.g., through the expansion of the total number of opportunities in conjunction with the introduction of sex quotas, it may render the widespread operation of a quota system extremely difficult.

A third objection is that the quota approach might have counterproductive results for females, such as "intrateam ostracization of the girls who dilute the overall performance, and interteam exploitation of the 'weaker' sex members of the opposing team."[34] This is a realistic concern, especially since the structure of many masculine$_d$ sports makes it more or less inevitable that relatively weak players will be resented by their teammates and exploited by those on opposing teams. The problem will probably be most severe in the case of the most extremely masculine$_d$ sports, such as football, in which size and strength are overwhelmingly important. As we have seen, there are other reasons for concluding that sex integration in these sports should not be a high priority. In the case of the less extremely masculine$_d$ sports, however, the quota system is often quite feasible. For in these cases the difference in effectiveness between the average male and female team member will usually be no greater than that between the best and worst male players, and hence no more serious a problem.

As our third option, the components approach usually represents an attempt to ensure equal status, support, and publicity for female athletes, without the perceived risks of integrated competition. However, one variant of this approach permits some degree of crossover between the female and male teams, e.g., such that up to 20 percent of the predominantly female team will be male, and vice versa. This permits exceptional female athletes to compete with males, but entails the risk that the "stars" of the predominantly female team might turn out to be males, thus largely vitiating the point of maintaining prima facie segregation.[35]

The primary drawback of the components approach is that it makes the success or failure of each team dependent upon that of the other. If one of the two teams is the best in its league, then it seems unfair that it should be held back by the relatively inferior performance of the other.[36] This objection must be taken seriously. For while the team's members need not be chosen entirely on the basis of (some single standard of) athletic excellence, the logic of the game --any game--demands that a team's success or failure depend on its own performance. On the other hand, to the extent that the two subteams function as a cooperative unit (e.g., by practicing together, sometimes exchanging members, etc.) the force of this objection is lessened. The encouragement of such intrateam cooperation would have to be a major goal of the components approach, which might otherwise share most of the drawbacks of simple segregation.

The separate-and-mixed approach, like the quota approach, is an attempt to (partially) integrate masculine$_d$ sports without sacrificing equal opportunity for females. Its apparent advantage over the use of quotas is that it allows the membership of each team to be determined on the basis of the individual performance of each prospective member vis-à-vis other prospective members of that team. Thus, the quality of the top team will not be diluted by a quota for females, yet females and males who don't make the top team will still be able to play in the segregated second-level teams. The drawbacks of this approach are 1) that since most of the members of the first team will generally be males, there will be a minimal degree of sex integration; and 2) that males will have almost twice as many opportunities to play as females. It is probably fairer to exceptional female athletes than is strict segregation, and fairer to males who can't make the first team than the one-way crossover option; but it does little to eliminate the male hegemony in masculine$_d$ sports.

In reply to this criticism, it might be argued that if there are at least twice as many males as females who <u>want</u> to participate in masculine$_d$ sports (as is apt to often prove true), then it is not unjust to provide males almost twice as many <u>opportunities</u> to participate. But this argument is valid only if <u>the system</u> itself does not act to unfairly discourage female participation, as in fact it might. If only the very best female athletes have any chance of making the first team, and if the second-level teams receive considerably less reward and recognition (which may be inevitable), then many females will probably be discouraged from participating. And this would certainly be an unfair situation--at least as long as most of the sports offered are masculine$_d$ sports.

We return, then, to the point from which we began: There can be no <u>fully</u> just way of settling the integration/ segregation issue as long as most widely supported and heavily subsidized school sports inherently favor the average male over the average female physique. It is important to realize just how arbitrary and unnecessary this bias towards male athletic superiorities really is. Sports which favor small size, limberness, agility and balance, rather than large size, strength, and the like, are perfectly feasible, and can be just as enjoyable for both participants and spectators as the currently dominant masculine$_d$ sports.

The compromise approaches to the integration of masculine$_d$ sports discussed above are all preferable in many cases to either strict segregation or a strictly sex-blind approach; but they do not address these fundamental problems. Nor do they do much to alleviate the elitism of school sports, i.e., the extent to which resources and attention are concentrated upon a few teams and individuals, rather than being used to make the benefits of sports participation equally available to all students. Nevertheless, sex integration is an important interim goal, and one which may pave the way for further progress.

Since the pros and cons of the various approaches to sex integration are complex and somewhat speculative, the decision to opt for one or another of these interim solutions must be made in the light of the particular context. The nature of the particular sport, the (clearly expressed and justifiable) preferences of female and male students, and the financial, institutional, legal and political realities may all be relevant to the decision. The quota approach will probably prove most useful in those sports which are masculine$_d$ to some degree, but not to the extent that sheer size and strength are (among) the most important requirements. The components, separate-and-mixed, and one-way crossover approaches may be preferable where the sport in question is one which is masculine$_d$ to this more extreme degree.

Summary and Conclusion

Schools, like other publicly supported institutions that sponsor athletic activities, are morally as well as legally obligated to provide equal opportunities to female participants. The arguments that purport to show that males have a greater need to take part in sports are implausible in the extreme. "There no longer is any excuse (if there ever was) for failing to provide half of the events, facilities, budgets, and leadership for half of the population."[37] But equal opportunity requires more than equal expenditures for female and male sports, teams, or athletes. Ultimately, it requires what might be called the sexual democratization of the pantheon of national sports-- i.e., the giving equal support to sports that favor female physical abilities and attributes, or that favor neither sex, as to those in which males are inherently advantaged. It also requires the provision of enough teams or competition classes, in each sport, to allow all students who are interested and able to take part.

Given these changes, we could safely adopt a policy of strict sex-blindness in determining team membership without jeopardizing equality of opportunity for either sex. Under existing conditions, however, such a policy would greatly reduce women's opportunities to participate in school sports, as compared with a policy of strict sex segregation. But strict segregation is also unacceptable in the majority of cases, both because it is unfair to individual athletes whose abilities might make them better suited to play on the opposite-sex team, and because it perpetuates misunderstanding, lack of communication, and invidious or chauvinist comparisons between the sexes. Thus, it is important to experiment with various compromise strategies, which combine some degree of integration with some degree of segregation or sex-awareness. Such strategies will give at least some students the opportunity to learn that women and men can both cooperate and compete with one another without undue trauma to either.

NOTES

1. *Sports Illustrated*, May 28, 1973, p. 88.
2. D. Stanley Eitzen and George H. Sage, *Sociology of American Sport* (Dubuque, Iowa: Wm. C. Brown, 1978), p. 280.
3. Elementary schools were given one year to comply with the regulations, while secondary and postsecondary schools were given three years.
4. Elizabeth R. East, "Federal Civil Rights Legislation and Sport," *Women and Sport*, ed. Carole A. Oglesby (Philadelphia: Lea and Febiger, 1978), p. 213.
5. Caspar Weinberger, (then) Secretary of Health, Education and Welfare, Statement on Release of Final Title IX Regulations, June 3, 1975, p. 2.
6. In February 1981, U.S. District Judge Charles W. Joiner of Michigan held that Title IX could not be used to force a high school to provide golf teams for female as well as male students, because the school's (male-only) golf team receives no direct federal assistance. A few months later, U.S. District Judge Barefoot Sanders of Texas ruled that the intercollegiate athletic programs of West Texas State University are not covered by Title IX, since, although the college receives federal aid for other educational programs, no federal aid is given to that particular program. (See *The Chronicle of Higher Education*, September 9, 1981, p. 8.)
7. Quoted by Margaret C. Dunkle, "Equal Rights for Women in Sports," in *Women's Athletics: Coping with Controversy*, ed. B. J. Hoepner (Washington, D.C.: AAHPER, 1974), p. 9.
8. Plato, *Meno*, excerpt in *Woman in Western Thought*, ed. Martha Lee Osborne (New York: Random House, 1979), p. 17.
9. See, for instance, Ann Ferguson, "Androgyny as an Ideal

for Human Development," Feminism and Philosophy, ed. Mary Vetterling-Braggin, Frederick E. Elliston, and Jane English (Totowa, N.J.: Littlefield, Adams, 1977), pp. 45-69; and Joyce Treblicot, "Two Forms of Androgynism," ibid., pp. 70-78.

10. Bem, Sandra L., "Probing the Promise of Androgyny," Beyond Sex-Role Stereotypes, ed. Alexandra G. Kaplan and Joan F. Bean (Boston: Little, Brown, 1976), pp. 48-61.

11. Mary Wollstonecraft was one of the first philosophers to emphasize this point; see A Vindication of the Rights of Women (New York: W. W. Norton, 1972; first published, 1792).

12. See, for instance, Konrad Lorenz, On Aggression, trans. Marjorie Kerr Wilson (New York: Harcourt, Brace, and World, 1966); and Lionel Tiger, Men in Groups (New York: Vintage Books, 1970), pp. 148-160.

13. Paul Weiss, Sport: A Philosophic Inquiry (Carbondale: Southern Illinois University Press, 1964), p. 217.

14. Simone de Beauvoir, The Second Sex, trans. H. M. Parshley (New York: Bantam Books, 1970); see especially pp. 26 and 146.

15. Jane English, "Sex Equality in Sports," Philosophy & Public Affairs, 7 (Spring 1978), 273.

16. Margaret Mead, Male and Female: A Study of the Sexes in a Changing World (New York: Dell, 1949), p. 168.

17. See, e.g., "Sex Discrimination in High School Athletics," Minnesota Law Review, 57 (December 1972), 369.

18. For instance, Brenda Feigen Fasteau, "Giving Women a Sporting Chance," in Out of the Bleachers: Writings on Women and Sport, ed. Stephanie L. Twinn (Old Westbury, N.Y.: The Feminist Press, 1979), pp. 171-172.

19. B. C. Postow, "Women and Masculine Sports," Journal of the Philosophy of Sport, 7 (1980), 58.

20. B. C. Postow, "Masculine Sports Revisited," Journal of the Philosophy of Sport, 8 (1981), p. 60; English, p. 275.

21. Postow, "Women and Masculine Sports," p. 56.

22. Examples include horseback riding and vaulting, archery, riflery and other tests of marksmanship, figure skating, bowling, and martial arts, all of which emphasize skill rather than size and strength. Horse and auto racing, stunt flying, sky diving, and hang gliding, though not typical school sports, are additional cases in point.

23. Quoted from the Lehighton Times-News, July 6, 1973,

by Jan Felshin, "The Dialectic of Woman and Sport," in Ellen Gerber, et al., The American Woman in Sport (Reading, Mass.: Addison-Wesley, 1974), p. 201.

24. A. Craig Fisher, in The Physical Educator, October 1972, p. 122; quoted by Jan Felshin, work cited in note 23 above.

25. Report on Experiment: Girls on Boys' Interscholastic Teams, March 1969-June 1970 (Albany, N.Y.: Univ. of New York, State Education Department, Division of Health, Physical Education and Recreation, 1972), cited by Carol L. Rose, "The ERA and Women's Sport," in Oglesby (ed.), Women and Sport, p. 237, cited in note 4 above.

26. "Sex Discrimination in High School Athletics," cited in note 17 above.

27. An example is the Boston and New York marathons, from which women were excluded prior to the 1970s; but now the fastest women have better times than thousands of the qualified male runners.

28. Wilma Scott Heide, "Feminism for a Sporting Future," in Oglesby (ed.), Women and Sport, p. 198.

29. Waneen Wyrick, The American Woman in Sport, p. 484. Cited in note 23 above.

30. Examples are the infamous quotas placed on the admission of Jewish students to certain universities earlier in this century, or the quotas limiting the admission of females to medical schools.

31. M. A. Warren, "Secondary Sexism and Quota Hiring," Philosophy & Public Affairs, 6 (Spring 1977), 240-261.

32. Richard Alan Rubin, "Sex Discrimination in Interscholastic High School Athletics," Syracuse Law Review, 25 (Spring 1974), 563.

33. Ibid., p. 564.

34. Fasteau, p. 172.

35. Rubin, p. 564.

36. Ibid., p. 565.

37. Gerber, The American Woman in Sport, p. 534. Cited in note 23 above.

QUESTIONS

(1) Warren attempts to refute various arguments which support the view that discrimination against females is justified in school sports. In your opinion, does she succeed in refuting them all? Why or why not?

(2) Warren says that "if the school is aided by tax money collected from women and men alike, then it is unjust to deprive female students of any significant class of benefits that male students enjoy."

a) Do you agree or disagree? Why?

b) If all taxpayers were men (because all women devoted themselves to caring for their homes and families without pay) would it then be justified to deprive female students of any significant class of benefits which male students enjoy, in your opinion? Why or why not?

c) If a school sports program is funded by gate receipts and/or alumni contributions rather than by taxes or tuition, might this justify providing less opportunity for females than for males to participate in the program, in your opinion? Why or why not?

d) What circumstances (real or imaginary) would clearly justify depriving male students of some benefits enjoyed by female students, in your opinion? What circumstances would clearly justify depriving the female students?

(3) Warren thinks that "the predominance of male-only or mostly-male sports in most school athletic programs" may convey the "implicit message that the most prestigious social roles may justly be reserved for males."

a) Do you agree that this is the implicit message? Why or why not?

b) If you disagree with Warren in question (a) above, describe a real or imaginary school athletic program (and its social context) that would convey this message in your opinion.

c) If you agree with Warren in question (a) above, describe a real or imaginary school athletic program (and its social context) that would convey the message that the most prestigious social roles may justifiably be reserved for females.

(4) a) Summarize Warren's reasons for the position that "simple justice requires that schools and colleges cease to discriminate against female students ... in the provision of athletic opportunities."

b) What other reasons can plausibly be given in support of Warren's position?

c) What reasons can plausibly be given against Warren's position?

(5) Suppose for the moment that sex segregation is needed to provide equality of opportunity for adults in masculine sports. Under this supposition, would Warren be correct that "there is

no legitimate basis for sex segregation at the elementary
school level" in your opinion? Why or why not?

(6) a) Present the most plausible argument you can in support of sex segregation in those sports in which neither sex
has a clear physical advantage.
    b) Is this a sound argument? Why or why not?

(7) Warren states that if there is a limited number of places
on teams, then sex-blind competition would be unfair to women
who happen to prefer masculine sports, since it would give
them less opportunity than men to participate in these sports.
Do you agree with Warren that this would be unfair? Why or
why not?

(8) Warren states that the best female players in masculine
sports may be just as excellent as the best males "relative
to the relevant standard of comparison."
    a) What are some different possible standards of com-
parison?
    b) Which of these possible standards do you think is most
relevant for judging who should be given access to a limited
school athletic program? Why?

(9) What else would you like to discuss from Warren's essay?

2. EDUCATION AND SPORTS:
A Reply to "Justice and Gender in School Sports"

Janice Moulton

In Chapter 1, Mary Anne Warren first undertakes the distasteful task of answering the arguments <u>against</u> equal sports opportunity for females. There are arguments that girls will not benefit from sports participation as much as boys, that boys need sports more, either to develop their characters or to master their bodies, and that boys will be psychologically damaged if they lose to girls. Warren points out that these claims are unsupported by any evidence and even if they were, they do not justify denying equal sports opportunity to females.

Warren explains that more is at stake than sports opportunities. She argues that sports occupy a special place in the world, functioning as a symbol of male domination in politics, business, and the more lucrative professions. "If there were other school-sponsored activities in which only females took part, and which brought equal status and recognition...," sports discrimination would not be so bad.

Warren goes on to argue, as English and Postow have before her,[1] that most existing sports have developed or been changed to emphasize physical traits in which males have an advantage over females. Therefore, full equality for females in sports will not occur until more sports and games have been developed that stress the physical traits in which females have an advantage over males. But until this has occurred, we need to consider how to do the best we can to provide females greater access to the sports that exist now, even those in which male physical characteristics are an advantage. The primary problem is whether these sports should be sex segregated, sex integrated, or some mixture of both. Warren points out that there are a number of ways to struc-

38

ture teams, matches, and tournaments so that females can participate in the existing male-advantaged sports.[2]

Much of what Warren says, and the strategies she proposes, assume that it is right to consider sports opportunities as a privilege reserved for the best players. Those cited by Warren who believe that ʀports opportunities ought not to be extended to females clearly accept the "privilege" view of school sports. They just want to reserve the benefits of sports for those who they believe deserve it most. Males, on their view, deserve it most because they are better people, or will become better athletes, or will benefit, appreciate, or use the sports opportunities to a better purpose.

Although Warren explicitly advocates sports programs for all students, when discussing team composition, she does not object to sports being treated as a privilege. Her question then is how to structure teams and tournaments so that students of both sexes can try out for them. I would like to argue instead that sports should not be thought a privilege, an activity for only the most talented. I believe that we do not need a team and tournament structure that allows equal participation of only the exceptional players from both sexes, but structures that allow equal participation of everyone, exceptional or not. In arguing for this I am not opposing Warren's claims, but rather extending the spirit of her remarks.

But how, you might ask, could anyone not consider sports participation a privilege? There is only so much money allocated to school sports, not enough to provide coaching, facilities, etc., to every student. To provide the coaching, facilities, and places on teams for everyone would require an enormous increase in funds allocated for sports. There isn't that much money available. So it has to be allocated somehow. Therefore the sports advantages available must be treated as privileges, given to some and not all, however one determines who the benefited will be.

To illustrate my alternative view, let's compare sports with another school activity: education. It would be possible to provide a much better education to some people by depriving others. We could certainly consider education a privilege--there is only a given amount of time and money dedicated to it--and parcel it out according to desert. And those who deserve it most might be those who would appreciate it most, or those who need it most, or those who would make the best use of it. The people who were candidates for an education would vary depending on the criterion of merit. Those who did not meet the criterion would get little or no education.

Most people believe that none of these criteria should determine who gets an education. We think everyone should get an education, regardless of individual differences in the ability to appreciate, benefit from, or use it. There may be advanced classes that only specially qualified students can take. But the primary responsibility of every school is to provide a basic education for all of its students. If school budgets or faculty are reduced, it is the specialized classes with smaller enrollments that are usually eliminated. Even higher education, once reserved for the well-to-do and a few with exceptional talent, is now available in some form for nearly everyone who has completed high school and even for many who have not. The increased accessibility of education is seen by most as a good thing, an improvement in society. [3]

But unlike education, the teams, coaching, and facilities of school sports are usually reserved for a few outstanding athletes. No similar movement to increase the accessibility of sports has taken place. If resources are plentiful, secondary teams may be supported. But it is usual to concentrate the resources in coaching, facilities, and extra privileges for a very small number of people, and neglect the large majority entirely.

I would like to suggest instead that sports should be treated like education: not as a privilege to be doled out on some criterion of merit but as a basic resource provided by every school for each student. I do not mean that high scores, medals, and trophies should be given to everyone, any more than A grades should be given to everyone. Nor is it necessary that everyone be able to participate in every game or tournament, any more than everyone is able to attend or qualify for every class in school. But the basic benefits of sports are important enough that they should be made available to everyone, and that includes instruction, coaching, team and tournament organization, supplies, and whatever else is necessary so that all students can participate in sports.

Some might think that existing physical education classes do serve this purpose. But these classes rarely provide training for or participation in a series of games

or meets that are taken seriously enough to have records
kept, teams organized, etc. (Moreover, the arbitrary sex
segregation of these courses tends to perpetuate the inferior
status of females. Arguments that different abilities justify
sex segregation are invalid. Such arguments would also apply to the sex segregation of many academic subjects on the
grounds that one can find sex differences in abilities. Different abilities might justify ability segregation--advanced and
beginning tennis courses, for example--but not sex segregation.)

Before giving the reasons for my view, I would like
to consider other arguments based on the benefits of sports
that favor extending sports opportunities, but not to the extent that I propose.

Let us look at one argument that would distribute some
benefits more widely, but not to everyone. Many of the benefits of sports participation that are available to the athletic
elite are extrinsic--Rhodes scholarships, extra money, special privileges such as free tutoring, better meals than at the
dormitories, free trips, etc. Sports stars are recruited, not
merely admitted like other students, and are treated better
to keep them happy and healthy. People who do not believe
that sports are more important than other school activities
are told: The alumni like it; it helps raise money; special
treatment of the stars will increase school spirit and make
everyone happier. These rationales deserve skepticism, but
even if they were true, we could argue that other activities--
theatre, music, debating--ought to receive the same special
treatment. Perhaps weekend television ought to broadcast
college theatre productions, and the result might be better
for the colleges, alumni, and other students, than the broadcast of college sports. In that case, talented school actors,
musicians, debaters, and anyone who can excel in anything
that can promote school spirit or please alumni or raise
money ought to receive special treatment. But this does
not produce the conclusion we want. We can conclude that
other talents and other enterprises besides sports deserve
the special treatment now reserved for athletes. But we
can't conclude that everyone, even the untalented, deserves
sports.

Let us look at another argument about equal opportunity in sports. Consider the intrinsic pleasures and benefits
of sports: physical fitness, learning and improving skills,
game strategies, practice in cooperating with others, the

pleasure of physical exercise and physical competence, the camaraderie with other players (including opponents), and the exultation of winning. If I were going to argue that the importance of sports is comparable to the importance of education on the grounds of these benefits alone, I can imagine a number of objections. Sports may provide individual pleasures and benefits, but there is no reason that society has to make any commitment to providing these pleasures for everyone. The personal pleasures and physical fitness that sports participants obtain do not amount to something a society has to provide its members. People ought to be free to seek such pleasures, but we don't have to commit public funds to provide them. We can still reserve these funds for the people with special talents in sports. On this view, we are not obliged to provide the pleasures and benefits of sports to everyone. School funds ought to be used to give everyone an education because an education is necessary for people to function in and contribute to our civilization, and because education is needed for so many occupations. To deny some an education is to deny them an essential part of civilization. Even if the personal benefits of sports are very important, I have yet to show that sports should be treated like education. I have to show that sports have a similar importance in our society.

Contrary to the view presented in this objection, many of those who would give males priority in sports want to argue that it is important. Among other things, it builds character.[4] The many clichés borrowed from sports to describe behavior expected and approved of in the business world are some indication that the things learned in playing sports are thought to be important. Sports participants learn how to be "team players," how to "play ball." They can be relied on to "know the score," to "touch base," to know how to "run interference" for their teammates. Even those who only participate as spectators in sports can quote "ballpark figures."

Warren argues for a different sort of significance that sports have in society. Even in school, male-dominated sports are a sign, she says, of dominance elsewhere in society. Having special school activities that feature only boys, and no activities of equal importance that feature only girls, makes male domination in the rest of society seem natural. That is, in Warren's view, the inequalities between boys and girls in school are particularly important because it teaches young people to view these inequalities as natural. Either equalize the access to sports or provide a separate-but-equal activity for girls in school. However, Warren would probably agree that the different status accorded males and females in the rest of society would soon be reflected in the status accorded the separate-but-equal activities provided for girls in school. Therefore, the only realistic remedy is to integrate girls into the activities now provided primarily for boys. Warren's argument does not address the question of the many girls and boys who now receive very little of the benefits from these school activities because they do not excel.

If these arguments for extending sports opportunities fail to support the conclusion that sports opportunities should be made accessible to everyone and not treated as a privilege, then what argument is needed? I have to show that sports participation is important enough that no student should be denied or discouraged from participating in sports. School sports are the beginning of the development of a form of life, a cultural practice, and we learn in school which sports are interesting, what kinds of players are interesting, and what we are going to play or watch later in life. More important, we learn whether we are going to be part of this aspect of civilization. It is not an accident that most of the spectators of professional sports are those who once, however informally, were participants themselves. Sports include not only the playing of games but the immense time and energy our culture spends on both professional and amateur sports--the organizing of recreational events and leagues; the regulatory agencies and facilities; the media space and time devoted to broadcasting, reporting and reminiscing about sports; the time people spend reading about, watching, and discussing games, statistics, and predictions about sports; and teaching sports to children. People who are denied sports opportunities in school are unlikely to develop the interest or the knowledge needed to participate in this pervasive cultural phenomenon. They will not even know enough or have the chance to develop the interest in watching sports. They won't know what it feels like to play the game, how difficult and exhilarating good plays are, the intricacies or purpose of game strategies. They will be deprived of participation in a widespread cultural phenomenon, not only as a player, but as a spectator, conversation sharer, and teacher.

A society comes with conventions and practices and rituals that constitute its civilization. If individuals who live in that society are excluded from important parts of the civilization, that is unjust, whether or not what they are excluded from has intrinsic value apart from its role in the culture. It will be unjust because they are excluded from an important part of the civilization and denied a chance to participate in the social structures, to form the bonds that come from common interests and common experiences, and to learn about such social interactions.

If schools provided sports facilities as they do educational facilities, then Warren's alternatives for integrating sports could all be used. We would not have to choose among them. There might be some skill-segregated teams, but there are good reasons not to structure all teams on the basis of skill. One can learn a lot more by playing with and against more skilled players. And one can have a lot of fun being the star on a lesser team and helping less skilled players. We can assume that outstanding athletes would want to participate in some of the lesser teams for additional practice. As it is now, many informal games are played with whoever shows up, and every school athlete has played in such games. There is no reason why school funds cannot be used to support such informal teams by providing coaching, refereeing, league organization, and facilities that are now provided only for elite rigidly structured teams.

NOTES

1. Jane English, "Sex Equality in Sports," Philosophy and Public Affairs, vol. 7, no. 3 (Spring 1978); B. C. Postow, "Women and Masculine Sports," Journal of the Philosophy of Sport, vol. 7 (1980). It is important to note that some sports have been altered to stress physical traits in which males are advantaged. The rules of men's lacrosse have changed from the original sport to make it more like American football, but women's lacrosse remains the original sport.
2. Let me add that these ways are used now in a number of sports. Relay races in many sports (running, cycling, swimming) are scored by adding the scores of individual performances. Municipal recreational leagues of softball usually have all female, all male, and mixed sex leagues. In intramural co-ed softball at least five players must be female. One person may belong to more than one league, and there is no stigma attached to any type of team. With a little more time and experience in integration it is likely that other ways of organizing teams and matches will be found.

3. There are many private schools and colleges with restrictive admissions standards. There are also
courses with prerequisites that exclude many students. I am not arguing against these restrictions
although, obviously, they could be misused. If the
only restrictions to sports participation were similar
to prerequisites and admissions requirements then although students would have to demonstrate some skill
in gymnastics or wrestling to join the advanced teams,
there would be many elementary level teams for the
less skilled and for teaching the more advanced techniques.
4. See Kathryn Addelson's article in this volume for an excellent discussion of this idea.

QUESTIONS

(1) See the skeleton of Moulton's argument given in the Introduction to Part I.
a) For each of premises (1), (2), and (4), answer the
following questions: Do you agree with the premise? Why
or why not?
b) On the supposition that premises (1) and (2) are true,
how strongly do they support premise (3)? (If necessary,
refer to the "Background on Arguments" in the General Introduction.)
c) Do you agree with premise (3)? Why or why not?
d) On the supposition that premises (3) and (4) are true,
how strongly do they support the conclusion, (5)?

(2) Moulton says that physical education classes rarely provide the same benefits as a school sports program. (For
the distinction between a sports program and physical education classes, see note 1 to the Introduction to Part I.)
a) In your view, can physical education classes do as
much as a sports program to provide students with access
to an important aspect of civilization? Why or why not?
b) In your view does every student deserve access to a
school sports program in addition to physical education
classes? Why or why not?

(3) What else from Moulton's essay would you like to discuss?

3. ATHLETICS, GENDER, AND JUSTICE*

Ramon M. Lemos

Although the title of Chapter 1 is "Justice and Gender in School Sports," Dr. Warren raises and discusses issues that have implications reaching far beyond the participation of males and females in school sports. The issues she discusses concern the general question of the requirements of justice with respect to the participation of males and females in organized athletics of all sorts. This includes not only school athletics but also professional athletics and organized amateur athletics not sponsored by any school, college, or university. I, too, shall address myself to this more general question or set of questions. In doing so I shall follow more or less her order of presentation. Since the first of the two major parts of her essay is devoted to a presentation of what she refers to as "the moral case for equal athletic opportunity," I shall begin by examining critically what she says about such opportunity and what it consists of and requires. I shall then examine critically what she says in the second part of her essay, which is devoted to a discussion of sex segregation and integration in athletics. Since, however, the topics of the two main parts of her chapter are closely interrelated, the discussion of what she says in the first part will unavoidably include references to what she says in the second part.

---

*Editor's note: The version of Warren's essay to which Lemos had access when writing this chapter did not contain some revisions that Warren made later. Some of the sentences of Warren's which Lemos accurately quoted in his essay were later changed in Warren's final revision, which appears in this volume. Lemos's main points are unaffected.

Dr. Warren assumes at the outset that "equal opportunity for women in school sports has yet to be achieved." To determine the truth or falsity of this assumption both an empirical or historical investigation and a philosophical analysis are required. Since in this paper I am concerned only with philosophical issues I shall not undertake the empirical or historical investigations but shall instead concentrate on the philosophical analysis. Such an analysis requires us to determine the meaning of the sentence "equal opportunity for women in school sports has yet to be achieved." As in the case of other assumptions or statements, the question of whether the assumption in question is true or false, indeed the question of precisely what it is, can be decided only after the meaning of the sentence used to express it is determined. In the sentence in question it is only the subject-expression, "equal opportunity for women in school sports," that is reasonably open to a variety of interpretations. Once we determine the meaning of this expression the truth or falsity of the statement can be determined by making the appropriate empirical or historical investigations. As I have indicated, I shall not undertake those investigations but shall instead confine myself to the philosophical issue, which is that of the meaning of the subject-expression.

We seek in vain if we look for anything approaching a precise definition of this expression in Dr. Warren's paper. Instead, she maintains that "equality of opportunity is a difficult notion to define." This claim might be true, but it seems unlikely that it can be true for the reason she gives, which is that equality of opportunity "is, to some extent, consistent with inequality of outcome." What inequality of outcome has to do with equality of opportunity she fails to make clear. She does say, apparently in an attempt to explain the connection between the two, that female and male students might have the same "apparent opportunity to take part in a certain sport, yet males might choose to do so more often than females, or vice versa." Why in this sentence she qualifies her use of the term "opportunity" by using the adjective "apparent" I do not know. Perhaps she intends to suggest that the opportunity of male and female students to take part in a certain sport is only apparent and not real if either more males than females or more females than males choose to do so. To say, however, that an opportunity is only apparent as opposed to real is to say that it is not an opportunity at all. Either an opportunity to do something exists or it does not. If it does, the opportunity is real rather than apparent. If it does not, something else may exist that might seem in certain respects to be an opportunity although in fact it is not. Such a phenomenon may be labeled an "apparent" opportunity, but if we do so we must be careful to avoid confusion. We must remember that apparent as opposed to real opportunities are not real or genuine opportunities in any sense at all but are only phenomena that might in certain respects resemble real opportunities. Therefore, either male and female students have the same opportunity to take part in a certain sport or they do not. Whether they do or not cannot be determined by considering whether more males than females or more females than males choose more often to do so. Instead, the fact that members of one sex choose more often to participate than do members of the other sex has no connection with the question of whether the members of both sexes have the same opportunity to participate.

Whether male and female students have the same opportunity to be active in school sports is to be determined, not by considering how many members of each sex choose to do so, but rather by considering whether there are factors that tend to prevent more members of one sex than of the other from participating. Perhaps the clearest instance of such a factor would be the existence of what Dr. Warren refers to as "rules, regulations, or prevailing practices or attitudes ... such that no, or fewer, females are permitted to take part in certain sports." Clearly, if either males or females are not permitted to participate in a given sport, then the members of the sex that is not permitted to participate in it do not have the same opportunity that the members of the other sex have. If male and female students are to have the same opportunity to participate in all sports, regardless of the nature of the sport, then the members of each sex must be permitted to do so. The nature of certain sports, such as boxing, wrestling, and football, is such that few if any females would want to participate in them against males. Nonetheless, if no one prohibits females from participating in such sports against males, they have the same opportunity as males, even though few, if any, of them choose to do so.

It seems, however, that for Dr. Warren it is not sufficient that females be permitted to participate in any sport in which males are permitted to participate if they are to have the same opportunity as males to participate. Instead, it is also necessary that females not be "wrongly discouraged" from wanting or choosing to take part. I think we can agree that they ought not to be wrongly discouraged from doing so.

Indeed, it seems analytically true that no one ought ever wrongly to discourage anyone from wanting or choosing or attempting to do anything whatever. If so, then the claim that females ought not to be wrongly discouraged from wanting or choosing to participate in certain sports is trivially true. The important question is what counts as wrongful discouragement. This question cannot be answered adequately without considering precisely what it is that females are discouraged from doing and the reasons that can be given in support of such discouragement. If better reasons can be given for discouraging than for encouraging females to participate in certain sports, then those who attempt to discourage them from doing so do not necessarily discourage them wrongly. That, however, there are any sports that females but not males ought to be discouraged from participating in seems doubtful, at least so long as they compete only against other females. The reason for this qualification is that there are certain sports (boxing, wrestling, and football, for example) the nature of which is such that females have little or no chance of competing successfully in them against males. In the case of such sports it does not seem to be wrong to attempt to discourage females from attempting to compete against males. But it seems doubtful that such discouragement is necessary to induce significant numbers of females not to want or choose to compete against males in such sports, since very few females seem anyway to want to compete against males in such sports, perhaps because they recognize that they have little or no chance of doing so successfully.

We have seen that attempts to discourage females from wanting or choosing to compete against males in certain sports do not seem to be wrong. In addition, these attempts to discourage females do not seem to constitute a denial of an equal opportunity to females to compete against males in such sports, so long as they are permitted to do so if they want or choose so to do. To attempt to discourage someone from wanting or choosing to do something is not necessarily to prevent that person from doing it. To some degree males also seem to be discouraged in various ways from wanting or choosing to compete against females in certain sports, yet this does not mean that they are prevented from doing so. It might be true that the degree to which they are discouraged from doing so is not as great as that to which females are discouraged from wanting or choosing to compete in these sports against males. It might also be true that this difference of degree, if it does in fact exist, is unjustifiable. Nonetheless, just as attempts to discourage females from wanting or choosing to compete in certain sports against males do not seem always to be wrong, so also attempts to discourage males from wanting or choosing to compete against females in these sports do not seem always to be wrong. In both cases the reason justifying such attempts at discouragement is the same--in such sports females have little or no chance of competing successfully against males.

Such discouragement, however, as was indicated above, does not amount to prohibiting or otherwise preventing males and females from competing against each other in such sports and in fact is compatible with permitting them to do so. So long as any males or females who want or choose to do so are permitted to do so, it seems that they have an equal opportunity, even though females more than males might be discouraged from doing so and even though few if any females have much if any chance of competing successfully against males. If far fewer females than males want or choose to compete against males in these sports the cause is probably not so much that they are more heavily discouraged than males by social pressures and customs as that they recognize that they have little if any chance of competing successfully. Given that few females want or choose to compete in these sports against males, there seems little if any point in attempting to prohibit those who wish to do so from doing so. The fact that few wish so to do means that the level of competition among males in these sports will not seriously deteriorate because of the participation of females, and those few females who choose to participate cannot rightly complain of being denied an equal opportunity to do so if they are permitted so to do.

To say, however, that females may rightly be discouraged from competing against males in sports such as boxing, wrestling, and football is not to say that they may rightly be discouraged from competing against females in such sports. The primary if not the only sense in which such sports may rightly be regarded as masculine is that few if any females can compete in them successfully against males. Although few females seem to want to compete in such sports even against other females, there seems to be little if any reason for attempting to discourage or prevent those few who might want to do so from so doing. Certainly there seems to be little if any reason to attempt to prevent them from participating through issuing prohibitions of various sorts. This last follows from the general principle, stated here very roughly, that people ought to be permitted to do what they want to do so long as they do not harm others or perhaps also themselves, taken in conjunction with the fact that competition between females in so-called masculine sports would seem to cause no more harm than competition between males in such sports. In fact, competition between males in such sports results, because of their greater bodily strength, in more serious bodily injuries than would probably result from competition in such sports between females. But if the occurrence of serious bodily injuries to males as a consequence of their competing against one another in such sports is not sufficient to justify attempting to prohibit such competition, and I do not think it is, then neither is the possibility of serious bodily injuries to females as a consequence of their competing against one another in such sports sufficient to justify attempting to prohibit such competition on their part. In this connection it might be mentioned in passing that Dr. Warren's claim that "women who participate in integrated contact sports may prove no more apt to sustain serious injury than their male comrades, or even less so," will doubtless seem ludicrous to those who have themselves participated in such sports or who know anything of any significance about them.

Thus far I have argued that males and females may rightly be discouraged but not prohibited from competing against each other in those sports in which few if any females have much if any chance of competing successfully against males. I have also argued that females may not rightly be discouraged or prohibited from competing against other females in such sports. If these conclusions are correct, then it would be wrong to discourage or to prohibit females from competing either against males or against other females in those sports in which good female athletes do have the ability to compete successfully against some males. Such sports, of course, are those in which successful competition does not depend significantly on the degree of bodily strength and speed that females usually lack. Given the preceding, I think we can correctly say that females have the same opportunity as males to participate in various sports against males or against other females if and only if the members of both sexes are equally permitted to do so and the members of neither sex are wrongly discouraged from doing so. This is not intended as an adequate exact definition of the concept of equality of opportunity between the sexes to participate in sports of various sorts--I agree with Dr. Warren that it is hard to define this concept adequately and precisely. It is instead intended only as a rather rough statement of the conditions that must be satisfied if such equality of opportunity is to exist. I hope this rough statement will suffice for the purpose of discussing the question of whether females have a right to such equality of opportunity and, if they do, of what is involved in their having such a right.

As was indicated at the outset, the first part of Dr. Warren's chapter is devoted to presenting "the moral case for equal athletic opportunity." This strikes me as a strange enterprise indeed. Although I cannot here attempt to show it, it seems to me that if there are any absolute moral rights at all one such right is the right to equality of consideration and that if there are any unconditional moral obligations one such obligation is the obligation to respect each person's right to equality of consideration.[1] In the present context this right can be respected and the corresponding obligation fulfilled only if we give the same consideration to females as we do to males in connection with the opportunity to participate in sports. That is, once the right to equality of consideration and the corresponding obligation are recognized, there is no longer any need to endeavor to develop a "moral case for equal athletic opportunity." Instead, all one needs do is to respond to objections to and arguments against providing such opportunity, and this, it seems to me, Dr. Warren does admirably. She repudiates convincingly, I think, claims to the effect that males have a greater need than females for athletic training because the former "have greater difficulty 'mastering' their bodies" and that males benefit more than females from participating in sports because such participation leads to the development of certain virtues and traits of character which are more important in males than in females. Since any virtues and good traits of character that such participation might develop are good-making properties of human beings and not simply of males as opposed to females, it is as important that females as well as males, if they are to be good human beings, develop such virtues and traits of character. Why, however, she refers to the recognition of this as a "feminist insight" escapes me, since one need not be a feminist to recognize what seems to me to be a rather obvious truth.

Good sportsmanship is one virtue which participation in sports might help develop. Such sportsmanship is the willingness to subject oneself to rules on terms of equality with others and to accept graciously the outcome of contests conducted in accordance with such rules. This virtue is re-

quired for the practice and viability of democracy, as I have
indicated elsewhere,[2] and for this reason if for no other it
is as important in females as it is in males. But the importance of fostering certain virtues in people regardless of their
sex is only one reason for the importance of female participation in sports. There are others. It is desirable that people, whether male or female, develop strong and healthy bodies. To the degree that participation in sports contributes
to this end it is as important for females to participate as
it is for males. In addition, since it is no more important
that males engage in activities they enjoy than it is that females do so, it is no more important that males participate
in sports because they enjoy doing so than it is that females
participate because they enjoy so doing.

If the preceding considerations are acceptable, I think
we may conclude that females have the same right to participate in sports that males have and that we have the corresponding obligation to permit them to do so. In this I agree
with Dr. Warren. She goes on, however, to draw consequences she seems to think follow from this right and the
corresponding obligation that seem to me not only not to follow from them but also to be incompatible with them. She
admits that "the moral arguments for providing equal sports
opportunities for females apply equally well to other athletically-
discriminated-against groups, such as the physically handicapped, or males who are relatively small, overweight, etc."
and that "it is not only females who have been excluded from
many sports opportunities." She does not, however, develop
consistently the implications of these admissions but instead
makes claims, suggestions, and proposals that are incompatible with them. I turn now to show that this is in fact the
case and that what she in effect proposes is not equal athletic
opportunity for males and females but rather preferential
treatment for females.

This can be shown by concentrating on what she says
concerning interscholastic and intercollegiate athletic competition. If courses in physical education are either required
or open to all students, whether male or female, then female
students have the same opportunity as males to take such
courses. And if grouping by ability in academic courses is
permissible, advisable, or obligatory, as I think it is, even
though few black students might place in the groups of highest
academic ability, then so also is grouping by ability in courses
in physical education, even though few female students might
place in the groups of highest athletic ability. Similarly, if

intramural sports programs are offered for all students, whether male or female, no injustice is done female students if certain among the sports offered are such that few if any female students can compete successfully in them against male students. If physical education courses are either open to or required of all students, whether male or female, then all students may participate in the sports offered in such courses. And if all students, whether male or female, are permitted to form intramural teams, then female as well as male students have an equal opportunity to participate in intramural sports.

The situation, however, is different in interscholastic and intercollegiate competition. Here only those students who are the best in the sports offered can become members of the varsity teams. Male and female students have the same opportunity to become members of such teams if competition for such membership is open to all students, whether male or female. Female students cannot then rightly complain that they are denied an equal opportunity or treated unjustly if few or none of them succeed in such competition. Such open competition without regard to sex satisfies any reasonable interpretation of the Department of Health, Education, and Welfare regulations implementing Title IX of the 1972 Educational Amendments that require all schools receiving federal aid to provide or move toward providing "equal opportunity for both sexes to participate in interscholastic, intercollegiate, intramural, and club athletic programs." Most male students, like most female students, lack sufficient athletic ability to compete in athletics at the varsity level. Those female students who lack such ability may no more rightly complain that they are treated unjustly if they fail in the competition for membership on varsity teams than may those male students who lack such ability. In certain sports, such as cross country, gymnastics, diving, swimming, golf, and tennis, some female students do have sufficient ability to compete successfully against males for membership on varsity teams. But in the case of those females who lack such ability, the obligation to respect their right to equal athletic opportunity does not require that separate female varsity teams in any sports at all be provided or supported. The establishment and support of such teams is an act of generosity or chivalry that exceeds the claims of justice. Similar considerations apply to professional female athletes. If professional female golfers or tennis players complain that the prize money for female tournaments is not as great as that for male tournaments, as some have in fact done, the just remedy is to open male tournaments to them. Such a move would doubtless lead most to a return to competition in tournaments open only to females.

I should like to end by making three brief comments about Dr. Warren's recommendation that sports in which males excel be de-emphasized. The first is that I think she exaggerates the importance of such sports for the formation of the attitudes and beliefs of most people concerning the abilities of males and females. Most people probably realize that the fact that certain males excel in certain sports does not mean that males generally are superior to females in other endeavors and areas of life. The second is that there is a certain paternalistic (or maternalistic), elitist, anti-democratic, or even totalitarian flavor to her recommendation. Rather than endeavoring in various ways to induce people to engage in and to watch only those sports the promotion of which contributes to the attainment of certain goals one might happen to have, respect for the autonomy of people seems instead to require that we leave it up to them to participate in and watch the sports they enjoy. After all, the sports in question are only games. The third comment is that her recommendation seems to manifest a certain envy of or resentment at male excellence in the sports in question. It seems no more reasonable to recommend that those sports in which males excel be de-emphasized than it would be to recommend de-emphasizing other areas of endeavor in which they excel, such as the composition of music to take only one example. Rather than being envious or resentful of such excellence as exists, it seems that we ought instead to rejoice in it, encourage it, and nourish it wherever it can be found. The excellence of what is at best only a few males in sports requiring a degree of bodily strength and speed that females usually lack does not in the least mean that females cannot excel in those endeavors that do not require such strength and speed.

NOTES

1. For a discussion of the right to equality of consideration and the corresponding obligation see my "The Concept of Natural Right," Midwest Studies in Philosophy, VII (1982), 133-150, and my "Human Rights and Moral Goals," forthcoming in Proceedings of the Tenth Inter-American Congress of Philosophy.
2. See my "A Moral Argument for Democracy," Social Theory and Practice, IV (1976).

QUESTIONS

(1) In your opinion, would a school's failure to provide sports which appeal to females constitute "wrongful discouragement" of females from participating in the school sports program? Why or why not?

(2) According to Lemos, in sports such as boxing, wrestling, and football, "the nature of which is such that females have little or no chance of competing successfully in them against males, ... it does not seem to be wrong to attempt to discourage females from attempting to compete against males."

    a) List the various ways in which females are or can be discouraged from attempting to compete against males in these sports.

    b) For each of the ways which you have listed, answer the following questions: Is the use of this type of discouragement for this purpose morally permissible in your opinion? Why or why not?

(3) According to Lemos, "if all students, whether male or female, are permitted to form intramural teams, then female as well as male students have an equal opportunity to participate in intramural sports."

    a) Do you agree or disagree with this statement? Why?

    b) Do you think Warren would agree or disagree with this statement? What would her reasons be?

(4) What else from Lemos's essay would you like to discuss?

4. REPLY TO MOULTON AND LEMOS

Mary Anne Warren

Professor Janice Moulton and I agree that the opportunity to participate in school-sponsored sports should be viewed not as a privilege but as a basic benefit to which all students are equally entitled. Like her, I consider it unfortunate that school athletic funds are often disproportionately spent on a few elite teams, rather than on a wider range of activities which would enable all interested students to take part. On the other hand, neither of us objects to the grouping of student athletes by ability--so long as the less skilled ones are not denied equal access to facilities, coaching, and so forth. Consequently, I am a bit puzzled about why she takes exception to my assumption that even in a fully egalitarian system there may still be some teams or competition classes for which students must try out competitively. Perhaps I failed to stress sufficiently the distinction between grouping by ability (which is not always objectionable), and excluding the less talented students (which generally is objectionable). In any case, I accept her comments as--at worst--friendly amendments.

There are, on the other hand, some serious disagreements between Professor Ramon Lemos and myself. He and I agree that all students should have an equal opportunity to take part in school athletics, but we disagree about what this entails. His position is that female and male students have equal athletic opportunities providing neither sex is actually forbidden to take part in any of the sports offered. In his view, a system of sex-blind competition for a limited number of participatory opportunities (e.g., the "varsity" teams), and the provision of other sports activities (e.g., intramural teams) would be fully sufficient to guarantee equality of opportunity. In my view, this system does not necessarily guarantee that the athletic needs and interests of female and male students will receive equal consideration.

Consider the hypothetical case of a school which offers no varsity sport except football and sponsors just one team; suppose that females are permitted to try out for this team, but that they almost never do, and that those who try out almost never make it--not because of prejudice, but because they are less effective football players than the males who make the team. Lemos would apparently not see in this situation any violation of female students' right to equal athletic opportunity; whereas I would see it as a denial of equal athletic opportunity not only to the majority of female students, but also to those male students (possibly also a majority) who have no interest or aptitude for football.

This difference is not a matter of semantics; the debate is not primarily about what the phrase "equality of opportunity" means in the abstract. The issue is, rather, what should all students have an equal opportunity to do, in the context of a school sports program? Lemos thinks that it is enough if they all have an opportunity to compete for the opportunity to participate in some sport or other. Moulton and I think that they are entitled to the opportunity actually to participate; and, if possible, in a sport suited to their interests and abilities. The primary argument for this more liberal construal of the demands of equality in this context is that sports participation is such an important component of a person's education that it ought to be freely available to all students; making it available only to some is just not good enough.

There are a few other points in Professor Lemos's essay that are worth a brief response. First, while I do not know which of my specific suggestions he is referring to when he says that I am advocating "preferential treatment" for female students, and therefore cannot give a specific reply, my general reply to this charge is that preferential treatment is not necessarily wrong; it all depends on the circumstances. Suppose, for example, that the cost of providing sports programs for physically handicapped students is slightly higher per student than it is for physically able students; this would be preferential treatment, but not, I think, objectionable. Preferential treatment for some is wrong if it leads to unjust consequences; but providing sports opportunities for those who would otherwise be denied them is not (normally) an injustice.

Second, I would deny that it is "ludicrous" to suggest that women and men might prove capable of participating together in even some of the so-called "contact" sports (though probably not the rougher "combat" sports, such as boxing), without undue risk of injury to either. Lemos thinks that no one who knows anything about contact sports would make such a suggestion; but I have both watched and participated in informally organized co-ed softball and volleyball, without observing any higher injury rate among female players. (It is true that volleyball is not usually considered a contact sport; but given the number of violent collisions that actually occur, it probably should be!) I cannot be certain that this observation is either accurate or typical; but it certainly <u>might</u> be. So why not continue to experiment with integrated play and find out?

Third, Professor Lemos wonders why I say that it is a feminist insight that the virtues which are supposed to be developed through participation in sports are human, rather than specifically masculine virtues. The reason is that feminists have typically (though not always) shared this view, while antifeminists--like the Connecticut judge quoted in my article--typically (but again not always) insist that these character strengths are unnecessary for women. I agree that it ought to be obvious that this sex stereotyping of virtues is a mistake; but unfortunately it has <u>not</u> been obvious to most people in our culture, at least un<u>til</u> quite recently.

Finally, I must protest Lemos's claim that my attitude towards sports in which males tend to excel ("masculine$_d$" sports) is "paternalistic ... elitist, antidemocratic, or even totalitarian"; and that I am "envious or resentful of such excellence." What I actually said is that if female students are to have equal athletic opportunities, we will need to continue to develop and give increased support to a wider range of sports in which neither sex is physiologically advantaged. I don't suggest that we should <u>replace</u> masculine$_d$ sports with feminine$_d$ sports, only that we should try to give more equal attention and support to the latter. To increase women's athletic opportunities is not necessarily to significantly decrease those available to men. Of course resources are limited, and schools which have in the past spent virtually all of their athletic budget on male athletes will not always be able to double their total expenditures in order to offer equal opportunities for females without reducing the amount spent on males. If providing equal athletic opportunities for females sometimes means providing less lavishly for male athletes than was formerly possible, that is unfortunate, but not necessarily unjust. Nor is it a goal to be desired for its own sake. Far from wanting to curtail men's athletic opportunities, I would like to see a continued expansion of sports participation for both sexes.

Thus, I fail to see what is elitist or antidemocratic about my enthusiasm for the current trend towards improved athletic opportunities for women, and for other groups who have had fewer athletic opportunities in the past. I would have thought that if anyone is guilty of elitist or antidemocratic thinking it is those who see no need for schools to support this trend, or who feel somehow threatened by it.

5. AFTERWORD ON EQUAL OPPORTUNITY

Betsy Postow

There are various ways to understand the words "opportunity" and "equal opportunity."[1] For example, someone might hold that if I do not have the means to travel to anyone who is offering cars for sale, then I do not have an opportunity to buy a car, but that if I do have transportation to a showroom, then I do have an opportunity to buy a car. Other people would disagree, saying that if I have no money for a down payment, then I really don't have an opportunity to buy a car even if I can get to a showroom. Both uses of the word "opportunity" are understandable, and a reason would have to be given for preferring one use to another in a particular context. The context would determine which obstacles were of particular interest; the removal of those obstacles would create an opportunity. A similar situation exists with the definition of opportunity to participate in a school sports program. Lemos says that one has an opportunity to participate in a program of team activities if one is allowed to try out for a team. Warren says that one doesn't really have an opportunity to participate in the program if one isn't skilled enough to make a team. A reason must be given for preferring one usage of the word "opportunity" over the other usage in the context of deciding when a school sports program offers equal opportunity to all students to participate. Now the obvious reason for preferring one usage over another is that the preferred usage is more helpful in stating the requirements of fairness. After all, the reason people are interested in determining what constitutes an opportunity in this context is that they think that equal opportunity is equivalent to fairness in this context. So we should inquire what makes a school sports program fair or unfair to potential participants.

If we agree with Moulton that participation in a school sports program is tantamount to a passport to participation in an important aspect of our civilization, then we will probably agree with her that every student is entitled to the removal of all obstacles to her or his participation in a school sports program. On this view, any obstacle to participation counts as a lessening of opportunity to participate, and unequal obstacles will constitute unequal opportunity. Thus, for example, if a low level of athletic skill lowers a student's probability of being selected for the program, then students with low levels of athletic skill are denied an equal opportunity to participate, by this view.

Not everyone will agree with Moulton, however, about the extreme importance of school sports for participation in our civilization. If we disagree with Moulton about this, we may also disagree with her view that every student has a right to participate in a sports program. (We may, of course, have some other reason to agree with this latter view.) Now if it is not the case that everyone has a right to participation in a school sports program, then such a program need not be unfair simply because it cannot accommodate all students. A program can be fair to prospective participants if it uses a fair criterion for selecting participants. Suppose, then, that the program does not make places available for all students, and that we are looking for a principle of selection to determine who will receive places. One selection principle which probably suggests itself immediately to most of us is this: Those who have achieved higher levels of athletic performance (as evidenced by open competitions) are more deserving of places than those who have achieved lower levels. We may be tempted to accept this principle without question, but as philosophers we need to ask why we think those who have achieved more are more deserving. It seems to me that our reasons for thinking so are these. One consideration which may lead many people to accept the criterion of athletic achievement is that actual proficiency in a sport seems to be analogous to possessing the qualifications for a job. Since it is presumably fair to hire the candidates with the best job qualifications, it also seems fair to choose the most proficient athletes to participate in a school sports program. A second consideration is this. Everyone has been led to expect that scarce places in a program (and other scarce benefits) will be awarded on the basis of achievement. If a school were to stop abiding by this policy it would disappoint legitimate expectations. Aspiring athletes could rightly complain of having been misled in their decisions and plans for the future. A third reason for thinking that the achievers deserve the scarce benefits is that, offhand, there doesn't seem to be any other criterion that could reasonably be used to award scarce places in a school sports program.

Let us step back and evaluate these reasons for accepting the criterion of athletic achievement for awarding scarce athletic benefits (such as a place in a school sports program). The first consideration rests on the premises that 1) it is fair to hire the best qualified candidates for a job, and 2) being an athlete in a school athletic program is like having a job. We shall defer consideration of the first premise until reading Ruth Heizer's essay (Chapter 6), when we shall see why some philosophers have disagreed with this premise. To evaluate the second premise we must look for relevant differences between being on a team in a school athletic program and having a job. One difference will be apparent to those who think that the primary purpose of a school athletic program ought to be educational. A more qualified job applicant can do the job better. This is important largely because it benefits the consumers and the employer. Now a more proficient athlete can also "do a better job," but the benefits which the "consumers" (i.e., spectators) and "employer" (i.e., school) receive from this better job (e.g., greater enjoyment or greater prestige) are of secondary importance if the primary purpose of the school athletic program is educational. So this is one possible reason to reject the premise that selecting participants in a school sports program is relevantly similar to selecting a candidate for a job. Evaluation of this possible reason and generation of other possible reasons will be left to the reader.

Let us turn now to an evaluation of the second suggested reason for accepting the criterion of athletic achievement. Certainly people have been led to expect that athletic achievement will be the basis for awarding limited athletic benefits. Therefore it would be unfair to change the ground rules suddenly without somehow compensating those who were misled. But although it is unfair to change the ground rules suddenly, it is not necessarily unfair to change them with adequate advance notice. If there were some other fair criterion which we could use for selecting those who will receive scarce athletic benefits, it, too, could become the basis of everyone's expectations.

But what other possible criterion can there be besides athletic achievement? One possible criterion is _effort_, reflected perhaps in the number of hours a student practices. Another possible criterion is <u>need</u>, defined perhaps as a deficiency in physical and/or social skills that could be remedied by participation in a school sports program. A third suggestion is that those be selected who show promise of using the skills they gain to help society. Other possibilities will undoubtedly suggest themselves to the reader. Perhaps several of the suggestions should be combined, and some places in the program made available on the basis of each of the factors involved, or on the basis of some combination of factors.

How shall we choose a criterion? Of course we should examine each suggestion carefully to see if the considerations in its <u>favor</u> stand up to scrutiny. (As we have seen, some considerations in favor of the achievement criterion do not stand up as well as we may have thought. Still, that criterion may recommend itself for other reasons, or because it seems intrinsically appropriate.) There are also some considerations which count <u>against</u> any criterion to which they apply. One such consideration is self-defeatism. A school sports program may not be able to provide the benefits which it is intended to provide if the number and quality of participants chosen by a given selection criterion prevents it. That would be reason to reject or modify that criterion. Thus, for example, if those who would be selected by the effort criterion were incapable of realizing the legitimate goals of the program, the criterion should be modified or rejected.

Another consideration which should lead us to reject or modify a suggested selection criterion is that using the criterion in question supports a socially undesirable result. For the purpose of illustration, I shall take for granted that a sexist society is an undesirable result--i.e., that it is undesirable that rights, privileges, and roles in a society be assigned on the basis of sex. Therefore, any suggested criterion for selecting participants in a sports program is itself undesirable if it supports such a sexist society. As we saw in Warren's essay, there are arguments in support of the view that the practice of selecting participants in a school sports program purely on the basis of certain types of athletic achievement does in fact promote such a sexist society. Thus, a case can be made for rejecting or modifying the criterion of athletic achievement as it is currently used, or for supplementing it with other criteria.

To summarize so far, we have seen that there are

various possible criteria for selecting participants in school sports programs (e.g., athletic achievement, effort, need). We have also looked at some factors that can count as considerations for or against adopting any particular criterion. It is left to the reader to apply the appropriate considerations and decide on a criterion which she or he thinks should be used for the fair selection of the participants in a school sports program.

Once we have decided on our criterion for fair selection of participants, this criterion will determine what we should count as equal opportunity to participate. Equal opportunity to participate consists of equal freedom from all hindrances to participation which are not approved of by the criterion that we have chosen. For example, suppose that we have chosen the criterion of athletic achievement. This criterion approves of hindering students from participating on account of their low level of athletic skill. Thus, if we have chosen this criterion we should not say that students who are hindered or prevented from participating on account of a low level of athletic skill have less opportunity to participate than their more skilled classmates. We should instead say that they had the same opportunity as everyone else, but they didn't make it. To change the illustration, suppose now that we have rejected the criterion of athletic achievement and have chosen instead the criterion of psychological need. The criterion of need does not approve of hindering students from participating on account of their low level of athletic skill. Thus, if we had chosen this criterion we should say that students who are hindered or prevented from participating on account of a low level of athletic skill have less opportunity to participate than their more skilled classmates. Thus different choices of a selection criterion for participants in a program can yield different conclusions about whether a particular program offers equal opportunity. (Of course different selection criteria can sometimes lead to agreement about whether a particular program provides equal opportunity. For example, both the criterion of athletic achievement and the criterion of psychological need would imply that a sports program which imposed a high equipment fee as a condition of participating would not provide equal opportunity for those students who could not afford the fee.)

Any selection criterion which we might choose would be compatible with a decision to segregate the players by sex (or ability groups, or effort groups) after they had been chosen as participants.[2] And any selection criterion which we might choose would be violated by a decision to set up sex-segregated teams with a predetermined number of places on each, for this would make a student's chances of participating partially dependent on sex. Sex-integration, on the other hand, would not be unfair in this way, for it would not lower women's chances of being selected for the program if selection were made solely on the basis of our approved criterion (whether achievement, effort, need, or anything else).

Let us turn now to the quality of the participation. It is not enough that there be equal opportunity to participate in a sports program if "participate" means just going through the motions. There must be equal opportunity to receive the benefits of the program through interested participation. A plausible case can be made that if a sports program is unappealing to a student, this lack of appeal hinders the student from receiving the benefits of the program even if she or he does participate. To take an extreme example, if track were the only sport offered, those to whom track is unappealing would not reap the benefits of wholehearted participation. For students to have completely equal opportunity to reap the benefits of a school sports program, the program should appeal to everyone equally. Thus a variety of sports should be offered, and features of the program which are aversive to some students should be minimized. Of course the appeal of a program depends on the interests of the students, and these can vary widely. The variety is of two sorts: purely individual differences in interest, and differences which depend in part on the student's social classification (racial, economic, or gender). A special effort should be made to accommodate these latter differences in interest in order to neutralize the insidious effects of social classification. Sports at which females can excel, for example, have a high potential for appealing to females. Thus a case can be made that these sports should be included in a school sports program in an effort to equalize opportunities to reap the benefits of interested participation in the program. Given these considerations, the reader is left to determine what features need to be designed into a sports program if it is to provide students of all social classifications with equal opportunity to reap the benefits of participation.

In summary, we have not arrived at a picture of what an equal-opportunity sports program would look like, but we have found a procedure for arriving at such a picture. The procedure is this: 1) List the different possible criteria which could be used for selecting those students who will receive the benefits of the program.[3] 2) Using relevant considerations described above, evaluate each of the listed criteria and identify the most plausible one. 3a) Identify the factors which can hinder a student from receiving the benefits of the program. (These will include lack of appeal.) 3b) Using the criterion chosen in (2), and the emphasized definition of equal opportunity, identify those hindrances which can be said to diminish a student's opportunity. If students are equally free of these hindrances, then their school has an equal-opportunity sports program.[4]

NOTES

1. This analysis of the notion of opportunity relies on concepts which were introduced by Gerald C. MacCallum, Jr., in "Negative and Positive Freedom," Philosophical Review, 76, no. 3 (1967), pp. 312-334.
2. This would not deprive anyone of equal opportunity to participate in the program, but it might still deprive some participants of equal opportunity to reap the full benefits of participation in the program. This is explained below.
3. A criterion may be such that all students would be selected if that criterion were used. Moulton, for example, suggests such a criterion: the criterion of membership in our society.
4. This essay would have been harder for the average reader to follow if I had not heeded some of the helpful comments of Dianne M. Meagher.

SUGGESTIONS FOR FURTHER READING

James C. Dick, "How to Justify a Distribution of Earnings." Philosophy & Public Affairs, 4 (1975), pp. 248-272.

Gerald C. MacCallum, Jr., "Negative and Positive Freedom," Philosophical Review, 76, no. 3 (1967), pp. 312-334.

QUESTIONS

(1) a) List all the (even remotely) plausible selection criteria you can think of for participants in a school sports program.

b) Pick the criterion that seems most plausible to you on an intuitive level.

    c) List all the considerations you can think of for and against the criterion which you chose in answer to part (b).

(2) Do you agree that "the primary purpose of a school sports program ought to be educational"? Why or why not?

(3) In your opinion, would it be self-defeating to use need as the sole criterion for selecting participants in a school sports program? Would any of the other suggested criteria be self-defeating? Support your opinions.

(4) a) In your view, is the procedure which is outlined in the conclusion a reasonable procedure? Why or why not? Suggest possible improvements.

    b) Carry out either the procedure which is outlined in the conclusion, or the improved procedure which you suggested in answer to question 4 (a) above.

    b') [Shorter version] For the purpose of this shorter version, assume that the criterion which you selected in your answer to question 1 (b) above really is the best criterion. On this assumption, what changes would the athletic program at your school need in order to make it an equal-opportunity program?

(5) What else would you like to discuss from Postow's essay?

SECTION B:

Fairness to Women in
Athletics-Related Employment

6. EMPLOYMENT FOR WOMEN IN ATHLETICS: WHAT IS FAIR PLAY?

Ruth B. Heizer

Are women getting their fair share of the good jobs in athletics? Are they being promoted and paid fairly? These questions presuppose that one knows what constitutes fair treatment. Does it mean equal? If so, equal in what respect or by what criterion? Does it mean preferential treatment? If so, why, and for how long?

The various courts and governmental agencies continue to kick around the legal football of affirmative action and its guidelines. Philosophers, on the other hand, continue to debate the morality of preferential treatment for women and the more general question of what constitutes justice.[1] This chapter will attempt to map the terrain of this debate by offering a general survey of the relevant discussions in recent philosophical literature. Once we have our philosophical bearings, we will apply our findings to the specific issue of the hiring of women in athletic administrative positions (including coaching). The discussion that follows, then, is concerned primarily with the moral question. We will consider the fairness of the practice of awarding jobs to the female candidate because she is female--i.e., the practice of preferential treatment or reverse discrimination. What is said about the awarding of jobs will also be applicable to questions of pay differentials, promotions, etc. The terms "preferential treatment" and "reverse discrimination" will be used interchangeably and neutrally. The choice of term does not imply a judgment of fairness or unfairness.

It should be made clear at the outset that the difficulties that may be found to attend reverse discrimination ought not to be assumed to apply to affirmative action proposals.

70

The latter are the non-discriminatory attempts to facilitate equal treatment. It is nevertheless important to be aware of the objections to reverse discrimination so that affirmative action can be shown to be free of these.

A few writers have argued that "all is fair" not just in "love and war" but also in the awarding of jobs. Since an employer "owns" the jobs, she or he may fairly give them to anyone she or he pleases, they say. Hence, discrimination in favor of women is perfectly justifiable.

Some others also argue that discrimination is fair, but they do so on the grounds that sex is a relevant factor in determining who should be hired or given better pay. Different writers offer different reasons to justify the claim that sex is relevant. Some examples of reasons are the following: "We need an integrated staff, and since all of our current employees are men, the next employee hired should be a woman." "Women make better coaches of women." "Women are economically disadvantaged, and therefore they need increased pay."

The positions above do not find discrimination to be morally objectionable in itself. Most of the recent philosophical literature, however, assumes that discrimination in favor of men and against women is unfair. Since such discrimination has occurred in the past, the issue then becomes whether reverse discrimination now in favor of women is justified and on what grounds. One side argues that if discrimination on the basis of sex is unjust, as assumed, then it is just as unfair to favor women now as it has been to favor men in the past. The other side argues that a principle of compensatory justice demands that the injured parties, in this case women, be awarded compensation for past employment injustices and hence given preference for jobs now.

A fact which is not always recognized is that not all arguments that could be offered in favor of preferential treatment for women are mutually compatible. The assumptions and justification backing one appeal can be in conflict with those backing another. For example, a person cannot consistently argue that Jane Roe was unjustly treated because she was better qualified for Job X than was Joe Doe who got it and at the same time insist that because Jane is a widow and has three children to provide for she ought to get Job Y even though candidate Jack Snow is better qualified for it than she is. The Job X judgment assumes that there are merit criteria which determine fairness; the Job Y one makes its appeal to need criteria. The person judging must make up her or his mind whether the societal benefit of jobs should be distributed according to merit or according to need or according to some other criterion. Of course, it is also possible to frame a criterion which grants some weight both to need and to merit, but such a criterion would have to include a formula for determining the relative weights of need and merit. It is hard to see how this could be done in any plausible way. It is important, therefore, to examine closely the justificatory principles appealed to by the various arguments. In what follows we shall classify possible positions on preferential treatment by the justificatory principles to which they appeal. Within this framework, appeals that count sex as relevant and those that view it as irrelevant will be distinguished.

"All's Fair" Because "It's Mine"

The first view considered accepts neither a merit nor a need criterion for just distribution, but claims merely that "all's fair." It is fair for private employers to bestow the benefits of employment on anyone they choose for any reason they choose because they "own" the jobs. Judith Jarvis Thomson has considered this approach. She claims that in a purely private college, for example, if the employer does not imply that he is giving an equal chance to all applicants, then he does not act unjustly if he gives preference to a black (or woman) just because she is black (or female).[2] The employer may act badly or even wrongly--by some standard-- but not unjustly. That is, applicants do not have a right to an equal chance at the benefits which belong solely to the employer. If, for example, a small private college wishes to hire a tennis coach and selects a female over a male-- just because she is female--the school is not being unfair to the equally or better qualified male candidate in Thomson's view. This is because the school "owns" the job and has a right to award it as it chooses.

Now some people, as Thomson acknowledges, may deny that anything is ever privately owned in this morally robust sense of ownership.[3] In any case, few persons would want to take this first "it's mine" route of justification for preferential treatment for women. At best it is applicable only in a very limited private sector. Furthermore, it automatically rules out any appeal to past employment injustices suffered by women, because discrimination against women in the private sector would also have been perfectly justifiable. Hence this view is incompatible with appeals to compensatory justice.

Merit Criterion with Sex Relevant

Those who adopt a merit principle assume that a just society will be one that awards jobs to those who by ability and training are best qualified to do them well. This is probably the most commonly accepted view in American culture.

One merit approach which considers sex to be relevant appeals to an "integration principle." This principle states that it is desirable to have diversity of sex in the work force, and for this reason sex is a relevant meritocratic consideration in hiring. Other things being roughly equal, the better qualified candidate for a job will be the one whose sex is the one needed to bring about the desired integration.

The integration principle is controversial; arguments to establish its validity are not obviously conclusive. It has been argued, for example, that it is desirable to have diversity of sex in educational settings because the variety of intellectual perspectives and life experiences it affords enriches the educational program. [4] But similar arguments might show that it is also desirable to have diversity of age, national origin, political affiliation, religion, etc. If all these were granted, one would then be faced with the difficult if not impossible task of deciding how to weigh each of these factors against the factor of sex in actual hiring situations.

But even if an integration principle is accepted, it has to be made more precise to be of any use in justifying preferential treatment. It must say how much integration or "mix" is desirable. Until it specifies this, we do not know how long it might be desirable to continue preferential treatment. Until one woman is hired in each occupation (that is, tokenism by occupation)? Until one woman is hired in each place of employment (that is, tokenism by factory, store, school, coaching staff, etc.)? Until a certain percentage is employed in each occupation or in each place of employment? If so, should this be a percentage proportional to the percentage of women in the total population, or in the candidate pool?

And, of course, the integration principle would not al-

ways support preferential treatment for women.   There are
situations where men would have to be added to a work situation in order to achieve integration, as is the case of secretaries in many businesses, male coaches for some women's
teams, etc.

A second justificatory attempt which considers sex to
be a relevant meritocratic job qualification is one that claims
that women can--because they are women--do certain jobs
better than men can.   A proponent of such a view might
claim, for example, that women are better teachers or better coaches, or at least that they are better teachers of
women or better coaches of women, or perhaps that they
are better role models for women.

A justification for preferential treatment on this ground
would require several things.   First, one would have to provide the empirical data to support the claim that women can
do certain jobs better.   Preference would then be justified
for those jobs only.   Further, one would have to allow the
justice of awarding preference to men in those areas where
their superior strengths could be demonstrated.   Of course,
if no superiority had been established but men had nevertheless been favored, then this preference would have been unjust.

Merit Criterion with Sex Irrelevant

A different approach is to espouse a merit distribution principle and count sex as irrelevant meritocratically.   This is by
far the most common stance and the perspective of most philosophers who have written on the subject.   Interestingly,
however, the position is adopted both by those who argue for
preferential treatment and by those who argue against it.
Both sides agree that jobs should be awarded to the best
qualified and that sex is irrelevant as a qualification.   They
are also agreed that in the past there has been discrimination, that is, that men have been awarded jobs because they
were men and not because their genuine qualifications were
superior.   They are further agreed that this was unjust.
One side argues, however, that this injustice warrants preferential treatment for women now, and the other side denies
this.

Those who argue for preferential treatment (or reverse
discrimination) do so by appealing to a principle of compensa-

tory justice. This principle specifies that if someone gets more than the distribution principle (in this case, the merit principle) warrants as his share, then this surplus should be taken from him and returned to the slighted party so that the scales of proper distribution are back in balance again. The obvious application of the principle being made is that men have robbed women of jobs in the past, and now these should be returned. Men have had preference in the past; now it is women's turn.

The other side, however, insists that if discrimination on the basis of sex is unjust, as both agree, then it is just as unfair to favor a woman for a job now as it was to favor a man at an earlier time. They grant that compensatory justice warrants returning a job to a woman by taking it from the precise man who has "taken" it from her unjustly. What they deny is that the principle warrants favoring women just because they are women and women generally have been wronged. The latter practice, they say, commits the same error that was committed earlier, and "two wrongs do not make a right."

One particularly interesting interchange was carried on by James Nickel, J. L. Cowan, and Alan Goldman. [5] Nickel finally decided that the inconsistency could be avoided if one admitted that sex was not the justifying basis for compensatory programs but could nevertheless be the administrative basis for them. [6] He sees a sufficiently high correlation between the wronged persons and their sex such that this characteristic can be used to administer compensatory programs without serious injustice. Persons are compensated because they have been injured, not because they are female. But since sex is highly correlated with injury and the former is easy to identify, the ease of administration warrants the use of sex in the compensatory programs.

But does this tactic solve the problem? It may remove a certain immediate inconsistency; but since it calls for the administration of a program on a basis which cannot be correlated precisely with the moral justification of it, new injustices are created, and for the very same reason as the original ones--because sex is used as a basis of judgments for which it really cannot provide a basis. Just as before, when maleness was erroneously supposed to designate the better qualified, so now femaleness is erroneously supposed to designate the injured. In fact, as Alan Goldman has argued, there is actually an inverse ratio between past discrimination and the beneficiaries of preferential hiring. This is so because the member of the preferred group to whom the job will go will be--still assuming merit criteria--the best qualified individual of that group. And most likely that best qualified individual is--as attested to by her qualifications--the one of the group who has suffered the least from past discrimination. [7]

In order to illustrate further the problems with the compensatory approach, let us suppose that Jane Doe has been discriminated against in employment because of her sex. A principle of compensatory justice will, without problems it seems, justify her reinstatement in that particular job at the expense of the employer and the man who benefited by her injury. With the blanket preferential practice under consideration, however, the compensatory principle is applied very differently. That application calls for an employer (not necessarily the offending employer) to give preferential treatment to any woman (not necessarily the offended one) at the expense of some man (not necessarily the beneficiary of the previous unjust act). This, surely, is a strange application of the compensatory principle. The principle as generally accepted calls for reimbursing the injured party in direct proportion to the injury and at the expense only of the wrongdoer, and perhaps the beneficiary. [8]

Are there ways, however, to apply the principle more loosely? The facts of the case are that many women over a long period of time have suffered employment injustices because they were women. There is no way to compensate these precise persons nor to exact the reparation from the ones who caused their injury or who directly benefited from it. One suggested loosening of the principle of reparation is to compensate the descendants of the injured parties. [9] But even if it were felt that the principle could be extended in this way, there are still problems. After all, the descendants of the injured woman as well as the descendants of the benefited man will be both male and female. Hence this interpretation of the principle could not justify the practice of giving job preference now to females generally at the expense of males generally.

Of course, one could disregard past generations and consider only those of employable age at the present. But here again the principle cannot be applied in a fair and reasonable way to members of whole groups because those who have suffered most will benefit least and those who have suffered least will benefit most. For example, a 50-year-old woman who has suffered more from discriminatory practices in employment will benefit less from preferential treatment (because of fewer remaining employable years) than will a 20-year-old female just entering the job market. On the other hand, the 20-year-old male will suffer more than the 50-year-old male, who has benefited more. This is not to say that the 20-year-old male has not profited from past practices at all nor that the 20-year-old woman has not suffered at all. It is merely to say that when one considers the relative weights--which in order to apply the principle properly it seems one should--then a compensatory justice principle is not reasonably applicable as a justification for reverse discrimination in the form under consideration.

Some would argue, however, that what is being done with a policy of preferential hiring is repaying an injured group, not individuals, by means of giving jobs to some of the group's members, and hence that the above objections do not hold. On this interpretation, one must first decide in what sense women constitute a group. Boris Bittker has argued that unlike Indian tribes, for example, there is no such black group to be a recipient of reparations. [10] The same probably holds true for women. Second, one must ask in what sense discrimination against individuals has injured the group. And further, one must justify making reparations to the group through its individual members, especially by means of jobs.

These waters are poorly charted, [11] but it would seem that the injury suffered by a group, assuming that there is such, when some of its members are discriminated against because of their membership in that group, is not of the same magnitude or quality as the injury to individuals. Thus, to try to compensate the group by giving job preference to its members--even assuming the appropriateness of the attempt-- is unjustified. The injury to the group that is being compensated is not as great as the injury to the individuals who will suffer from the reverse discrimination.

Need Rather Than Merit

Having considered merit appeals of types which do and do not treat sex as a relevant characteristic, we turn now to the arguments that are based on a need distribution criterion, or what is sometimes called an equality of result approach.

The battle lines are not so neatly drawn here, probably because American society has not generally acknowledged that its benefits were to be distributed on a need basis. That is, Americans have generally felt that jobs should go to those best prepared to do them well (merit) rather than to those who are poorest or most disadvantaged (need), i.e., those whose low status needs to be raised to the point of equality of result. Nevertheless, there are writers who point to data of the following sort when they argue that women deserve preferential treatment in the employment arena: The median salary for women is only 57 percent of that for men.[12] Many women are heads of households with heavy financial responsibilities. Our culture has discouraged women from preparing for certain jobs, hence they are not prepared to compete. And so on.

The only way that women will be able to catch up, these people argue, will be if preferential treatment in employment is given to women. The writers sometimes speak of their "catch up" programs as "compensatory." Perhaps the use of the same term "compensatory," which was employed above in connection with appeals to compensatory justice, has masked the subtle shift in justification that has taken place. The earlier appeals were for a correction of past injustice which abused a merit distribution. These latter appeals are to a related but distinct sense of compensation which is roughly characterized as "making up for a disability or deficit." This latter appeal is not for a corrective in a case where a distribution principle has been violated, but rather for a change in the distribution principle itself. Jobs should be awarded to those most in need of them. The notion at work is similar to that employed in some sports where players are given a handicap advantage.

Let us be very clear about this distinction. With the earlier appeal to a principle of compensatory justice, it is still assumed that jobs should ordinarily be awarded proportionally to merit. Since people in their commerce with one another have violated this principle, it is claimed, the injured parties deserve a corrective--in this case job preference for a period of time with the eventual restoration of a balance between reward and merit. There need never be a balance of reward to need. With a "catch up" principle, on the other hand, there is no appeal to past violation of the merit principle. Rather the merit principle itself is rejected, and it is claimed that a just distribution of the goods of society is distribution according to need.[13]

If the above characterization is correct, then, although "catch up" appeals avoid the problems discussed earlier, they call for embracing a different conception of distributive justice. And our society must be viewed as unjust, not because it has allowed unjust acts of discrimination against persons because of their sex, a characteristic which is meritocratically irrelevant, but because the criterion for job distribution should never have been merit in the first place. Without trying to assess the acceptability of a need distribution principle, let us merely examine some of the implications of accepting it. In particular, what would be the implications for the preferential treatment question?

Need Criterion with Sex Irrelevant

As with the merit principle, one could take either the stance that sex is relevant or the one that it is irrelevant in ascertaining distribution according to need. If sex is irrelevant, then it cannot reasonably be used as a basis for preferential treatment. If sex does not designate the most needy, then to treat one sex preferentially is to act unjustly by the very principle which is being invoked because in some cases it would be "catching up" persons who were not disadvantaged over those that were, as would happen any time a privileged woman was hired in preference to a needy male.

Need Criterion with Sex Relevant

On the other hand, if one were to take the stand that sex is relevant and that women should receive preferential treatment, one would be claiming that by nature or by circumstance women are deficient or disadvantaged and that women are universally or generally the needier sex. Although some may wish to try to demonstrate women's inferior status, it would be difficult and also probably undesirable to try to argue for natural deficiency. Most claims, therefore, are to a circumstantial deficiency. It is claimed that women have been held back, or mistreated, and are therefore disadvantaged.

It may be tempting to point to women's disadvantaged position as warrant for preferential treatment, but this approach seems to be as fraught with difficulties as the other approaches. This is so because one must first accept the principle that jobs should be distributed on the basis of need, and then one must show that this need is so correlated with sex that the neediest candidate for a job will always be a woman; but this surely cannot be done. Although unemployment figures are higher for women and their median income is lower, sex surely does not in any individual hiring instance designate the needier job candidate.

Promoting Future Justice

In discussing the merit criterion, we rejected reverse discrimination because 1) the individuals whom it would favor are not those who most deserve compensation according to the merit criterion, and 2) it would wrong innocent men by denying them the rewards of merit. Consideration (1) all but nullified the major moral reason in favor of reverse discrimination, and consideration (2) provided a potent moral reason against it. Mary Anne Warren has suggested a new reason in favor of reverse discrimination while offering an ingenious argument to nullify the potent moral reason against it. [14] The new reason in favor of reverse discrimination is that it will help destroy practices which subtly perpetuate sexist discrimination, thus promoting future justice. The argument to defuse the moral reason against (a limited form of) reverse discrimination is that it does not lower the rewards of individual men below what these rewards would be in a society which was just according to the merit criterion. Let us examine both these arguments in more detail.

Warren's new reason in favor of weak reverse discrimination in the form of quotas is the claim that it will ultimately lead to an elimination of all sexual discrimination. This will result, she thinks, because employers will be faced with the alternatives of meeting their quotas of women employees either by getting rid of subtle forms of discrimination against women or by practicing a more blatant reverse discrimination against men. Since the latter is so distasteful, she thinks that society will choose the former and will consequently move toward a more just merit system. Ultimately, jobs will be awarded according to genuine merit, not according to pseudo-merit skewed by what she calls "secondary sexism," which she defines as "comprising all those actions, attitudes and policies which, while not using sex itself as a reason for discrimination, do involve sex-correlated factors or criteria and do result in unfair impact upon (certain) women." An example of secondary sexism would be preferring the job candidate who has a family to support.

Since this is usually the male candidate, the practice has the effect of discriminating against women, even though the characteristic of "having a family to support" is itself sex-neutral.

Warren's defusing argument claims that her quota proposal is not unjust to individual men who "lose out." This is so because the quotas are set according to the numbers of women that could be expected to quality on merit if secondary sexism were eliminated. Thus, by definition, the male candidates have the same chance at a job as they would have if society were just. Thus, how can it be said that they are treated unjustly? This defusing argument makes sense statistically. Obviously, if employers were to eliminate secondary sexism and if the quotas have been based on correct estimates, then by definition the quotas could be met without injustice to individual men. But Warren seems to have the cart before the horse. In her reasoning in favor of reverse discrimination, she assumes that reverse discrimination in the form of quotas will cause the elimination of sexism; whereas in fact it is only if the quota is met because sexism has been eliminated that the defusing claim can be made. This is so because if the quota is met through the alternative of blatant reverse discrimination instead of through the elimination of secondary sexism, then individual men will be treated unjustly. The victim of blatant reverse discrimination cannot be told that his chances are what they would have been in a just society, because this is not so. His chances in a society free of sexism would have been greater.[15] Warren's goal is a worthy one, but the means used to reach it is unjust, at least to the extent that it allows blatant reverse discrimination.

Unjust but Justified

It is possible, of course, to admit that reverse discrimination is unjust because it violates a principle of equality (where sex is irrelevant meritocratically) and yet to maintain that such a practice is morally justifiable by appealing to other generally accepted principles. Tom Beauchamp, for example, argues that this is the case.[16] The other principles that he appeals to are those of compensatory justice and utility. He claims that women have been mistreated and continue to suffer from invidious discrimination, and further, that the only effective means of eliminating some of this is through reverse discrimination. Thus, reverse discrimination is morally justifiable.

By way of illustration, suppose that conference rules allow only 13 players to dress for tournament play. Two players are equally qualified for the thirteenth spot. It would be unjust to select either over the other, given the usual criteria for selection. But if dressing only twelve players could jeopardize the effectiveness of the team, then a principle of utility could justify the unfairness of choosing one player over the other. Or, if one player were deserving of compensation for some past action, then a principle of compensatory justice could justify awarding her or him the spot. This example is intended to illustrate Beauchamp's claim that although a practice may violate one principle of justice, it may well be justified by appeal to other standards. Specifically, reverse discrimination violates the principle of equality but fulfills those of compensatory justice and utility. Beauchamp sets forth factual evidence of discrimination against women that he feels will yield only if met with reverse discrimination. The social value of eliminating the discrimination and its effects on women is sufficient to justify reverse discrimination, even though reverse discrimination violates a principle of equality. The practice has social utility and serves a compensatory function.

Beauchamp's argument in favor of reverse discrimination is probably the strongest one considered here. Its weaknesses lie in its claim that the practice will fulfill the requirements of compensatory justice and utility. Would reverse discrimination in hiring really compensate women in a manner which even roughly approximates the degrees to which they have been disadvantaged? It would surely benefit women generally, but the individuals benefited most would no doubt be those who have suffered least, as was noted earlier in this chapter. Thus it is highly questionable that an appeal to compensatory justice will justify the practice since that principle calls for rectifying injuries in a manner commensurate with the injury.

The appeal to a principle of utility is also problematic. The goal of a society in which women are not disadvantaged is unquestionably desirable. But the claim that reverse discrimination is the only means or even the best means of achieving the goal is questionable. Settling questions of utility is always difficult because of the necessary appeal to factual matters and predictions about the future. No definitive answer will be attempted here, but it will be noted that the negative consequences of reverse discrimination must be taken into account as well as the positive ones. If the negative outweigh the positive, then the principle of utility argues against the practice rather than for it. Some negative consequences include the resentment of males, the loss of self-esteem in some favored females, the loss of efficiency due to the inferior performance of the lesser qualified candidates, etc. In light of such negative elements, it is certainly questionable whether utility appeals can really justify the injustice.

What Is Fair?

We have considered the major options for justifying preferential treatment and have found all of them subject to serious criticism. Most readers will find this a frustrating conclusion because it seems so obvious that women have been discriminated against, that they continue to be discriminated against, that the effects of this discrimination linger on, and further, that all this is surely unfair. If preferential treatment for women is not fair, what is fair?

First, it needs to be made clear that not one of the objections raised against preferential treatment for women in any way speaks against equal treatment for them. Rather, they support the cause of equal treatment. This is so because what was objectionable about preferential treatment was that it assumed that one's sex can be a fair basis for discrimination. But if sex cannot play such a role, this means that neither should the male sex receive preference. Sex must be irrelevant and the sexes treated equally. But women are not yet being afforded such equal treatment. Therefore, as a minimum, it is fair that steps be taken to insure non-discrimination in employment. It would be fair to impose heavy penalties on those who continue to discriminate and to give significant compensation to individuals who have been discriminated against.

The sorts of subtle discrimination which operate before one gets to the actual hiring office can likewise be eliminated. In athletics, provision for equal athletic experiences for young girls, equal opportunity for admission to educational programs, and equal encouragement to compete and excel are examples of other levels at which equality must also be insured. Nearer to the hiring stage it is essential that women have an equal chance at learning about job openings and an equal opportunity to meet the people that do the hiring. All of these are the sorts of handicaps that affirmative action programs are designed to counterbalance, and none call for reverse discrimination.

In addition, it should be remembered that merit, as
generally understood, includes not only actual training and
experience but also ability, which means potential for producing if given an opportunity for training and experience.
A wise employer naturally has a preference for an employee
who can begin producing immediately, but the employer is
also wise if she or he can recognize undeveloped talent which
can be cultivated with a minimum investment to produce over
the long term. Thus, it need not be a violation of merit criteria to select candidates with less training and experience if
there is evidence that they have potential which has gone undeveloped because of lack of opportunity due to discrimination.
Since this is very often the case with women, it is not discriminatory to look at the individual women and to take into
account their individual histories. In fact, this is precisely
what constitutes fairness, it seems. The candidate should
not be looked at as male or female and assumed to have
other qualities automatically accompanying that characteristic. It should not be automatically assumed, for example,
that a male candidate for a coaching position is inherently a
more aggressive competitor than a female candidate. Nor
should it be automatically assumed that a female candidate
has undeveloped talent just because she is female. Nevertheless, it is not unfair to be alert for the possible presence
of these characteristics in an individual.

Although progress toward something resembling an
equal result will no doubt be slower by means of a non-
discriminatory policy, surely the long term advantages are
greater than by pursuing preferential means. One thereby
not only acts fairly, but also avoids male backlash and preserves female self-esteem. Productivity and efficiency are
maintained for the benefit of all while still moving the disadvantaged forward. And the ultimate achievement of the desired goal of a non-discriminatory society, when reached,
will not have been hampered by policies which, though well-
intended, are themselves discriminatory.

All that has been said about these issues generally
also applies specifically to women in athletic positions.
Women here have been discriminated against and are at a
disadvantage in seeking posts. A book which is particularly
helpful on this question is Equality in Sport for Women, edited by Patricia Gaedelmann, et al., and published by the
American Alliance for Health, Physical Education, and Recreation.[17] It notes that the new laws, which are improving
the sports situation for women generally, have not always

improved the status of women in the administrative positions. There has been a sudden growth of women's athletics, so the coaching market is increasing, but the job market is working more to the advantage of the men. This is the case because men have had the opportunity to be both high-level competitors and well-qualified coaches, while women have not. Thus men can present better merit qualifications than women who have often served merely as volunteer coaches of semi-competitive teams. The authors note that this is particularly true where male and female athletics programs have merged. The female coach often finds herself in the assistant coach role.[18] The same thing is happening with regard to athletic director jobs. The women often end up as the assistant athletic directors when departments are combined.

The AAHPER book also provides an interesting checklist whereby one can assess the fairness of employment practices in an institution. A sample of the questions follows:

1. Are men and women given equal opportunities to apply for open positions?
   a. Is news of vacancies as readily available to both women and men, i.e., are jobs advertised in places where women would have easy access to them as well as in places where men would have such access?

2. Are men and women paid the same salaries for essentially the same work for teaching and coaching?

3. Do both sexes have equal opportunity to assume coaching of supervision duties (including selling and taking tickets, keeping score, conducting open recreation programs, etc.) for extra pay?

4. Are men and women given the same decision-making power regarding the conduct of physical education and athletic programs?

5. Do men and women in physical education and athletics have comparable teaching loads and/or released time?

6. Are both sexes represented in administrative positions for the programs?

7. Are men and women given similar contracts with regard to length of appointment, fringe benefits, etc.?

8. Are monies for professional travel, coaches clinics, scouting trips, recruitment, etc. distributed equally between men and women?

9. Are secretarial help and clerical assistance available equally to men and women teachers and coaches?

10. Do both sexes have equal opportunities for teaching at preferred hours of the day?

11. Do men and women have equal opportunities to schedule their practice and competitive events at the preferred times?

12. Do both sexes receive the same fringe benefits with regard to insurance, retirement contributions, etc.?

13. Are men and women given comparably sized, located, and equipped offices?

14. Are numbers of men and women distributed equitably throughout the professional ranks?

15. Do both sexes receive promotion and tenure after like years, performances, etc.?

16. Do men and women both have access to the same number of support staff in their positions, e.g., assistant coaches, trainers, information directors, teacher aides, student teachers, graduate assistants, managers, custodial help?

17. Do women and men share equally in the "extra duties" expected of school personnel, e.g., committees, supervision?

18. Are men and women given equal opportunities to assume leadership positions within the department?

19. Do both sexes have equal access to such fringe benefits as coaching or teaching uniforms, use of school owned vehicles, access to recreational facilities, passes to athletic contests, membership in golf and country clubs, discounts on clothing and sporting goods, etc.?

20. Does the institution have an affirmative action plan? Is it available for public examination? Has the institution activated this plan?[19]

The range of questions points up very clearly that fairness in employment reaches far beyond the point of just obtaining a job. Fairness also touches an employee at many other levels. The basic issue remains the same, however. Discrimination is unfair. What is fair is equal treatment.

The foregoing discussion has been directed toward the moral issue of fairness. A few words can now be added on legal and practical matters. There are a variety of legal regulations concerning non-discrimination, the major ones being the Equal Pay Act, Title VII, Title IX, and Executive Order 11246 as amended by 11375. Different government agencies are entrusted with the job of enforcing compliance with the regulations. An excellent summary of the regulations, compliance agencies, complaint procedures, and court histories are given in the AAHPER book previously cited.

Some of the regulations not only work for non-discrimination but are also affirmative in nature along the lines mentioned earlier in this chapter. Unfortunately, the backlog of complaint cases in some of the agencies has rendered the regulations ineffective.

The reader is also referred to the organization SPRINT, the athletic branch of WEAL (Women's Equity Action League). The organization provides information and assistance to women and to institutions who have concerns about fair practices in athletics. They operate a tollfree hotline (800-424-5162), and their address is 806 15th Street, N.W. Suite 822, Washington, D.C. 20005.[20]

NOTES

1. Several important books devoted to this debate are Barry R. Gross (ed.), Reverse Discrimination (Buffalo, N.Y.: Prometheus Books, 1977. This work contains a choice selection of essays and an extensive bibliography); Marshall Cohen, et al. (eds.), Equality and Preferential Treatment (Princeton, N.J.: Princeton University Press, 1977); Barry R. Gross, Discrimination in Reverse: Is Turnabout Fair Play? (New York: New York University Press, 1978); and Alan H. Goldman,

Justice and Reverse Discrimination (Princeton, N.J.: Princeton University Press, 1979).

2. Judith Jarvis Thomson, "Preferential Hiring," Philosophy and Public Affairs, 2 (1973), 369-374. It should be noted that much of the literature discusses this issue in terms of both race and sex. The sources cited in this essay may be discussing it with respect to either or both.

3. Ibid., p. 371. "If anyone thinks that I don't own the apples, or, more generally, that no one really or fully owns anything, he will regard what I shall say in the remainder of this section, in which I talk about what may be done with what is privately owned, as an idle academic exercise. I'll simply ask that anyone who does think this be patient: we will come to what is publicly owned later."

4. Such a claim is made in a journal of the American Association of University Professors. Marx Wartofsky, et al., "Affirmative Action in Higher Education: A Report by the Council Commission on Discrimination," AAUP Bulletin, 59 (1973), 180-181.

5. James W. Nickel, "Discrimination and Morally Relevant Characteristics," Analysis, 32 (1972), 113-114; J. L. Cowan, "Inverse Discrimination," Analysis, 33 (1972), 10-12; Nickel, "Classification by Race in Compensatory Programs," Ethics, 84 (1974), 146-150; Nickel, "Should Reparations Be to Individuals or to Groups?" Analysis, 34 (1974), 154-160; Alan H. Goldman, "Reparations to Individuals or Groups?" Analysis, 35 (1975), 168-170.

6. Nickel, "Classification," pp. 147-148.

7. Goldman, op. cit., p. 169.

8. See George Sher, "Justifying Reverse Discrimination in Employment" in Cohen, op. cit., pp. 49-60. Sher would say that this misses the point. The issue is not whether the male who is discriminated against is responsible for the original injury to females but whether unless reverse discrimination is practiced he will benefit more from its effects on his competitors. He will benefit more unless he is restrained and they given the edge, because he will use his advantage to get the job they would otherwise have gotten. Sher has in mind here a notion of compensation which is different from reparations, which are backward-looking. Reverse discrimination would, on Sher's view, be forward-looking. It would be justified on grounds of neutralizing competitive disadvantages. Sher proceeds, however, to say that although many blacks suf-

fer from such disabilities, that this is far less true
of women. He also concludes by saying, "Strictly
speaking, however, the account offered here does not
allow us to speak this way of either group. If the
point of reverse discrimination is to compensate for
competitive disadvantages caused by past discrimination, it will be justified in favor of only those group
members whose abilities have actually been reduced;
and it would be most implausible to suppose that every
black (or every woman) has been affected in this way"
(p. 59).

9. Boris I. Bittker, The Case for Black Reparations (New
   York: Vintage, 1973), pp. 91-104. Bittker sees no
   problem in a reparations program which could identify
   as beneficiaries the children who had been forced to
   go to inferior segregated schools, for example. Nor
   would there be any conceptual difficulty in compensating
   the descendants of a deceased student. He does, however, see difficulties arising if one must resort to racial classifications in order to identify recipients.

10. Ibid., pp. 71-85, especially p. 75.

11. See the Bittker pages cited above and also a more gen-
    eral discussion: Michael D. Bayles, "Axinn, Kant and
    Rights of Collective Persons," in Human Rights:
    Amintaphil I, ed. Ervin H. Pollack (Buffalo, N.Y.:
    Jay Stewart Publishers, 1971), pp. 411-415. Also
    Paul W. Taylor, "Reverse Discrimination and Com-
    pensatory Justice," Analysis, 33 (1973), 177-182.

12. Robert Livernash, Comparable Worth: Issues and Al-
    ternatives (Washington, D.C.: Equal Employment Ad-
    visory Council, 1980), p. 38. This work quotes U.S.
    Department of Labor figures, noting that the gap is
    widening. In 1955 the women's median full-time earn-
    ings were 64 percent of men's but had fallen to only
    57 percent in 1973.

13. I shall not try to define the term "need" precisely.
    Very roughly, I mean a criterion of distribution aimed
    at an equal result. It would thus call for giving more
    to those who are farthest behind or most disadvantaged.
    For a general discussion of merit versus need criteria
    see Joel Feinberg, Social Justice (Englewood Cliffs,
    N.J.: Prentice-Hall, 1973), pp. 107-119.

14. Mary Anne Warren, "Secondary Sexism and Quota Hir-
    ing." Philosophy and Public Affairs, 6 (1977), 240-
    261.

15. Warren's "primary reason for weak quotas is to increase
    present fairness of competition" (op. cit., p. 259).

She recognizes that individual departures from a merit principle might even be doubled on her proposal. "But since it would no longer be women who are repeatedly disadvantaged by those departures, the overall fairness of the competition would be improved. The average long-term chances of success of both men and women candidates would more closely approximate those they would enjoy in an ongoing just society" (p. 256). It is evident that Warren's appeal is to long-term statistical chances, whereas our objection is based on short-term cases. Surely, however, it would be small comfort to tell the victims of discrimination that maybe somewhere down the way things will even out for them--or at least for some of their fellows--and therefore that they have not been treated unfairly.

16. Tom L. Beauchamp, "The Justification of Reverse Discrimination," in Social Ethics, eds. Thomas A. Mappes and Jane S. Zembaty (New York: McGraw-Hill Book Company, 1977), pp. 183-193.

17. Patricia Gaedelmann, et al., Equality in Sport for Women (Washington, D.C.: American Alliance for Health, Physical Education, and Recreation, 1977).

18. Christine Grant, "What Does Equality Mean?" in Gaedelmann, p. 18.

19. Patricia Gaedelmann, "How Can I Determine if Equality Exists?" in Gaedelmann, pp. 27-28. These questions are reprinted here with the kind permission of the American Alliance for Health, Physical Education, Recreation, and Dance, 1900 Association Drive, Reston, VA 22091.

20. The author wishes to acknowledge the assistance of the National Endowment for the Humanities in her study of this general question through a Summer Stipend in 1973 and a Summer Seminar with William Blackstone at the University of Georgia in 1975. Valuable editorial assistance on this essay was provided by Betsy Postow.

SUGGESTIONS FOR FURTHER READING

In addition to the works listed in the notes, the following are suggested:

Bayles, Michael D. "Compensatory Reverse Discrimination in Hiring," Social Theory and Practice, 2 (1973), 301 ff.

Black, Virginia. "The Erosion of Legal Principles in the Creation of Legal Principles," Ethics, 84 (1974), 93 ff.

Blackstone, William T. "Compensatory Justice and Affirmative Action," Proceedings of the Catholic Philosophical Association, 49 (1975), 218 ff.

_____. "Reverse Discrimination and Compensatory Justice," Social Theory and Practice, 3 (1975), 253 ff.

_____, and Robert D. Heslep, eds. Social Justice and Preferential Treatment: Women and Racial Minorities in Education and Business. Athens: University of Georgia Press, 1977.

Feinberg, Joel. "Noncomparative Justice," Philosophical Review, 83 (1974), 297 ff.

Fried, Marlene G. "In Defense of Preferential Hiring," Philosophical Forum, 5 (1973), 309 ff.

Goldman, Alan H. "Affirmative Action," Philosophy and Public Affairs, 5 (1976), 178 ff.

Hare, Robert P. Affirmative Action in Higher Education: A Selected and Annotated Bibliography. Monticello, Ill.: Council of Planning Librarians, 1977.

Held, Virginia. "Reasonable Progress and Self-Respect," The Monist, 57 (Jan. 1973), 12 ff.

Katzner, Louis. "Is the Favoring of Women and Blacks in Employment and Educational Opportunities Justified?" in Joel Feinberg and Hyman Gross, eds. Philosophy of Law. Encino, Calif.: Dickenson, 1975. 291 ff.

McGary, Howard, Jr. "Reparations and 'Inverse Discrimination,'" Dialogue, 17 (1974), 8 ff.

Martin, Michael. "Pedagogical Arguments for Preferential Hiring and Tenuring of Women Teachers in the University," Philosophical Forum, 5 (1973), 325 ff.

Newton, Lisa H. "Reverse Discrimination as Unjustified," Ethics, 83 (1973), 308 ff.

Sher, George. "Reverse Discrimination, the Future, and the Past," Ethics, 90 (1979), 81 ff.

Shiner, Roger A. "Individuals, Groups, and Inverse Discrimination," Analysis, 33 (1973), 185 ff.

Simon, Robert. "Preferential Hiring: A Reply to Judith Jarvis Thomson," Philosophy and Public Affairs, 3 (1974), 312 ff.

Thalberg, Irving. "Reverse Discrimination and the Future," Philosophical Forum, 5 (1973), 294 ff.

Vetterling, Mary. "Some Common Sense Notes on Preferential Hiring," Philosophical Forum, 5 (1973), 320 ff.

Wasserstrom, Richard. "The University and the Case for Preferential Treatment," Philosophical Quarterly, 13 (1976), 165 ff.

QUESTIONS

(1) Suppose a private employer uses the "all's fair because it's mine" approach to justify his own discrimination against women in employment.

a) Construct the most plausible argument you can either to support the employer's position or to undermine the employer's position. If necessary, review the "Background on Arguments" section of the General Introduction.

b) For each premise of the argument which you have just constructed, say whether you agree with it or disagree with it, and why.

c) For each statement which is supposed to be supported by previous statements in the argument, say how strongly the previous statements support it. (Each statement which begins with the word "therefore" is supposed to be supported by previous statements.)

(2) a) Construct the most plausible argument you can either for or against the view that being a woman is, in itself, a relevant job qualification for some coaching jobs.

b) Evaluate the argument which you have just constructed. Follow the directions given in question #1 (b) and (c).

(3) a) In your own words, explain why Heizer believes that a program of preferential treatment does not satisfy the compensatory principle.

b) What is the strongest objection you can think of to Heizer's position?

c) How would Heizer reply to that objection?

d) In your view, would that reply be satisfactory? Why or why not?

(4) In your view, does it make sense to compensate women as a group for past discrimination? Why or why not?

(5) In your view, do widening gaps between employment "results" of men and women of the sort cited in note #12 justify preferential treatment? Why or why not? Would Heizer agree or disagree with you? Why?

(6) Assume that the qualifications for a given job are not correlated with sex, and that 30 percent of the applicants for the job are female. Suppose that there is a quota which requires that 30 percent of the many employees who will be hired be female.

a) According to Warren, as reported by Heizer, this quota would not lower a male applicant's chances of being hired below what his chances would have been in a society with no sex discrimination at all. In your own words, explain Warren's reasoning.

b) In your own words, explain why Heizer disagrees with Warren.

c) In your view, what is the correct answer? Why?

(7) a) Construct the most plausible argument you can to support Beauchamp's view that preferential treatment programs will bring about results which are important enough to justify the unfairness which they create.

b) Evaluate the argument which you have just constructed. Follow the directions given in question #1 (b) and (c).

(8) Do you agree with Heizer that affirmative action of the sort she describes can bring about fair treatment of women in athletics-related employment? Why or why not?

(9) What else would you like to discuss from Heizer's essay?

SECTION C:

Fairness to Female Athletes in
Media Coverage

7. SPORTS, SEX-EQUALITY, AND THE MEDIA

Raymond A. Belliotti

Alternative concepts to the more traditional notions of the
role of women in society have flourished in recent years and
promise to do so in the future. Among the more laudable
victories of this movement has been an increased awareness
of the right of women to participate in athletic activities.
This chapter is concerned with a corollary issue: Should
female and male athletes receive equal media coverage in
recognition of their respective achievements? To answer
this question other issues must be examined: Why do and
why should the various media cover athletic events? Why
in the past has coverage of women athletes been less extensive than that afforded men athletes? Are the moral notions
of desert and entitlement relevant to this discussion? Does
unequal media coverage violate the rights of women? Is any
alternative proposal both practical and more fair than the
status quo?

I. Basic Distinctions

Engaging in athletics can result in two major kinds of rewards: basic rewards such as enjoyment, improved health,
an increase in self-respect which occurs when one recognizes
that she has done her best, the stimulation that occurs when
one tests her skills against opponents and works with teammates to achieve common goals, lessons of sportsmanship
which often accompany the thrill of victory and the agony of
defeat, and an increase in self-confidence which occurs when
one perceives oneself as physically competent; and scarce
rewards such as fame, glory, money, and national or international recognition. [1]

96

Athletic activities can be classified into four main
types: 1) recreational activities, where the primary motive
of the participants is the attainment of basic rewards, where
there is no or little spectator attendance and media attention,
and where the level of skill need not be very high.   Sandlot
games, stickball, intramurals, and non-league bowling, golf,
and tennis are all examples of recreational activities; 2) competitive activities, where organized leagues are accompanied
by a small, although often significant, number of spectators
and limited local media coverage, and where the relative
level of the skill of the participants begins to increase vis-
à-vis their non-participating peers.   High school sports,
little-league baseball, pee-wee football, league bowling, organized tennis, and tournament play in all sports are examples of competitive activities; 3) quasi-professional activities,
where spectator and media interest is very high, where participants have a very high level of skill, and where scarce
rewards are sought.   The Olympic games and big time college football and basketball are examples of quasi-professional
activities; and 4) professional activities, where the level of
skill and spectator attendance is highest, extensive and often
insufferable media attention is lavished upon the participants
and the events, and where the best participants are rewarded
handsomely with high salaries and national or international
recognition.   Games sponsored by the National Basketball
Association, the National Football League, the Professional
Golf Association, and so forth are all examples of professional activities.

Obviously, not all athletic activities can be classified
easily into one of the four main types.   Small time collegiate
wrestling and football, for example, would seem to fall somewhere between competitive and quasi-professional activity, for
the level of skill of the participants and the degree of spectator and media attention are all higher than they are in high
school athletics, but lower than they are in big-time collegiate
football.   It is helpful to imagine a continuum which classifies
athletic activities on the basis of the level of skill of the participants, the extent of media, advertising, and spectator attention which the event commands, the motives of the participants for engaging in the event, and the extent to which
scarce rewards accompany success in the event.   On one extreme of the continuum--purely recreational activity--we can
imagine a small child throwing a baseball against a brick
wall and retrieving the ground balls that result; on the other
extreme of the continuum--purely professional activity--we

can imagine an adult who is employed by a professional sports team and who engages in the activity only because of the financial remuneration or national attention which accompanies his or her participation. Every athletic activity will fall somewhere within the continuum, although many will not correspond exactly to any of the four main paradigms described above. The Olympic games, which have been classified as quasi-professional, may well be classified as professional, at least for participants of those countries which subsidize their athletes and which further reward victors with additional privileges upon their return to the homeland.

II. Media Attention and Allocation

Why do the media cover certain athletic events but not others? The sports departments of newspapers are limited by considerations of space, while sports directors of television and radio stations are limited by considerations of time. They claim to cover events on the basis of perceived reader or viewer interest. This interest is gauged by the number of spectators who attend the event, the level of skill of the participants, and whatever explicit requests that readers and viewers have made in response to previous coverage. Presently, the various media make no effort to parcel out space and time on the basis of inculcating certain societal values or on the basis of compensating for past deprivations.

It seems clear that women athletes have received less media coverage for a variety of reasons. First, they are generally at a biological disadvantage when competing in such popular sports as football, baseball, basketball, and tennis in which upper-body strength or size is of paramount importance.[2] Even the acceptance of an extreme feminist ideology cannot alter the fact that the most highly skilled males competing in such sport are vastly superior to the most highly skilled females. Second, the sports in which the most highly skilled females have a biological advantage--such as balance beam gymnastics and floor exercises which emphasize the importance of flexibility and balance--have been of minor interest to sports fans. Third, society has until recently regarded athletics as being somewhat inappropriate for females. It has been thought that women who engage in such activities are unfeminine and risk permanent injury to vital female organs. Moreover, there is an aesthetic aspect to the problem. The traditional model of feminine beauty has emphasized a body-type (36-24-36) which is not generally found

among the better female athletes. Although it is clear that
such proportions are not generally possessed by many women
at all--athletic or not--it has been thought that athletic conditioning only serves to increase the gap between the desired
model and the female sports enthusiast. Finally, there is
the suspicion that female athletes are "freaks" who must suffer from a hormonal imbalance or from homosexual desires.
All of these factors have no doubt contributed to the relative
lack of spectator interest in women's athletics. This, in
turn, has resulted in relatively little media coverage of these
events.

But such rationales must be questioned. Do the media
cover female athletes less because there is less fan interest
in their activities, or is there less fan interest in their activities because the media cover female athletes less? Surely,
at least to some degree, media attention leads rather than
follows spectator interest. Super Bowl Sunday mania is the
best example of this phenomenon. For decades prior to the
first Super Bowl a National Football League championship
game which purported to determine the "world" champion of
professional football existed. The emergence of the American
Football League provided another such "world" championship
contest. Both games held significant fan interest, but once
the winners of the two contests played each other in the first
Super Bowl the real hoopla began. Advertisers, public relations hucksters, and the media, in actions which have almost
conspiratorial undertones, "tub-thumped" the Super Bowl into
an event of heroic proportions. For weeks prior to the playing of the game we are all bombarded with newspaper, television, and radio coverage so lavish and extensive that media
coverage of World War II almost pales in comparison. Para-
doxically, with few exceptions, the games themselves have
been dismal and dreary events. Super Bowl pageantry far
exceeded original fan interest, although now the event has
become in a short time almost an American tradition.

It also seems clear the new conceptions of possible
female roles in society have served to dilute the force of
many of the other reasons cited above which purport to justify less media coverage of female athletes. Olga Korbut
and Nellie Kim have stirred increased interest in the "feminine" sport of gymnastics; women's bodybuilding and power-
lifting are enjoying a surge of participant and spectator interest, as is women's collegiate basketball; women's long-
distance running has become extremely popular and downright
chic; and much the same can be said for female participation

in racquet sports and swimming. Societal perceptions of female participation in sports have changed radically; the traditional model of the beautiful female body may be changing, although somewhat more slowly; and female participation in almost every sport has surged remarkably.

Several points emerge from this discussion: a) changing societal perceptions of the roles of women augur a trend toward more female participation in sports; b) it is too facile for the media to claim that they simply follow fan interest in determining their sports coverage since where there has been media coverage of female athletes increased fan interest has often followed; and c) the media cannot claim to be value-neutral in their approach, since by refusing to allow extensive coverage to female athletes they would in effect be reinforcing traditional societal perceptions and this is as much a value-laden decision as would be the choice to pursue an activist path which would reinforce changing societal perceptions of women.

III. Why Should Media Coverage Be Equal?

Jane English has argued in the following manner that women athletes have a justified demand for equal media coverage and prize money:[3]

An Argument from Self-Respect

(1) Members of disadvantaged groups identify strongly with each other's successes and failures.
(2) If women do not attain roughly equal fame and fortune in sports, then it leads both men and women to think of women as naturally inferior.
(3) When there is a wide disparity in such attainments between men and women, this is damaging to the self-respect of all women.
(4) All women have a right to self-respect.

Therefore, the right to self-respect justifies the demand for equal press coverage and prize money for women.

English considers scarce athletic rewards on the same basis as any other occupational benefit and concludes that women have a justified demand for equal media coverage as a derivative of their right to self-respect. This argument, although initially appealing, is not convincing.

Premises (2) and (3) are not persuasive. Even if the performances of the most capable women in sports in which objective performance measurement is possible--such as golf and bowling--are below the performances of the most capable men, we should not conclude that women are naturally inferior. Past cultural conditioning and social inequalities may well account for at least some of the disparity. If women do not attain equal fame and fortune because of performance disparity attributable in part to such discriminations, then women should draw no conclusions about their natural athletic capabilities. Therefore, premise (2) is questionable.

Why should all women lose self-respect because of a dearth of female athletic stars or because professional women athletes receive less prize money than men receive? It is only when society teaches us that our self-respect is connected integrally with the professional athletic attainments of our group that this might occur. It is one thing to say that members of disadvantaged groups identify strongly with each other's successes and failures, and quite another to say that unequal financial attainments in athletics will result in a loss of self-respect for all members of that group.

Moreover, we should not respect ourselves because of our own or our group's attainments of scarce rewards in professional sports. We should respect ourselves and those with whom we identify on the basis of the kind of people we are, the kind of moral life we lead, and the character we possess. All women may have low estimates of themselves as athletes without losing respect for themselves or their sisters as people. There simply is no necessary connection between a person's athletic attainments and that person's degree of self-respect. Again, there is an empirical connection only if society as a whole or the major social group itself teaches that athletic fame and fortune is an important aspect of the group's or an individual's self-respect. Therefore, there is no necessary connection and there should be no empirical connection between scarce athletic attainments and a group's self-respect.

Finally, there is no empirical connection. Do all women really lose self-respect because Chris Evert Lloyd does not earn as much money as Bjorn Borg, or because Nancy Lopez Melton is in a lower tax bracket than Tom Watson? It strains the imagination to conjure a vision of millions of American women dressing in black and hanging their heads in despondency over the disparity in prize money which occurs when Lloyd and Borg win their respective divisions of a tennis tournament!

We may assume that in any occupation--professional athletics or otherwise--if females demonstrated that they could perform comparably to the top males, then unequal recognition and pay would clearly be unjustified absent some compelling market conditions. Suppose that women could demonstrate this parity of performance but they were still denied equal recognition and pay. How might women respond? Rather than losing self-respect, they would be outraged, angered, and indignant. Women under such circumstances would have no reason to lose self-respect, since they would have proven they were just as capable as comparable males. No one would conclude that women were naturally inferior in any respect. The connection between thinking women naturally inferior and losing self-respect concerns inferior athletic performance and not inferior athletic fame and fortune. And even this connection is very tenuous since, as has been argued previously, inferior performance in athletics need not lead anyone to conclude that women are naturally inferior athletes or inferior human beings.

But let us suppose that women could be shown to be inferior performers to comparable males in all occupations in which both groups labored. What would be the response of women in such a case if they were recognized and rewarded less? The response might well be a loss of self-respect since they might be led to conclude--rightly or wrongly--that women were naturally inferior to men in certain important skills. But note three things: 1) this loss of respect would be connected with inferior performance much more than with the disparity between the fame and rewards women and men receive; 2) this loss of self-respect would not occur if women were judged inferior in only one or a few occupation(s), since they could point to other occupations in which they equalled or surpassed comparable male performers; and 3) no loss of self-respect need occur at all if the society in which we live valued different aspects of human personality, such as moral goodness, more highly than it seems to do presently. A capable athlete is a poor substitute for a compassionate and morally sensitive human being. And society should recognize the proper source of self-respect.

English argues that scarce athletic rewards should be dispensed on the basis of the proportional attainments of the major social groups.[4] But this would lead to paradoxical results. In men's athletics it is clear that there is an inverse relationship between the amount of media coverage allocated to the major social groups and the accomplishments of such groups in other societal spheres. For example, in the early and middle parts of this century Italian, Jewish, and Irish surnames were prominent in sports such as professional boxing. As these groups began to improve their standing in more important societal spheres their influence became less prominent in boxing.[5] So desperate are New York City boxing promotors for a "Jewish Hope," for example, that they encouraged former light-heavyweight titleholder Mike Rossman to accept the monicker of the "Jewish Bomber" even though his father is an Italian-American and "Rossman" is his mother's maiden name. Currently, blacks receive a disproportionately large amount of media coverage in men's professional sports because of their relatively large numbers and superior achievements. Yet they are surely a group who can most convincingly claim that they have been disadvantaged in larger societal contexts. The point is simply that in the area of men's athletics those groups which have been disadvantaged the most in other areas seem to turn in larger numbers to professional sports where they receive the most fame and prize money. Therefore, correlating scarce athletic rewards to the proportional attainments of the major social groups would have the ludicrous result of further depriving already disadvantaged people. Professional athletics has been one place where disadvantaged groups have received disproportionately greater rewards. To dispense scarce rewards suddenly on the basis of social group membership would exacerbate further an already deplorable situation, since so doing would eliminate one of the few areas where disadvantaged groups have an edge. The case of women (and the case of blacks in the earlier part of this century) may seem different because professional athletics, rather than being a refuge which offered a path to financial success, was yet another area from which they were excluded. But, again, the importance of equality of media coverage to the self-respect of all women seems dubious.

IV. Equality, Entitlement, and Desert

Often appeals are made to what people deserve or to what they are entitled when we argue about the distribution of benefits and burdens in our society. We can begin with an initial presumption of equality. That is, any unequal distribution of burdens and benefits must be justified by evidence which indicates that some relevant difference exists between those treated unequally. Such a presumption may seem like a very weak starting point since differences between people often are discernible so easily, but its importance lies in placing the burden of persuasion upon the party who champions unequal treatment rather than placing it upon the one who espouses equal treatment. Any unequal distribution must be scrutinized seriously in order to determine whether it is justified by relevant differences among those so treated or whether it serves merely to advance the self-interest of the powerful and influential segments of our society. "He deserves it more than she does" and "She is more entitled to it than he is" are two very common claims which are made by those trying to justify an unequal distribution of benefits.

The following general principles apply to the concept of personal desert:[6]

> If X (a person) deserves Y, then she does so on the basis of some prior action which she performed;

> If X deserves Y then there is a good reason for giving Y to X, but not necessarily a sufficient or conclusive reason for doing so;

> The nature of Y--whether it is a prize or a reward or blame or punishment--will determine to a large extent the nature of the prior action which warrants X's claim to Y.

For a characteristic or reward to be deserved, the individual possessing it must be able to point to some prior act that she performed by virtue of which her claim gains validity. It would be absurd for the winner of the New York State Lottery to prance gleefully about the state pontificating about how he deserved to win. For what prior action did he perform, that others did not, which warrants this claim? So, too, it is just as senseless for an individual born with immense natural abilities to preen before the rest of us and explain why he deserved these natural talents or his initial social position. He did not perform any prior act at all in securing such goods, much less one that would warrant his claim of deserving them. Because of all this some think that it is folly to distribute the primary social goods of society on the basis of innate talents or initial social status. [7]

But claims of desert do not constitute our whole notion of just distribution. Suppose the New York Giants play the Podunk Pallbearers for the right to enter the Super Bowl.

The Giants prove beyond a shadow of a doubt that they are the team which put forth the most effort on this particular Sunday. We need not delineate how these facts are known, but we shall assume that a calculus to determine them is possible. Because of an incredible series of good breaks and fortuitous circumstances, the Pallbearers win the game 21-20. Again, we need not specify the nature of the good luck that the Pallbearers received. Under these circumstances we might well claim that the Giants deserved to win the game. Doesn't the team which puts forth the most effort always deserve to win? But the Giants are certainly not entitled to go to the Super Bowl, nor do they have a right to go to the Super Bowl. Podunk, although they did not deserve to win, is entitled to go to the Super Bowl and does have a right to do so. By the same token, the winner of the New York State Lottery did not deserve to win, but still is entitled to the prize. The following pair of precepts display this difference:[8]

> X is entitled to prize Y if and only if X has fulfilled the qualifying conditions specified by the rules which determine who receives Y; and

> X deserves to win prize Y if and only if X manifested to a higher degree than all other competitors the possession of effort set forth as the basis of the competition.

So, one may be entitled to Y but not deserve Y and one may deserve Y but not be entitled to Y. Although one's initial starting position in society and natural abilities are not deserved, some have thought that people are entitled to these things, and hence justified in keeping them.[9]

A man may slave feverishly to support his incapacitated brother and we might want to say that he deserves a reward, but there simply may not be a reward for which he qualifies and therefore none to which he is entitled; another man may be entitled to a $1 million inheritance which he simply does not deserve from any inspection of past performance. Desert and entitlement, then, are two distinct claims of justice. They will sometimes weigh on opposite sides in determining what one ought to receive as her due in a just system of distribution. The disappointed Giants, although they deserved to win, cannot claim legitimately that they are entitled to go to the Super Bowl or that they have a right to go to it. The right to go to the Super Bowl is conferred upon that team

which fulfills the condition of winning the game and not necessarily to the team which deserved to win the game. Therefore, it is false that if X deserves Y then X has a right to
Y, but it is true that if X is entitled to Y then X has a right
to Y. Again, X may deserve Y but not be able to claim that
he has a right to Y, either because there is no Y to be
claimed in the first place, or because X has not fulfilled
the qualifying conditions for Y and is thereby not entitled to
Y.

Although it is easy to claim that the notions of desert
and entitlement are often in conflict, it is difficult to delineate the proper domain of each. Some situations, such as the
professional football game example, are governed totally by
the notion of entitlement; other situations, such as the grading
of student essays, are thought often to be governed by both
entitlement and desert since instructors sometimes reward
industrious, but not brilliant, students in recognition of the
superior effort they expended. Still other situations are governed totally by desert. When private employers confer jobs
to which nobody possesses a right, fairness and justice require that the more deserving candidates be given preference.[10] In such situations--those in which the notion of entitlement is irrelevant--the notion of desert is paramount in
determining just distribution.

It is not necessary to explain fully when and to what
extent the notions of desert and entitlement ought to be employed, to see that both are needed if the requirements of
justice are to be met. Moreover, rewards based on both
desert and on entitlement also serve an instrumental value:
both the industrious and the talented are encouraged to strive
toward excellence.

V. Proposals

There are at least six possible courses of action which can
be prescribed as a solution to the problem of how media coverage should be allocated to women and men athletes:

a) De-emphasize media coverage of all athletic events
and attack the problem of equal coverage by making
media attention of little importance at the outset;

b) Use a gender-blind criterion of perceived spectator
interest as the basis of allocating coverage;

c) Treat female and male participants in any given
sport with equal media attention;

d) Give equal media coverage to the sexes in general
(but not necessarily in each particular sport) by
starting to emphasize sports in which females have
a biological advantage over males;

e) Give media attention proportional to the number of
athletes of each sex in a sport;

f) Give equal coverage to the sexes in competitive athletic activities but continue present coverage in
quasi-professional and professional athletic activities.

Solution (a) has the advantage of making short shrift
of a seemingly complex problem, but those of us who reach
eagerly for the sports section of our daily newspaper will be
much dismayed at the dearth of coverage of our favorite athletic events.   This solution ignores the tremendous impact
that athletic contests have on a considerable sector of the
populace.   Moreover, advertisers and the media are already
so committed to extensive coverage that this solution is very
impractical.

Solution (b) pretends to use merit-based and neutral
criterion in determining the allocation of media coverage.
In fact, however, it seems only to reinforce past cultural
conditioning, for as I showed in Section I, media coverage
creates spectator interest to a considerable extent.   Proposal (b) is woefully conservative at a time when many perceive the need to encourage females to take advantage of existing athletic opportunities and to create new ones.

Solution (c) would allow unequal coverage of, for example, baseball and tennis, but would require that the amount
of coverage allocated to tennis be divided equally between
males and females.   An initial determination would have to
be made concerning the amount of coverage to be allocated
to a certain sport, but once this determination was made the
amount of coverage would be divided equally between the sexes.   One of the difficulties with such a radically egalitarian
approach is that it totally ignores differences between the
sexes in perceived spectator interest, relative athletic abilities, and number of participants.   Moreover, it has the ludicrous implication that, for example, male and female base-

ball players must be allotted equal media coverage. Given
the amount of attention already directed toward Major League
Baseball, what group of female baseball players can even
plausibly demand equal coverage? Alternatively, is the public really prepared to see media coverage of Major League
Baseball be radically curtailed?

Solution (d) cures some of the defects of (c) by requiring, not equal coverage of the sexes in each sport, but
equal coverage in general. Hence, females would receive
more media attention than males in some sports, less in others, and the overall totals would be roughly equal. This
solution also requires the introduction and promotion of sports
in which females have a natural advantage, or at least no natural disadvantage. This solution may be a noble ideal toward
which to strive, but given the limited amount of media space
and time allotted to sports, it does not seem immediately
feasible since many of the sports now considered "major"
would discover that their media coverage had withered in
deference to the increased coverage of "minor" sports. Is
the public really prepared to see major league baseball and
NFL football covered equally with women's gymnastics?

The implementation of solution (e) would call for proportional representation by, and media coverage of, the sexes in sports. But as I showed in Section III, this solution,
if practiced consistently, would eliminate one of the few areas
in which disadvantaged groups (e.g., blacks) presently have
an edge.

As the reader must have by this time surmised, solution (f) is my preferred proposal. It distinguishes two categories of athletic activity for the purpose of allocating media
coverage. In the first category--competitive events--media
attention would be allocated equally to male and female participants. In the second category--quasi-professional and professional events--media attention would be allocated essentially as is, although with an increased sensitivity to the need
for covering sports in which females have a biological advantage and for allocating more coverage to females than is currently expended for those sports in which they have a biological disadvantage. This solution would also commend more,
although not absolute, equality of media attention among various sports within the first category. Competitive baseball,
swimming, gymnastics, and tennis, for example, should all
receive roughly equal coverage, and the total coverage of
male and female participants within these sports should be

equal where possible.[11]   In second-category events--quasi-
professional and professional sports--neither equal media attention among the various sports nor equal total coverage of
male and female participants is prescribed.

    Are such distinctions merely arbitrary and do they
amount to no more than a mealy-mouthed compromise among
the other solutions which were found to be lacking?   Or can
a principled rationale be advanced for the differences prescribed for first and second-category athletic activity?

    The notions of desert and entitlement may be helpful
here.   Remember that the primary reasons for engaging in
first-category activities involve basic rewards.[12]   The notion
of desert seems very relevant in first-category sports, since
effort and participation are the more important goals we try
to cultivate by promoting first-category activities.   Gender
equality seems appropriate, since basic rewards should be
available to all without regard to gender.   The notions of entitlement and rights seem less important because we do not
wish to cultivate a competition for fame and money in first-
category events.   If we wish to cultivate consistently those
goals which first-category activities purport to seek, then
media coverage of these activities should be proportionate
to effort and participation (not achievement) and should be
available equally to both sexes.

    Note that no prescription has been offered for the
quantity of coverage that should be extended to first-category
events.   Because no notion of a right to coverage is involved,
strictly speaking, no participant can claim that he or she has
been deprived of that to which he or she is entitled where
no media coverage at all is afforded to a first-category event.
But where such coverage is extended it should be so done on
a desert-basis, which is also a gender-equal basis.

    It might be argued that my proposal is vulnerable to
the same objections which were raised against the previous
proposal which advocated equal media coverage for the sex-
es--namely, that the proposals ignore spectator interest and
the already extensive impact which certain sports have on the
national consciousness.   But we must bear in mind the reasons why media interest in first-category events exists: the
participants' desire to get some ink in recognition of their
achievements; the desire of friends and relatives to take pride
in the accomplishments of the participants; and the felt need
to inculcate school or community spirit by forging a sense of

identity among spectators and participants. Media coverage
of first-category events is almost always narrowly provincial
in character. And since the goals of coverage can be achieved
by attending to females and males equally, our presumption
of equality suggests that, where effort and participation are
to be rewarded and cultivated by an activity, the best way
to do this is by extending media coverage on a gender-equal
basis. To do otherwise would exclude from coverage some
members of one sex who were as deserving as those members of the other sex to whom coverage was extended. Such
an outcome would be contrary to the purported goals of first-
category athletic activities.

In sum, this solution maintains that the goals of first-
category athletic activities and the reasons underlying media
coverage of such events, along with the notions of desert and
equality, all suggest that where media coverage of such events
exists, it should be extended on a gender-equal basis.

We must now turn to second-category events. On my
proposal neither equal media attention for the sexes within
particular sports nor equal total coverage of females and
males is required in second-category sports.

The goals of second-category events involve scarce
rewards, most notably fame and money. The purpose of
media coverage is not primarily provincial in character, but
is concerned more with singling out the most highly skilled
national and international participants. There is, of course,
a provincial element which affects the focus and extent of
media attention, but it is not the raison d'être for covering
particular second-category sports. Media coverage of
second-category events--unlike that of first-category events--
reflects the national or international newsworthiness of the
events more than it involves the desire to serve provincial
interests. Consequently, the promise of money and fame is
held out to participants[13] in second-category events as the
main reward for successful participation. This type of quasi-
contract yields a basis for unequal coverage of the genders.
The notions of entitlement and rights are more appropriate
here than they are in first-category activities. Because the
amount of money and fame a participant receives is integrally
related to the amount of media coverage lavished upon him
or her, media coverage itself is yet another scarce reward
for which participants are in competition. Media attention
should be meted out on the basis of entitlement, with level
of proficiency (as opposed to effort) being the main criterion.

It is very clear that the most skilled males are more proficient than the most skilled females in sports such as basketball, baseball, football, hockey, boxing, tennis, golf, and bowling. These, coincidentally or not, are the sports which have most captured the public's fancy and which thereby command the majority of media coverage. Hence the additional coverage that males receive in such sports is that to which they are entitled based on superior skills. The adoption of an entitlement model for the allocation of media coverage, whereby different sports compete on the basis of perceived spectator interest and individual athletes compete on the basis of their skills and personalities, is most consistent with the goals of participation in second-category events. In contrast, the adoption of a gender-equal model is most consistent with the goals of participation in first-category events, as has been stated previously.

It may be objected that my distinction between first and second-category events is untenable because these categories are connected much more closely than I have suggested. Specifically, almost all participants in second-category activities begin their careers as participants in first-category activities, and if a gender-equal criterion is used where allocating media coverage of first-category events then many male participants who desire entry into the second-category echelon will be hindered by a lack of media attention. The problem is especially endemic where high school athletes need a certain amount of coverage to secure college scholarships.

My response to this objection has three parts: 1) the current system already discriminates against females in the same way in which the critics fear men will experience discrimination, since female athletes who wish to secure athletic scholarships are often denied adequate media coverage, so my proposal at worst only spreads the deleterious effects of limited media coverage more evenly; 2) the importance of big-time male college sports is so well entrenched that, for better or worse, college scouts will find the best male athletes regardless of the dearth of local media attention; and 3) the percentage of male and female first-category participants who enter second-category activities is so small in comparison to the total number of first-category participants that any detriment that the former might suffer by gender-equal media coverage is substantially outweighed by the values promoted by such coverage.

The proposal which I have recommended is much more practical than several of those discussed previously, in that it is immediately implementable where the will to do so exists. The question still remains, however, whether my proposal hinders or promotes the development of a non-sexist society. It might be argued that unequal media coverage of the sexes in second-category sports hinders this development, and that this consideration outweighs the considerations of entitlement to which I have appealed. In reply I would recall that unequal media coverage of women's athletic events does not and should not damage women's self-respect. Unless it is shown in some other way that unequal media coverage promotes sexism to a degree that outweighs considerations of entitlement, my conclusion stands. This objection does underscore, however, the fact that what is at stake here is not merely the postulation of isolated solutions to seemingly trivial athletic concerns. For these solutions both reflect the society which currently exists and either hinder or promote the society that we might create. [14]

NOTES

1. Here I follow a distinction set forth in Jane English, "Sex Equality in Sports," 7 Philosophy & Public Affairs 269, at 270-271 (1978).
2. See, e.g., B. C. Postow, "Women and Masculine Sports," 7 Journal of the Philosophy of Sport 51, at 52-53 (1980).
3. English, p. 273. For a more complete treatment of the topic of this section of the essay see Raymond A. Belliotti, "Women, Sex, and Sports," 6 Journal of the Philosophy of Sport 67 (1979). This material is used here by permission of the Philosophic Society for the Study of Sport and the Journal of the Philosophy of Sport.
4. English, p. 271.
5. This is not to suggest that the influence of such groups has disappeared totally. Gerry Cooney and Sean O'Grady currently carry the Hiberian banner and inspire remembrances of the past, while Vito Antuofermo, Ray Mancini, and John Verderosa continue to stir Mediterranean hearts.
6. See Joel Feinberg, Doing & Deserving (Princeton, N.J.: Princeton University Press, 1970), pp. 58-61; and James Rachels, "What People Deserve," in Justice and Economic Distribution, ed. by John Arthur and

William H. Shaw (Englewood Cliffs, N.J.: Prentice-Hall, Inc., 1978), pp. 150-163.

7. See, e.g., John Rawls, A Theory of Justice (Cambridge, Mass.: Belknap Press of Harvard University Press, 1971), p. 15.

8. Feinberg, p. 64.

9. See, e.g., Robert Nozick, Anarchy, State, and Utopia (New York: Basic Books, 1974), pp. 225-226.

10. See Rachels, p. 152. For a contrary view, see Judith Jarvis Thomson, "Preferential Hiring," Philosophy & Public Affairs 2 (1973), pp. 364-384.

11. Here we must take into account the relative number of female athletes. Until an equal number of male and female participants in first-category events is achieved, absolute equality in media coverage will not be accomplished.

12. Here I put aside consideration of those who engage in first-category events only as a way of developing those skills which are necessary for entering the second-category echelon. The number of such individuals is very small in comparison to those who remain as first-category participants.

13. I include Olympic contestants here because in socialist countries they are subsidized directly and in capitalist countries they are subsidized indirectly through under-the-table deals, and they often achieve enough fame to insure future financial success.

14. I wish to acknowledge the aid of my friend Gerald F. Casbolt, a professional journalist, who shared his thoughts on this topic with me. I also wish to acknowledge the aid of Betsy Postow, whose suggestions concerning both style and content proved indispensable.

SUGGESTIONS FOR FURTHER READING

The works cited in notes 1 and 6 above (English, Feinberg, and Rachels) are recommended. In Feinberg's book, see especially Chapter 4, "Justice and Personal Desert."

QUESTIONS

(1) a) In your own words, explain the distinction between desert and entitlement.

b) Give your own example of a real or imaginary case in which someone deserves something without being entitled to it. Give your own example of a real or imaginary case in which someone is entitled to something without deserving it.

(2) a) Can you add any proposals to Belliotti's list (a)-(f) of alternative methods of allocating media coverage of sports?

b) For each of Belliotti's proposals (a)-(e), and for each suggestion which you added in part (a) of this question, answer the following: What reasons are there for adopting this proposal? What reasons are there for not adopting it? In your view, should it be adopted? Why or why not?

(3) a) Construct the most plausible argument you can in support of the view that media coverage of competitive athletics should <u>not</u> be proportional to the effort of the participants. (If necessary, review the section of the General Introduction entitled "Background on Arguments.")

b) For each premise of the argument which you have just constructed, say whether you agree with it or disagree with it, and why.

c) For each statement which is supposed to be supported by previous statements in the argument, say how strongly the previous statements support it.

(4) Review the section entitled "Formulating Arguments on Our Own" in the General Introduction.

a) If you think any of the three arguments from Belliotti which are presented in the Introduction to Part I can be improved, then either make the appropriate changes or construct your own improved argument.

b) Choosing from the three arguments from Belliotti which are presented in the Introduction to Part I and from the argument which you presented in answer to part (a) above, select the argument which seems most plausible to you.

c) Evaluate the argument which you have just selected. Follow the directions which are given in question 3 (b) and (c).

(5) a) Construct the most plausible argument you can either in support of or in opposition to the conclusion that media coverage of professional and quasi-professional sports should be proportional to the proficiency of the athletes.

b) Evaluate the argument which you have just presented. Follow the directions given in question 4 (a) and (b).

(6) What else would you like to discuss from Belliotti's essay?

PART II:

WHAT IS THE PROPER PLACE OF
COMPETITION IN SPORTS?

INTRODUCTION

Sports competition is often said to build character: it provides a beneficial toughening up, a way to sublimate aggressive impulses, an occasion to practice good sportsmanship, an opportunity for camaraderie, and a motivational spur to higher levels of performance, among other benefits. But there is also said to be a dark side to competition: it engenders a "macho," aggressive stance, an attitude of enmity towards one's opponents, the feeling that a person's worth is determined by the outcome of a contest, and the withering of playfulness, among other things. Some advocates of competition (one thinks of some professional football coaches) might embrace and affirm these "dark" consequences. Others might deny that they are necessary consequences of competition. "Competition has bad results," they might say, "only when it is carried to excess--only when winning is overemphasized." At this point a critic of competition might respond "What do you mean by 'overemphasized'? Competition is the striving of two opposing sides to beat the other side and win. Competitiveness is a devotion of one's energies to the goal of winning. If we are honest," the critic of competition might continue, "we must admit that the logical consequences of allowing oneself to be engrossed in competition are that the goal of winning becomes paramount and that one's opponent becomes an enemy, if only for the duration of the contest. And these predictions are borne out by serious competitions in professional sports." The advocate of competition would then try to show that these are not the logical consequences of competition, but a corruption of it.

The chapters in Part II should enable us to settle this debate. They explore the different ways in which competition can be defined and experienced, and they examine the desirable and undesirable aspects of different sorts of competition. The last essay, Chapter 11, also investigates reasons for the

117

failure of modern sport to reach the ideal of competition and considers possible remedies.

In the first chapter of Part II, Mary Vetterling-Braggin presents two conflicting models of the sort and amount of competition which ideally ought to be present in sports. The first is a purely competitive model--popularly associated with Vince Lombardi--according to which (among other things) winning is the only goal and opponents are enemies to be crushed. The second is a purely cooperative model--associated with women's play days--according to which (among other things) winning is of no importance and opponents are respected and admired comrades. Vetterling-Braggin argues that each of these models has unacceptable elements: the cooperative model is wrong in asserting that winning is of no importance and that competitions are undesirable; the competitive model is wrong in asserting that winning should be the only goal and that opponents should be regarded as enemies to be crushed. She presents a third model of cooperative competition which she believes includes the desirable elements of both the previous models. This model rests on the belief that there is little or no tension "between being cooperative and having a properly channeled competitive drive."

In Chapter 9 Kathryn Pyne Addelson distinguishes three different types of competition: competition as cooperative challenge, competition in a ranking, and competition as combat. To be engaged in competition as cooperative challenge is to be spurred on or challenged to higher levels of performance by the performance of one's fellow participants. In sports that involve games, the efforts of the opposing players spur one on to higher levels of performance as one tries to win as defined by the rules of the game. To be engaged in competition in a ranking is to be in a situation in which our performance is ranked according to some criterion and rewards are assigned on the basis of this ranking. (In sports, the rewards can range from momentary glory to a greatly improved standard of living.) The requirements of the game itself do not impel players into competition in a ranking, as they do impel players into competition as cooperative challenge. It is possible to be in a situation defined as a competition in a ranking without aiming for the rewards, but it is also possible to aim for them. Wanting to win a game in order to receive the extrinsic rewards is different from wanting to win in order to meet the challenge set by one's opponents, and both are different from wanting to win in order to dominate or subdue one's opponents. Addelson's third sense of competition, competition as combat, is connected with the image of dominating and subduing opponents.

Addelson provides a social context for the different senses of competition. For example, she explains how competition in a ranking is woven into the ideological history of our country, intertwined with economic and evolutionary justification for inequality of wealth and power. And she points out that the picture of competition as combat is used to deny women equal access to sports on the ground that war is men's sphere--a ploy that appeals to the sexual division of labor which pervades our society and which gives the lion's share of resources to males. An ideal society, in Addelson's view, would practice competition as cooperative challenge in all phases of life, would be free of competition as combat, and would include a purified form of competition in a ranking which justly rewarded ability at an activity.

Addelson's conceptual scheme differs somewhat from Vetterling-Braggin's, but there are also important areas of correspondence. The most striking difference is that competition in a ranking lacks a correlate among the models of competition sketched by Vetterling-Braggin. Also, Vetterling-Braggin's purely cooperative model lacks a correlate among Addelson's senses of competition--but that is not surprising, for the purely cooperative model rejects competition. The most important areas of correspondence are these: Vetterling-Braggin's model of cooperative competition endorses competition as cooperative challenge as defined by Addelson. The first two theses of the model of cooperative competition roughly characterize the attitude of a player while she or he is engaged in competition as cooperative challenge. The remaining theses of the model can plausibly be taken to express views that would be held by an advocate of this sort of competition. In a similar way, Vetterling-Braggin's purely competitive model endorses competition as combat. Vetterling-Braggin and Addelson agree that a concern with winning is quite separable from a desire to crush or dominate an opponent. And, of course, they agree on the substantive point that competition as cooperative challenge is desirable, and that it should not be limited to sports.

Drew A. Hyland deals with two types of competition in Chapter 10: competition that leads to friendship and competition that leads to alienation. The first type is obviously compatible with Addelson's definition of competition as cooperative challenge, and the second type is obviously compatible with her picture of competition as combat.   Arguably, competition that is motivated primarily by a concern for extrinsic rewards should also be considered a case of competition that leads to alienation, since we neither appreciate nor engage our fellow participants fully when our primary concern is an external reward.   Hyland does not commit himself on this point.

Addelson, as we have seen, takes the perspective of society.   She holds that the sort of competition that we should promote is the sort that would lead people to develop the kind of character needed in a democracy.   In contrast, Hyland looks directly to human nature (as opposed to the requirements of an ideal democratic society) to determine the ideal form of competition.   According to Hyland, a human individual by nature is a) neither wholly monadic nor wholly relational; b) capable of reconciling in a non-contradictory unity the stance of dominance and the stance of submission; and c) characterized by a tension between incompleteness and the capacity for overflowing.   Competition of the sort that breeds alienation from one's competitors represents a deficient realization of human nature because it a) accommodates only our monadic and not our relational aspect; b) is undertaken from the stance of dominance; and c) fails to acknowledge the incompleteness which is one source of our erotic natures.   Competition of the sort that breeds friendship, on the other hand, has its source in the stance of play or assertive openness.   This stance embodies a reconciliation of the stance of dominance (pure assertiveness) with that of submission (pure openness). It also allows expression of both our incompleteness or striving for fulfillment and our capacity for overflowing.   Both sexes share the elements of human nature which make friendly competition the ideal form of competition, according to Hyland.   He therefore holds that this is the desirable form of competition for both sexes.

According to Hyland, the source of the competitive urge is definitely not the desire to dominate; it lies instead in our striving for fulfillment and our capacity for overflowing.   If we agree with Vetterling-Braggin that there is little or no tension between properly channeled competitive drive and cooperativeness, then we may well want to accept Hyland's account of the source of the competitive drive.   At any rate, we cannot agree with Vetterling-Braggin (or, of course, with Hyland) and also hold that a "properly channeled" competitive drive is merely a sublimated or controlled desire to subdue others.   Addelson, on the other hand, has

less reason to agree with Hyland.   She is not committed to
accepting any single source of "the competitive drive" since
there may be separate competitive drives, corresponding to
the distinct sorts of competition that she describes.

Hyland agrees with Vetterling-Braggin and Addelson in
holding that the desire to beat an opponent is separable from
the striving to win, but he goes even farther than they do in
this.   Addelson and Vetterling-Braggin distinguish the desire to
crush or humiliate an opponent from the desire to win a game.
This distinction is quite plausible, since one may win a game
without crushing or humiliating an opponent.   But one cannot
win a game without one's opponent losing the game.   Hyland
holds, however, that one can strive to win without desiring that
one's opponent lose.   "In this case," he says, "conceptual logic
must be superseded by phenomenological evidence [i.e. observation and description of our own experiences]."

Near the end of his essay, Hyland observes that "we
should be very interested [to know] what conditions ... bring
it about that athletic competition so often fails to be what it can
be."   This question is one to which Joan Hundley devotes most
of her essay, presented here as Chapter 11.   She argues that
the failure of athletic competition is embodied in the overemphasis on winning.   She then presents three different social theories
insofar as they are relevant to the philosophy of sport and draws
from each theory its explanation of the overemphasis on winning
in modern sport.   By the neo-Marxist theory, she tells us, success of any kind is predictably scarce under capitalism.   Winning in sport is a commodity which can be exchanged for money
(e.g., by the selling of time to those who wish to sponsor
broadcasts of winning teams).   The overemphasis on winning
in modern sport is explained by neo-Marxists as a consequence of the fact that winning is a valuable commodity.

On the view of play theorists, an irrational overemphasis on the value of work in general has led to the deterioration of the play spirit in all areas of life.   Among the
absurd consequences of this deterioration is the fact that
games are played for the sake of accomplishing something,
such as winning.   The brutality with which winning is often
pursued is due to the brutality and alienation which flow from
the general deterioration of the play spirit.

The third social theory which Hundley presents is radical feminism.   According to this theory, all social institutions, including sport, are used and adapted to maintain the

power of men over women. Sport is useful for this purpose because it can reinforce the ideal of physical dominance, aggression, and violence, which is part of the ideology that supports men's power. The overemphasis on winning in sports is required by the ideal of physical dominance, aggression, and violence.

Rejecting the view that sport cannot be reformed until all of society is reformed, Hundley draws on all three theories for ideas on how to counteract the overemphasis on winning in sport. The measures that she discusses include the discouragement of rigid time structures in games, the discouragement of statistical records, the encouragement of pick-up games, the inclusion of more women in sports, the inclusion of more woman-oriented sports in the athletic repertoire, and the direct encouragement of a healthier attitude in sport through play days.

8. COOPERATIVE COMPETITION IN SPORT

Mary Vetterling-Braggin

I. Brief History of the Debate

Stephanie Twin acquaints those of us who were not around in
the 1920s and 1930s with a debate of crucial significance to
the history of women's sports. On one side were those who
advocated what has come to be called the "competitive" model
of sport, on the other were "cooperative" model supporters.
The competitive model advocates advanced at least five key
ideals for all sports participants:

> (1) Winning is the end (in the teleological sense
> of the term) of sport; the means (the "way the
> game is played") of arriving at that end is of sec-
> ondary, or no, importance.

> (2) It is proper (indeed, functional) to view the op-
> ponent as an enemy to be "beaten" or "crushed."

> (3) Sports competitions, i.e., contests governed
> by rules and scored such that there ultimately
> emerges a winner and a loser, are more impor-
> tant than non-scored sports activity.

> (4) Competitive sports are "masculine" (i.e., ought
> to be engaged in by males) and "unfeminine" (i.e.,
> ought not to be engaged in by females).

> (5) Unbridled competitive spirit is functional for
> athletes and should, for that reason, be valued.

The cooperative model advocates, in the main, denied (1)-(5)
above:

(1') Comradeship and joy in physical motion is the end of sport and winning is of no importance.

(2') It is proper to view the opponent as an individual to be respected and admired.

(3') Non-scored sports activity is superior to sports competitions; the latter ought to be eliminated entirely.

(4') Competitive sports ought not be engaged in by anyone.

(5') Competitive spirit ought to be discouraged wherever it occurs.[1]

Because defenders of the competitive model were usually (although not exclusively) male physical educators who coached all-male teams and because defenders of the cooperative model were usually female physical educators who coached all-female teams, the debate came to be characterized by some writers in "battle of the sexes" terminology. Theses from the cooperative model were often dubbed "the women's" ideals, those from the competitive model "the men's."[2] But the debate turned out to be both literally and figuratively academic; the cooperative model never gained much of a following among female, much less male, athletes themselves. Many found alienating the cooperative model supporters' unqualified opposition to sports competitions and competitive spirit:

> Athletic women who went to college in the late 1950s remember with horror the "play days" that took the place of competition for women. The field hockey teams of, say, Vassar and Smith would meet, but rather than squaring off against each other, the players would intermingle for an afternoon's "recreation." Most women found it unbearably frustrating. "We'd be out there playing what should be a competitive game, but we weren't allowed to take it seriously or take any pride in winning," says one woman who is now a college administrator. "You could never develop a sense of teamwork because your teammates were always changing."[3]

Now, as then, it seems unreasonable to expect persons who engage in sport as a profession or serious hobby to support the abolition of competitions and the total suppression of competitive drive. But, in addition to the fact that the co-operative model is unlikely to be adopted, there does not seem to be sufficient reason for claiming that it ought to be, either. To see this, let us consider the four key arguments the advocates of cooperation used to urge the abolition of competitions in sport.

II.   The Arguments for Abolishing Competitions

One of the arguments was advanced against competitions for women in particular, and it amounted to the claim that we just "aren't up" to competitions, either physically or emotionally:

> They claimed that women were being pushed beyond themselves physically and emotionally to satisfy crowds. They predicted that nervous instability, premature pelvic ossification, narrowed vaginas, difficult deliveries, heartstrain and spinsterhood were the high prices women would pay for being serious contenders. [4]

Given all the data available to us now in the 1980s, [5] this point of view can summarily be dismissed; not one of the predictions described above has been borne out in fact.

A second argument rested on the moral claim that all sport ought to be a form of play. Competitions, said the cooperative model supporters, make sport work, not play, and for that reason, competitions ought to be banned from sport entirely. [6]

Ordinary notions of "play" usually involve reference to a form of activity that is both non-serious and engaged in separately from all material interest:

> [play is] a free activity standing quite consciously outside ordinary life, as being "not serious...." It is an activity connected with no material inter-est.... It proceeds within its own proper bound-aries according to fixed rules.... [7]

If the second argument is right, then, sport ought to be a form of play, i.e., both non-serious and connected with no material interest. If competitions really are what make sport serious, as the cooperative model supporters claimed, and if they are always connected with material rewards (money, medals, trophies, fame leading to paid advertisements, etc.) it follows, they say, that competitions ought to be eliminated from sport altogether.

There is good reason to question the second argument. It need not be morally undesirable to engage in sports in a spirit that is not purely playful. Sports may permissibly be engaged in for physical fitness, for example, or for other morally acceptable reasons, such as meeting the challenge of doing well something one enjoys doing. Competition does not necessarily add a morally undesirable purpose to sports.

A second reason to question the second argument is that competitions need not be designed in such a way as to make winning of paramount importance to the entrants. An example of how a competition might be designed otherwise is provided by the Colgate Women's Games.[8] A promotional poster for the 1982 Colgate Games reads in part, "You don't need to be a pro, or have experience to participate. You will meet famous athletes, celebrities, make new friends ... [sic] and maybe earn a grant towards your education." And this orientation has carried over in practice:

> The main point of the Games is that everybody plays. Six-year-olds with baby fat waddle around the track, and girls twice their age get tips on race style and strategy from young women twice their age.[9]

Although it is true that excessively prized competitions can make a sport so serious to coaches and athletes that they will go to almost any lengths to win (leading to the corruption of that sport), there simply is no evidence to the effect that moderately or low-prized competitions have such an effect[10] or that excessively prized competitions need have such an effect. Were the social emphasis placed on the comradeship and joy in physical motion equal to that placed on winning, for example, it is doubtful that the corrupting influence of excessive prizes would persist.

A third argument offered by cooperative model advocates in opposition to competitions is more compelling than either of the first two. Whenever there are competitions, it goes, there are winners and losers. Since losing can cause serious psychological harm (a sense of self-depreciation and lack of worth) to some sports participants, it concludes, competitions ought to be banned from sport.

That losing can have such a psychological effect on some sports participants is not a matter of dispute:

> Girls who lose too often may find their careers abruptly halted by disappointed mothers or financially troubled fathers. To understand the path that women's sports are rumbling down, I spent some time one summer at the junior national championships. At one of them, in Shreveport, Louisiana, some of the finest teenagers of tennis gathered. "If you do well here, you get a good ranking," explained a small, dark-haired girl named Karen, "and everyone is nice to you because they think you'll end up rich. If you get a bad ranking, you feel like junk."[11]

But that competitions must have such an effect is not as obviously so. It may be the case that the real cause of psychological harm is the socially-reinforced belief on the part of those close to the athlete (coaches, parents, co-participants) that losing is shameful. If competitions were maintained and social attitude towards them altered such that the losers score-wise became victors in experience, for example, it is doubtful that such psychological fallout from competitions would continue.

The fourth argument against competitions was based on the claim that competitions promote unbridled competitive spirit in some sports participants, a highly intense "do-or-die" style of play, a desire to "defeat someone." To discourage this sort of competitive spirit in sports, it was argued, competitions must be banned. But once again, as Barnard College's Agnes R. Wayman pointed out at the time, competitions themselves need not promote this type of "battleground mentality" in competition entrants;[12] a change in the social values associated with competitions could have a moderating influence on competitive spirit, channeling it properly to within morally acceptable bounds.

Indeed, three current tennis superstars seem to provide convincing evidence for the view that competitions and properly channeled competitive drive can coexist. Martina Navratilova, an undeniably competitive athlete, does not describe her opponents as "enemies" to be "beaten" or "crushed," nor does Billie Jean King or Chris Evert Lloyd, also undeniably intense competitors. They unanimously characterize their opponents in terms of respect and admiration while simultaneously admitting that their competitive spirit provides the drive to attain (or maintain) an excellence at their craft greater than that which their opponents exhibit. Competitions and high quality opponent performance provide these sports figures with goals to strive for, and their competitive spirit provides the desire to meet these goals. For these athletes, at least, competitions and well-channeled competitive drive are both valuable and functional.

To summarize, the cooperative model adherents failed to advance sufficient grounds for the total abolition of competitions in sport. They did, however, offer sufficient grounds for arguing that competitions mated with social values as we know them today can have adverse effects. If competitions are to persist, then, those who are likely to suffer psychological distress from losing should be discouraged from entering them until current social attitudes toward losing at competitions, toward opponents, and toward "the way the game is played" have been radically and systematically altered.

III. Cooperative Competition

There is another model, the key elements of which have been proposed by others,[13] which seems to me to avoid the excesses of the competitive model without entailing the cooperative model's total rejection of competitions and competitive spirit. It is one to which both serious and recreational athletes could assent and is being offered here as a feasible model for all sports participants:

(1") Both winning and how the game is played are of equal and primary importance in sports competitions.

(2") It is proper to view the opponent as an individual to be respected and admired.

(3") Both sports competitions and purely recreational sports ought to be valued and encouraged in our society.

(4") Competitive sports ought to be encouraged in

some, discouraged in others (depending on the psychological fallout they are likely to have, given current social values).

(5'') Properly channeled competitive spirit ought to be encouraged in all.

(6'') The social values currently associated with some competitive sports ought to be discouraged wherever possible and other, more positive, values encouraged in their stead.

This model concedes the cooperative model supporters' fundamental claim that none of the key theses of the competitive model are, as they stand, acceptable. On the other hand, it rejects the cooperative model's unqualified denial of the value of sports competitions and competitive spirit. It says that cooperative and competitive elements of sport can and should coexist, ideally under conditions of an altered social value system.

Cooperative competition, like the other models, will have its detractors. Adherents to both the cooperative and competitive models, for example, are likely to object that cooperation and competitive drive are contradictory traits: that it is impossible for one and the same individual to be both competitive and cooperative at the same time. (Or, at the very least, that the tension between the two sorts of traits is so strong that to encourage both in one and the same athlete is to promote frustration in that athlete.)

This objection would be forceful were the sort of competitive spirit advocated by the cooperative competition model the same kind of competitive spirit as that promoted by the competitive model. (Clearly, tension would result from trying to be cooperative with an opponent whom one wishes to "beat" or "crush.") There is, however, little if any tension between being cooperative and having properly channeled competitive drive. The latter is not a "do-or-die" sort of drive, but is to be more closely aligned with a personal striving for excellence which is promoted by those same strivings in, and excellences of, one's opponents. When one has this sort of drive, one is more likely to hope that opponents will perform well (so as to spur good performance in oneself) than is one to hope for opponent failure; one is more likely to accept opponent challenge honestly and straightforwardly than to "psych out" an opponent or take advantage of opponent weaknesses;

and one is more likely to do whatever one can in practice to help opponents perform at their best than to wish for conditions which support their mediocre or poor performance. Empathy[13] is both a cause and effect of the spirit of cooperative competition and the model under discussion encourages its development in all athletes.

The cooperative competition model need not be limited to sports applications. The very doing of philosophy itself could only stand to benefit from a move away from its current competitively modeled structure toward cooperative competition. The formal practice of commentators disclosing and discussing their remarks with speakers and authors in advance of speaking engagements or journal publications would facilitate cooperative truth seeking.

In closing, it is worth noting that those involved with some sports seem already to be well underway toward applying the cooperative competition model in practice, most notably in non-body contact sports such as tennis, swimming, gymnastics, and volleyball. Body contact sports (wrestling, football, and boxing, for example) are still, for the most part, bastions of competitively modeled sport. Since women in our society are far more likely to adopt non-body contact than body contact sport and since body contact sports are, for the most part, male-dominated, sports in which women participate in numbers are likely to serve as the best vehicles for cooperative competition in the future.[14,15]

NOTES

1. These models were not advanced as units (as they are here) by any one group or individual participating in the debates of the 1920s and 1930s. They represent, rather, a compilation of the sorts of ideals advocated by people who identified with one group or the other. This particular set was extracted from the history of the debate provided by Stephanie Twin in the introduction to a book she edited, Out of the Bleachers: Writings on Women and Sport (Old Westbury, N.Y.: The Feminist Press, 1979), from characterizations of the two models provided by Jack Scott in his "A Radical Ethic for Sports," pp. 182-97 in that same volume, and from Bonnie A. Beck's "The Future of Women's Sport" in Jock: Sports and Male Identity, Donald F. Sabo and Ross Runfola, eds. (Englewood Cliffs, N.J.: Prentice-Hall, 1980).

2. Twin, p. xxxii.
3. Janice Kaplan, Women and Sports (New York: Viking Press, 1979), p. 165.
4. Twin, p. xxx. Although it is easy to understand why the medical disabilities predicted would be high prices for women to pay (premature pelvic ossification sounds the worst!), it is not clear why "spinsterhood" would be a high price, too.
5. See, for example, Twin, Part I: Physiology and Social Attitudes (pp. 2-75) and Kaplan, Ch. 2: Physiology (pp. 17-51).
6. Twin, p. xxx.
7. John Huizinga, Homo Ludens, A Study of the Play Element in Culture (Boston: Beacon Press, 1955), p. 13. Other definitions of "play" are provided by Paul Weiss in his Sport: A Philosophical Inquiry (Carbondale: Southern Illinois University Press, 1969), pp. 132-51, and by Harry Edwards in his Sociology of Sport (Homewood, Ill.: Dorsey Press, 1973), pp. 43-61. Since these definitions do not significantly enhance the case for a cooperative model, however, I shall avoid repeating them here.
8. The Colgate Women's Games, sponsored by the Colgate-Palmolive Company, is an annual series of track and field events for women and girls. It is open (and free) to all female residents of New York City, Nassau or Suffolk Counties in New York, and Hudson County in New Jersey. Further information is available from Colgate Women's Games, 300 Park Avenue, New York, NY 10022. "Colgate Women's Games VIII: Rules and Regulations" (n.p., n.d.), pp. 1, 9, 10.
9. Kaplan, p. 174.
10. Witness again the Colgate Games; in 1982 the first prize in each event was a $750 educational grant-in-aid.
11. Kaplan, p. 171. (What astute perceptions!)
12. Agnes R. Wayman, "Let's Take It in Our Stride," The Sportswoman, 10, no. 7 (March 1934): 14.
13. See Jack Scott, op. cit.
14. For an excellent discussion of the positive moral implications of empathy in a context other than a sports-related one, see Elizabeth Lane Beardsley's "Legislators and the Morality of Their Constituents," in Ethical Issues of Government, Norman Bowie, ed. (Philadelphia, Pa.: Temple University Press, 1981), pp. 83-89.
15. I am grateful to Betsy Postow and to Adele Laslie of Lehigh University for their creative responses to earlier drafts.

QUESTIONS

(1) a) For each of the theses (1''), (2''), (3''), and (6'') of the model of cooperative competition, answer the following: Is this thesis compatible with the view that one's opponent is an enemy to be beaten or crushed? Why or why not?

    b) Present and support your own opinion about whether it is indeed <u>functional</u> to view one's opponent as an enemy to be beaten or <u>crushed</u> in each of the following types of sports: professional sports, quasi-professional sports, competitive recreational sports, purely recreational sports. (The categories correspond to Raymond A. Belliotti's classification in Chapter 7 of this volume.)

    c) If your opponent in a purely recreational game regarded you as an enemy to be crushed, what would you do? Why?

(2) Do you agree with Vetterling-Braggin that there is no sufficient reason for urging that competitions in sport be abolished? Why or why not?

(3) According to Vetterling-Braggin, people who are likely to suffer psychological distress from losing should be discouraged from entering competitions until social attitudes are changed.

    a) In your view which groups, if any, should be discouraged from entering competitions until social attitudes are changed? Why?

    b) What sort of discouragement would be appropriate?

(4) For each thesis of the model of cooperative competition, answer the following: Do you agree or disagree with it? Why?

(5) What else would you like to discuss from Vetterling-Braggin's essay?

9. EQUALITY AND COMPETITION: CAN SPORTS MAKE A WOMAN OF A GIRL?

Kathryn Pyne Addelson*

I. Equality and Difference

> In no country has such constant care been taken as
> in America to trace two clearly distinct lines of
> action for the sexes and to make them keep pace
> with one another, but in two pathways that are dif-
> ferent. (Alexis de Tocqueville, Democracy in
> America, 1835-40)[1]

Competition in sports, as well as in education, business, politics, and the arts, has often been closely connected
with equality. "Competition" may be understood in several
different ways, and so there are several ways of connecting
it with equality.

Competition has sometimes been closely connected
with equality of opportunity. For example, after the University of Georgia, Athens, was investigated under Title IX
in 1978, its president wrote in protest,

> Athletics provide one of the purest examples of
> equal opportunity left to us. Everyone competes
> on the basis of individual ability and desire to par-
> ticipate. College and university athletics, funded
> through voluntary support of spectators, provide
> every student with the opportunity to achieve his
> or her full potential. Intercollegiate sports have
> thrived for decades under this creed. The current

> incursion of the Federal government into college
> athletics can only lead to the destruction of sports
> programs as we know them and result in a loss of
> opportunity and enjoyment for both men and women.
> (Davison, 1979:   37)

Title IX is concerned with insuring that both men and women
have fair access to athletic resources in educational institutions.   The college president understands equal opportunity
to mean that those people who are interested in sports should
be allowed to compete for a share of the resources, and the
share is to be determined on the basis of their ability.   Outstanding athletes get special training and opportunity while
the less able get to attend gym class or play pickup games.
The focus is on "career athletes"--people of considerable
ability who are interested in making a major commitment to
sport.   Through competition, they receive a lion's share of
the athletic resources.

Understanding competition and equal opportunity in this
way has in the past made it seem easy to explain away the
fact that men have the greatest amount of sports resources.
It seemed easy to say that women could have the opportunity
to compete for resources but they just weren't as interested
in sports as men were, or if they were interested, they just
didn't have the same sports ability as men.   People who
thought in this way noticed that men and women had very
different kinds of lives in our society, but they attributed it
(in part at least) to questions of individual interest and talent
rather than to a sexual division of labor or systematic differences in social opportunities.   The recent concern with equal
opportunity, in Title IX and elsewhere, shows more concern
with systematic differences.

At times, some people have understood competition in
a second way--as competition in a battle that requires aggression to win the victory over the enemy.   Some people
who thought this way also argued that, for biological reasons,
men are aggressive and suited for war and women are nur-
turing and suited for the home.   In sports competition, they
said, women are naturally less able than men.   This argument defends the unequal distribution of both work and sports
resources by arguing that a sexual division of labor is natu-
ral--men naturally fight the battles of the sports, business,
and political world and women naturally tend children and
home.

There is a third way of understanding sports competition and the question of equal access to sports resources. Competition is said to be intrinsic to most sports and the very reason that sports contributes to building good character. In this way of thinking, sports builds the kind of character that is essential to the citizens of a democracy. For example, in the 1950s, General Douglas MacArthur proclaimed that sport is

> a vital character builder ... that molds the youth of our country for their roles as custodians of the Republic. Fathers and mothers who would have their sons be men should have them participate in sports. (Twin, 1979: 190)

Women became full citizens and were acknowledged politically equal to men when they were given the vote in 1920. It would seem that parents who would have their daughters be women--and custodians of the Republic--should have them participate in sports as well.

There are differences of opinion on this point, of course, and sometimes in high places. For example, in 1971 a Connecticut Superior Court Justice denied a female student's suit to be allowed to compete on the high school cross country team, saying "Athletic competition builds character in our boys. We do not need that kind of character in our girls" (Parkhouse, 1980: 66). This argument also rests ultimately on presuppositions about a sexual division of labor. However, if our girls are citizens, then they, too, need the kind of character sports competition builds.

In this essay I shall be particularly interested in sports competition as it contributes to building character in citizens of a democracy, for this is a sense in which sports is important to all of us, whatever the age, sex, creed, color, or level of "natural" ability. Focusing on this aspect of sports requires separating different senses of competition. In Section II below I distinguish "competition as cooperative challenge," which seems important to building character, from competition as a ranking of individuals according to ability. In Section III I discuss competition understood as battle.

Interestingly, presuppositions about the sexual division of labor greatly affect our understanding of competition and

equality. That is the second theme of this paper--not equal
opportunity to compete, but citizens' access to sports resources for building character in a society in which a sexual division of labor has been and still is an important feature. In Section IV I reflect upon some ways in which differences in men's and women's lives under a sexual division
of labor results in unequal access to character-building sports.

As a beginning, a historical look at the sexual division
of labor is helpful. Sports as we know them in the United
States began to be developed in the mid-nineteenth century,
a development that was intensified after the Civil War. Their
development was one aspect of the great social changes which
shaped life as we know it today.

In the wake of the Industrial Revolution, and the opening of the West, industrialists, bankers, politicians, rail-
roaders, and even doctors and ministers saw themselves at
war in a competition with each other and with nature.
Barker-Benfield remarks upon the "social breakdown" that
followed the Civil War:

> Among the identifiable symptoms were the failures
> and corruption of the Reconstruction, the longest
> depression in American history, insatiable trusts,
> swarms of what were held to be sexually potent
> and racially inferior immigrants, and a govern-
> ment discredited at all levels.... The Civil War
> had perhaps dramatized the crudest source of iden-
> tity, the sexual distinction between fighting men
> and nonfighting women, a line that had already
> been sharpened as a reaction to the women's
> rights movement. [Barker-Benfield, 1976: 84]

The movement for women's rights had begun in the 1840s
but it was greatly intensified after the Civil War.

In the years when sports were expanding and developing, higher class women had begun attending public and private colleges, and many were active in doing volunteer reform work. Some supported themselves by writing. A few
were entering (or trying to enter) professions like medicine
and law. Two thirds of the teachers in public and private
schools were women. Women constituted a considerable part
of the work force in many industries. Very large numbers
of them did paid and unpaid labor on farms and on the fron-
tier: some ran boarding houses, cared for other women's

children, or worked as domestics; some supported themselves
as prostitutes; some were nurses and midwives; and many
worked in the family shop.

Despite the fact that large numbers of women did paid
or unpaid work outside their homes, "women's work" was
believed to lie in the domestic sphere of home and hearth.
And, of course, working or not, women did have the responsibility, heavier then than now, of seeing that the house was
cleaned, the meals properly attended to, the linens and clothing washed, and all the social necessities taken care of.
They were responsible for nursing the elderly and the sick,
but in terms of moral obligation, theirs was the task of giving birth to many, healthy children and raising them with a
proper moral training. At least this was the task of women
of the "better" classes, for there was considerable worry
that immigrant women were having too many children. Men's
special responsibility was to sally forth into the public sphere
of politics and the free market of business and industry.

Many men argued against women entering public life,
particularly in the more prestigious occupations, by claiming
that women were by nature unsuited for competition.[2] Arguments against giving women the vote often took this form.
Here are the words of New York's Senator Freylinghuysen,
spoken shortly after the Civil War.

> It seems to me as if the God of our race has
> stamped upon [the women of America] a milder,
> gentler nature, which not only makes them shrink
> from, but disqualifies them for the turmoil and
> battle of public life. They have a higher and a
> holier mission. It is in retiracy to make the char-
> acter of coming men. Their mission is at home,
> by their blandishments and their love to assuage
> the passions of men as they come in from the bat-
> tle of life, and not themselves by joining in the
> contest to add fuel to the very flames. [Flexner,
> 1968: 148]

The senator is using religious grounds for stating that men
and women differ in nature. However, others used "scientific" grounds in biology, psychology, and medicine. Even
some feminists claimed a difference--but they declared that
women's natural moral superiority argued for giving them the
vote to drive out immorality from the public, male realm.
Few feminists at that time would argue that women were
suited for the dog-eat-dog fray.

The distinction of "proper spheres" which men and women naturally fulfill served as a justification for a sexual division of labor. The division of labor existed in fact-- though not quite as Senator Freylinghuysen put it. Women (not men) were responsible for household and childrearing duties. Men (not women) went out to hold leadership posi- tions in politics, business, industry, and the military. But while nearly all women had the duties of their sphere, only a few men were leaders. However, even when women went out to work, they were for the most part channeled into lower paid and less skilled "female" work categories, working un- der male foremen.

In 1920, the Nineteenth Amendment to the Constitution was passed, giving women the right to vote. It is not just suffrage that is important here since with it came the recog- nition in the Nineteenth Amendment that men and women are created equal in that they should take active parts in govern- ing their society. According to Thomas Jefferson--and to our public policy almost from the beginning--voting citizens must have an education and a life that fosters common sense, in- dependence, responsibility, and other important human capa- cities. Being given the vote means being given the opportu- nity to share in the resources that allow us to develop the virtues needed to be citizens of a democracy.

In granting women the right to vote, the Nineteenth Amendment also recognized that women should be given a greater chance to develop their human capacities. Many philosophers, political theorists, and educators have argued that democracy is the best form of government because it is only by participating in governing their own society that peo- ple can fully develop. Citizens must have a good education to govern themselves and this is the basic justification for public projects from the public schools and state universities to recreational programs and the public park systems. But democracy itself offers them opportunities to exercise and develop their judgment and character.

Of course, recognizing that all men and women are created equal doesn't mean that they are equal in everything they do. Some people are better at doing some things. How- ever, our policy has been to allow everyone to compete for benefits above and beyond those needed for good citizenship, giving the basics to all. If sports build character in citizens of a democracy, then those "basics" must include access to sports resources for men and women.

Interestingly, some of the people most involved in shaping women's sports activity have also felt that women should not engage in athletic competition as men do. For example, in the 1920s and 1930s, the Women's Division of the Amateur Athletic Federation opposed women's taking part in intercollegiate sports and lobbied against women being allowed to take part in track and field events in the 1932 Olympics.[3] They discouraged competition between men and women:

> Girls, because of anatomical and physiological differences, cannot run as fast, jump as high, or swim as far as men; and no amount of striving or training will enable them to equal or break men's records in fields requiring strength and endurance. [Sefton, 1941: 27]

The Women's Division went through various bureaucratic transformations, eventually becoming the Division for Girls and Women's Sports (DGWS), and (in 1974), the National Association of Girls and Women in Sports. The attitude against women competing changed little. What it meant to young, athletically interested girls is shown in volleyballist Mary Jo Peppler's remarks:

> Sports in school weren't very competitive for girls, just what they called "play days." We'd play all different sports without even keeping score. It was felt that competition was bad for girls. They wouldn't allow any men to get involved in our sports as coaches or officials because then they'd bring with them the idea of competition. It was something women were afraid of. Sports for girls, then, were just a way to get exercise. [Jordan, 1977: 168-69]

The Association for Intercollegiate Athletics for Women, which is apparently in the process of being absorbed into the (heretofore men's) National Collegiate Athletic Association, has been less restrictive than earlier organizations, but it, too, has subscribed to a philosophy that women's sports should be different in important ways from men's.[4]

Those who set the principles of the women's athletic associations cannot be labeled sexist in the straightforward way that we would label Senator Freylinghuysen a sexual bigot--and in fact many of them were courageous fighters for women's equality. However, they argued that sports competition as it existed for men corrupted character and that equality for women should not mean that women's characters became corrupted through the same unsavory sorts of competition. They helped restrict women's access to sports resources.

In order to understand how sports competition can be an important character builder as well as an important corrupter of character we must distinguish between different senses of competition that are relevant to sports.

II. Competition

One way we talk about competition has to do with the nature of many athletic activities. According to the rules of many games, one person or one team competes with another. Simply to decide to play tennis or handball or racquetball with someone else, for example, involves trying to place the ball where they cannot return it and to return it wherever they place it, with the aim of achieving enough points to win. Competition in this direct context presupposes cooperation-- everyone involved has to cooperate in playing the game according to the rules. Competition becomes a kind of cooperative challenge for each. In this sense,

> [o]ne must play against the opponent during a competitive experience, but at the same time one plays with the opposition. As we have said, the opponent is not just an obstacle to surmount in order to win, but a human being who has offered to pit his or her talents against your talents in order to have competition. In a sense, one must cooperate if one is to compete. There can be no experience of facing the struggle unless your opponent gives you something to struggle against. Consequently, the athlete should be grateful for the opportunity to compete against another. One is therefore both with and against another during competition. [Neal and Tutko, 1975: 171]

Games like softball, field hockey, badminton, soccer, and football, or sports like fencing and boxing offer prime examples of competition as cooperative challenge.

Moving away from these prime examples, there is a continuum of cooperative challenge. In some sports like golf, bowling, or archery, the competitors perform parallel activity, but a cooperative challenge may still be involved. For example, a person may play golf alone. In a "friendly game" he or she may be spurred on to play better. In a tournament, or if a bet is placed, the cooperative challenge becomes explicit in that one player takes the other player into account in plotting strategy--by trying a longshot on the last hole, for example, if it offers a chance to win.

Other sports give their benefits in the training for the challenge. For example, running in itself is a physical activity that people and many other animals simply do. It becomes a sport when there are rules defining the competition and requirements that affect training (for example, the need to learn proper starting technique). In the longer races, the cooperative challenge is fairly direct, for the runner must plot strategy to use his or her own special abilities against those of the opponents. However, the cooperative challenge in track events seems more to come from the larger collective activity that includes team membership and practice and culminates in the meets.

Perhaps a limiting case of competition as cooperative challenge occurs in some athletic activities we don't call sports. For example, people doing aerobic dancing or exercising often find they do better in a group than alone because they are challenged to rise to a higher standard. I call it a "limiting case" because it doesn't involve rule-constituted competition, though it does seem to offer the basic social-psychological element of cooperative challenge that is an aid to excellence.

It is this first kind of competition that has been said to develop ability, strong character, discipline, and all the things athletic experience is said to foster. Winners and losers, occasional players and serious athletes in training all gain from cooperative challenge.

At another extreme of the continuum, competition may be extended beyond a game in which individuals or teams face each other to a set of games in a playoff or even a whole season. Then the challenge changes, and even in a recreational league, there may well come to be more emphasis on winning, if, for example, the teams want to make the playoffs or if someone is keeping records. For serious athletes, competition is extended beyond the game of the moment because they have individual careers. According to Olympic gold medalist Patsy Neal,

> When one is very young and is in love with move-
> ment experience and with play, the controlling eth-
> ics is probably that, "It's not whether you win or
> lose, but how you play the game." And even though
> this basic concept is still paid verbal homage at the
> Olympics, as competition becomes more skilled and
> more refined, the individual gradually rejects this
> concept although he or she may continue to say it
> is still paramount.
>
> Most athletes are trained and coached physically
> and emotionally to win. [Neal and Tutko, 1975:
> 169]

If winning is the goal of the game by the rules, then playing
a game properly means playing to win. However, winning
may have implications outside the game of the moment, particularly for serious athletes.

Consistent winning is one way in which better athletes
are recognized on any level. It is one way of sorting people
into "peer groups" of players with comparable ability so that
everyone gets an appropriate challenge. Used properly, it
is a way of letting everyone develop their abilities, and it is
a way of giving the best athletes the opportunity to become
outstanding ones. The challenge is greater and they accept
it. However, Neal remarks,

> These [highly coached] athletes are torn between the
> values of society and the intrinsic values they have
> derived from the game itself. They want to win
> but they realize the importance of the process and
> the method of winning. [Neal and Tutko, 1975:
> 169]

When it is a part of the rules of the game, winning is part
of the cooperative challenge of competition. But when Neal
speaks of the "values of society" she may be referring to a
different kind of competition, which I shall call "competition
in a ranking." The most widespread example of competition
in a ranking is in our educational system. Individual students
are given grades to measure how much they have learned and
grade point averages are calculated. Prizes are awarded on
that basis. But students need not choose to compete, nor
(in many cases) do they offer a challenge to each other.
They simply go to school and do the required work and the
teachers rank them. The ranking may have enormous consequences. For example, in the late 1960s it meant the dif-

ference (for many men) between staying at home and going into the armed forces. It makes a difference between getting into medical school and spending one's life in an interesting, prestigious, and lucrative profession rather than spending one's life in some other way. The ranking is extrinsic to the learning, and every high school student knows honor roll grinds who "aren't all that smart."

In sports, individuals or teams may compete in a ranking. Neal speaks of athletes being trained and coached to win, and in fact career athletes are those for whom the results of competition are important because the career, in most sports, is intrinsically associated with ranking competition. A ranking measures inequality, and career athletes are those of superior ability.

In recreational sports--for example in pick-up games or in Sunday morning shirts and skins basketball--the cooperative challenge is predominant. There is no official ranking structure, and although some individuals on the teams may be intensely competitive, they are usually the sort who compete in non-sports activities as well--to have the best-looking date or the fanciest car or to mow a lawn or paint a wall faster than someone else. Ranking enters even in recreational leagues when there is a grading system by wins and losses over the season, with the reward of being in the playoffs or the brief glory of being league champion. However, this is very far down on a continuum that has the complex ranking methods and the extraordinary rewards of professional baseball, football, hockey, golf, or tennis. In between are school sports, and they range from college football, which sometimes resembles the professional sports, to fencing, which is more often done for the love of it.

Bearing all these differences in mind, we might take a career athlete as one who is committed to a sports activity in which he or she not only competes in a cooperative challenge but in a ranking as well.[5] The career athlete may or may not be a competitive person, of course.

The justification for cooperative challenge lies in the joy of the game and the contribution to health and good character. The justification for competition in a ranking is much more complicated and much more confused. Patsy Neal was right to speak of the "values of our society," for in our society differences in rank very often mean differences in reward. Understanding ranking requires understanding changes in our theories about the world and human nature, and the changes in our lives that underlie them.

The development of sports was part of the social process that included industrialization and urbanization, and a growing specialization in jobs and the development of the professions. The ideas of competition helped explain how it is that all men are created equal in a democracy in which there are very great inequalities of wealth, power, and influence.

One idea of competition was very important in the economic theory that was current in nineteenth-century America. In a free market, workers are supposed to compete for jobs and capitalists are supposed to compete for a piece of the market. This competition is what is supposed to fuel the engine of progress and make a vigorous free market through which the wealth of the nation grows. The image of free market competitors is one of energetic people with know-how, people who are willing to try a little harder and work a little longer.

A second idea of competition came from theories of biological and social evolution. The metaphor that many people took from these theories was that life on this planet is a competitive struggle in which the fittest win out. To speak of "survival of the fittest" led some people to think of "winners" in the competition as fitter or better--a thought which went along with the mistaken idea that some species are "higher" than others. [6]

The economic and evolutionary ideas together seem to justify the unequal distribution of wealth and power in a democracy: those people who win out in the economic competition rank higher on the fitness scale. They deserve to be on top. And since economic competition is for greater monetary rewards (how else would the market mechanism run?) they deserve their fortunes. [7] So the stratified social organization seems just. This image of competition also seems to explain how to build a strong nation. If high positions are given out to winners in competition, then we will excel in politics, industry, science, and sports because the competition will select those who are the most able, those who merit the high position and reward. Meritocracy is called just because it rewards the deserving, and it is said to be in the interest of the nation because it rewards the best. Or so goes this story about competition in a meritocracy.

To complete the picture we need yet another sense of competition: competition as combat.

III.   Competition As Combat

> The most striking differences in instinctive equip-
> ment consists in the strength of the fighting instinct
> in the male and of the nursing instinct in the fe-
> male.... The out-and-out physical fighting for the
> sake of combat is pre-eminently a male instinct,
> and the resentment at mastery, the zeal to surpass,
> and the general joy at activity in mental as well as
> physical matters seem to be closely correlated with
> it. [E. E. Thorndike, 1914][8]

Sports events often seem to be taken as battles by re-
porters and fans. In international soccer, fans show that
when their team wins, they feel they have symbolically con-
quered the nation the other team represents. Some television
announcers treat the Olympics as part of a cold war that will
show American free enterprise is superior to Soviet socialism. Football, basketball, and hockey fans sometimes behave as though the honor of school or region turns on whether
their team wins or loses. In some sports, fans may be
abusive to the visiting team, treating their opposition as
enemies, not as competitors.[9] This is sports competition
as combat.

In combat, the fighting team serves as a symbolic
champion for its home group. In real war, of course, the
results of victory are not simply symbolic, for the victors
get not only the fame but fortune as well. Americans in the
nineteenth and the twentieth centuries overwhelmingly considered war a male activity, so much so that when some of
them wanted to exclude women from something they described
it as battle. The New York Senator whom I quoted in Section
I of this chapter used this ploy in arguing against giving
women the vote.

Although many fans participate, there are few people
who would explicitly endorse the national and regional chau-
vinism that comes from taking athletes as champions and
sports events as battles. Most of us would deplore the fact
that the National Council of Secondary School Athletic Directors had to develop a publication called Crowd Control (see
Miller, 1974: 176). However, there are some among us

who take warlike competition in sports to be particularly male--some deploring it and others saying it serves good purpose.

Mary Jo Peppler distinguishes male competition from female competition in a way that sheds light on arguments against women competing as men do. She says,

> [m]en compete differently [from women]. They're aggressive. Their satisfaction comes from dominating their opponent rather than striving toward perfection.... Men wouldn't dare help another man who might beat them. They have this ego problem that women don't.
>
> Sport has been a male domain for so long that it's the men who have defined how one should compete. The problem for the woman athlete is that we've accepted these definitions and tried to copy them. But since it's not consistent with our natures, the best we can become is just a poor copy of aggressive male models. [Jordan, 1977: 195-6]

This argument on the basis of men's and women's natures sounds suspiciously like nineteenth-century arguments. Certainly the majority of men are not ego-smashing, aggressive competitors. To speak of "natures" in a context in which not all men and women show the characteristically "natural" behavior is to speak of norms, not natures.

Some contemporary writers have tried to argue that there is a genuine biological basis for male aggressiveness. For example, popular writer Steven Goldberg has argued in The Inevitability of Patriarchy that due to hormones, human males are naturally aggressive and that when they compete among themselves this competition operates as a kind of natural selection in which weaker and less able men lose out and better ones win fame, fortune, and leadership in the great battle of life--not only to their own benefit but to the benefit of the species.

The military metaphor has been common in describing evolutionary competition. Darwin himself uses it at the close of the chapter on natural selection in his Origin of Species. He there uses the then common comparison of the relations of species to a "great tree":

The green and budding twigs may represent existing

species; and those produced during each former
year may represent the long succession of extinct
species. At each period of growth, all the growing
twigs have tried to branch out on all sides, and to
overtop and kill the surrounding twigs and branches,
in the same manner as species and groups of species have tried to overmaster other species in the
great battle of life. [Darwin, 1950: 129]

Overmastering others in the battle of life hardly suits (for
example) the survival of dandelions, mitochondria, or even
those perennial winners, the cockroaches.[10] In fact, survival for a species very much depends on fitting comfortably
with others into an environment (as Darwin's own example of
finches adapting to different niches shows). Even predators
depend on the survival of their prey species. The military
metaphor connects competition with dominating and subduing
opponents--an image that is not present in the idea of sports
competition as a cooperative challenge or a ranking.

Darwin, of course, was talking about competition
among species and Steven Goldberg was talking about competition among individuals within a species. However, human
society isn't a battlefield any more than nature is, and human
survival can't be said to depend on the more aggressive
males' competing for fame, fortune, and leadership. We
would do better to choose leaders of wisdom and ability for
the task at hand. Experience seems to bear this out, for
as a nation we are far more in debt to the scholarly Thomas
Jefferson, who made such a poor showing as war governor
of Virginia, than we are to rough-riding Teddy Roosevelt.

Competition as battle among aggressive males also
contradicts the idea of competition as cooperative challenge.
Patsy Neal says,

Probably the two most important factors that
determine whether an athlete is ethical are:
(1) how the athlete sees his or her opponent in
relation to the competitive process and (2) how
the athlete sees himself or herself during the competitive process. [Neal and Tutko, 1975: 171]

She goes on to discuss playing against an opponent while playing with him or her--the passage I quoted as the basis of the
definition of cooperative challenge in Section II above. To
take sports competition as battle is to take one's opponent as

an enemy and oneself as bent on being victor and champion.

Of course, Steven Goldberg's argument is little more than a renewed effort to justify the sexual division of labor, warning us that men and women are biologically different and that the human race will come to nought unless women stay home and leave the battle of public life to men. He confuses winning a battle over an enemy with qualifying for a higher rank because one has merit.[11]

There are some, however, who seem to argue for male superiority on the basis of criteria for measuring merit.

> In sports, male and female are placed in their historical biological roles. In sports, strength and speed do count, for they determine the winner. As in premechanized combat, women are usually second place to men in sports. They can compete against one another and they can cheer their men on, but a quick review of the record books comparing the achievements in sports of men and women confirms the distinctness of the sexes here. [Beisser, 1977: 189]

Like many group comparisons, this argument hints that biological differences are the basis for men's higher rank. But we must ask carefully what that alleged "higher rank" amounts to. After all, although men finish first in the Boston Marathon, the top-placing women beat out the vast hordes of the male runners.

To rank men over women in sports because the best statistics in record books belong to males is to take those top-ranking males as champions who symbolically win the battle for all males. This makes even less sense than does ranking American's free enterprise over Soviet socialism because our hockey team beat theirs. It ignores the fact that sports excellence is judged for individual and team performance, and that in some leagues, women have outperformed men.[12] It ignores the fact, that is, that competition in sports ranks individuals and teams, not ideologies or nations or sexes. The meritocracy includes all the women who do well, and all the men who do well, even though women and men alike might not come up to the top male record in some sports.

If we take the ranking competition in sports seriously, then all people--men and women, boys and girls--should have opportunity to compete on grounds of their individual merit. If women and girls are held back from competing because men and boys get the lion's share of resources, that seems to be discrimination. However, if we seriously describe sports competition as combat, and believe firmly that war is men's business, then sports seem men's business, too. Describing sports or politics or industry or banking as battle has been one traditional way of ruling women out of the competition. It is an argument that relies on a sexual division of labor to give the greatest portion of resources to males.

It is a mistake to understand sports competition as a war, as combat against an enemy. Unfortunately, a major part of our problem in understanding what equal treatment of women in sports would be, in school or outside it, comes from the fact that we live within the traditions of a society in which a sexual division of labor has existed and still exists today. In the last section of this essay I would like to look at some of what that means, not so much for equal opportunity to compete in a ranking but for the opportunity to gain the character that cooperative challenge in sport is said to build.

IV.   Making a Woman of a Girl

Having sorted out the various kinds of competition, we can now turn to asking how participation in sports helps build the character that citizens of a democracy need.

One former high school and college athlete I interviewed felt sports was a prime influence in his life:

> Sports taught me how to communicate with others and how to work and play with others. How to follow directions and communicate, and how to think. As well as hand-eye coordination and the things you usually expect to get from sports.

Olympic gold medalist Ann Henning said,

> I owe a lot to sports. If I didn't get into athletics, I have this feeling, I don't know why, but

> I just do, that I wouldn't be too neat a person. I'm
> lazy.... I know there are things I can have and
> be, which I never would have realized if I hadn't
> gone into athletics. [Jordan, 1977: 56-66]

Sports can be centrally important in the lives of both men
and women. In our society, however, men's and women's
lives may be different in many ways.

If we ask about differences in what men and women
have the opportunity to do, we see that difference in opportunity begins when they are boys and girls. The college athlete I quoted above said this about his sports participation:

> I played baseball in the second grade and swam
> from the time I was seven. There were elementary
> school intramurals that I was part of. In high
> school, I played all the intramural sports and at
> Saturday Rec I played on teams with my friends.
> And I was on the high school track team.
> I wasn't in the academic or the social clubs in
> the high school. But people knew I was a regular
> guy. That's why when I talk about athletics as so-
> cializing me ... well I knew people because of ath-
> letics but people knew me too. Senior year I was
> the fastest kid in the high school. Senior year in
> college I was captain of the track team.

Ann Henning set an Olympic record in speedskating in 1972,
and she certainly outranks that college athlete in athletic ability. Still, she did not have the same opportunity.

> [Often] she competed successfully against boys
> her own age, although those successes were con-
> fined to casual pick-up games at the local park.
> She was prohibited, by her sex, from competing
> against those same boys in more officially sanc-
> tioned contests such as the local Little League Pro-
> gram.
> "That didn't really bother me," she says, "I
> knew I could beat the boys and they knew it, too."
> [Jordan, 1977: 59]

Henning's experience was a common one.

Mary Jo Peppler was once voted the best women volleyball player in the world. She has this to say about her
girlhood experiences.

> Everywhere I went ... I was inclined to get into
> sports. It's always been a part of my life since
> I can remember. I played all the sports with the
> boys--I was the quarterback on our neighborhood
> football team--until about the sixth grade, when
> my parents told me I shouldn't be out there play-
> ing football with the boys, taking off my t-shirt
> and all, you know. It was a tough day for me
> when they told me that....
>
> By the time I got to high school it was obvious
> I had talent compared to the other people in school.
> But nobody directed me. If I had had any kind of
> encouragement at all, I would have been smart to
> go into a more recognizable sport, like tennis,
> rather than volleyball. [Jordan, 1977: 168-69]

Ann Henning, Mary Jo Peppler and the former college
athlete I interviewed were career athletes of exceptional ability. Even though the women had better athletic capacities
than the man, he had access to sports resources that they
did not. The reason is not so much discrimination on the
part of school or little league officials (though that sometimes exists) but the fact that our educational and sports institutions originated in a society in which a severe sexual
division of labor held sway. They exist today in a society
in which boys and girls are, for the most part, raised to
live different sorts of lives. The importance of this becomes clear if we consider ordinary people, not just career
athletes. I'll say something about boys and girls first, and
then take a very brief look at the access to sports resources
which ordinary citizens have.

In 1972, sociologist Janet Lever studied fifth grade
children, aged ten and eleven, from one suburban and two
city schools in Connecticut. Her study doesn't tell us what
all boys and girls do, for the children were mainly white
and middle class, and boys' and girls' lives are very different in different parts of the country, in rural areas, and in
different ethnic or racial communities. But it's helpful even
to discuss such a limited group of East Coast children.

Lever spent a year observing the children, and she
interviewed them, and had them keep play diaries. She found
that boys did more things outdoors, and they played more in
large groups of children of diverse ages. Their games were
more often competitive ones with a clearly defined winner,
lasted longer, had more complex rules and a higher ceiling
of skill. Lever felt that the games the boys played let them

develop organizational skills and offered them experience in understanding rules and settling disputes. She felt the boys may have improved their ability to deal with interpersonal competition. Some of them received training in leadership skills because of the kind of games they played. [Lever, 1976: 484]

Some girls played games with the boys sometimes. But as we saw in the remarks by career athletes above, opportunity for boys to play these games was much greater. Lever says,

> Boys in all three schools could play daily, depending on the season, in ongoing basketball, football, or baseball games involving ten to twenty-five or more persons....
> Most boys reported regular participation in neighborhood sports games. In addition, at the time of the study, 68% said they belonged to some adult-supervised teams, with a full schedule of practice and league games. [Lever, 1978: 478-79]

However, if we focus too closely on equal opportunity, we may overlook some of the facts that are important. Lever says,

> Boys grant much more importance to being proclaimed the winner; they virtually always structure their games, be it one-on-one or full team basketball, so that the outcomes will be clear and definite. [Lever, 1978: 479]

In contrast, she reports that the girls often participated in their games "for the fun of the turn, not to win" (Lever, 1978: 478). And in general, she says, the girls were satisfied to keep their play loosely structured. The girls' games tended to be cooperative. In their one-on-one play, the girls learned how to relate in an intimate way to "best friends."

In describing the children's play, Lever speaks of "boys' games" and "girls' games." In fact, many of the games the boys played (basketball, hockey, football) are adult games played mainly by men. The games girls tended to play (hopscotch, jumprope, jacks) are not adult games played by women but rather children's games. Further-

more, the games the boys played were largely those introduced after the mid-nineteenth century, those suitable for
organized sports. Lever says,

> Historical analysis of children's games confirms
> that boys are playing more team sports now than
> ever before. Equally important, boys have drifted
> away from loosely structured play toward more
> formally organized competitive games.... Evi-
> dence presented here supports this picture. It ap-
> pears that the growing cultural emphasis on sports
> and winning has carried over to non-physical ac-
> tivities and made them more competitive and that,
> to date, it has had this effect to a far greater ex-
> tent for boys than for girls. [Lever, 1978: 480]

Given the concern that competition by ranking is emphasized
over competition as cooperative challenge, we may want to
question the trend in boys' sports rather than simply ask for
equal opportunity for girls.

On the other hand, Lever also suggests that the skills
one learns in the games boys play may be important to the
careers many men have in business, industry, and the professions. If this is so, then the old sexual division of labor
shows in the way boys' and girls' play is organized, with
boys in training for the fray of career competition and the
girls learning the intimacy, cooperation and indifference to
winning needed to be a man's helpmeet.

There are two factors that must be separated in considering Lever's observations. One concerns equal opportunity for women and girls. Courts, legislatures, and government bureaus are concerned that all citizens should have an
equal opportunity to compete and be ranked and receive rewards according to their ability, within existing institutions.
Equal opportunity is very important for extraordinary athletes, and Ann Henning and Mary Jo Peppler did not have it.
They lacked it not because wicked people discriminated
against them but because the social, educational, and sports
institutions that existed in the 1960s were historically developed from a society in which a severe sexual division of
labor existed. Our organized sports originated not only with
the industrial and urban revolutions, but also in the separation of home from work and the division of men's and women's
"spheres." Times have changed and women now have careers
in men's sphere. Court orders and legislation are needed to
give them equal opportunity to compete in the rankings.

Lever's results indicate that equal opportunity for ordinary girls may also be important to their career goals--not only for girls who want to have a try at being a career athlete but those who want careers in the worlds of business and politics. If the games boys play give them organizational and other skills important in business and politics as they now exist, girls should perhaps play them, too.[13] Courts and legislatures are of less help in this regard because it is a question of what boys and girls <u>choose</u> in a sex-divided society.

The second factor concerns educating citizens. Organized sports were developed in a society in which men's work in business and politics was considered to be a competitive battle in which the victor showed himself <u>fitter</u> than the vanquished and thus deserving of the spoils. Even if some of those sports do give boys skills to survive in our present world of business and politics, it is <u>far</u> from clear that citizens in a democracy should be encouraged to have that kind of character. In fact, this is very like the objection that the earlier women's sports organizations had to modeling women's athletic programs on men's. Those organizations were right in their criticisms, but unfortunately they retained presuppositions of a sex-divided society. They felt the social, business, political, and sports worlds needed changing, but their strategy was wrong.

What would be a better strategy?

A philosopher is not the one to decide on a better strategy. However, whatever the strategy, it must include an understanding that women of extraordinary ability, who wish to become career athletes, must be given opportunity to do so within our existing institutions. They must be given opportunity to compete in rankings, to develop their excellence, and to reap the rewards. However, <u>all</u> women need sports as it builds character for citizens in a democracy. Not just girls or college students but mothers and working women and golden agers. So do all men. There is ample reason to believe that sports that dominate because they get good gate receipts or because they develop skills useful for a competitive, stratified business and political world may <u>not</u> be the best ones for this purpose.

The answer to whether sports can make a woman of a girl is the same as the answer as to whether sports can make a man of a boy. It is an answer we do not yet have, for it requires understanding how to change our social, business, and political worlds so that the ideal of cooperative challenge replaces that of aggressive and ruthless battle with an enemy. It requires understanding a competition that ranks and justly rewards ability at an activity rather than a competition that perpetuates inequality and gives some groups the lion's share of resources that should be available to all citizens. Understanding how sports can make a woman of a girl means understanding what sports competition must become to build the kind of society in which the citizens of a democracy make their home.[14]

NOTES

1. The quotation is from Democracy in America, ed. Phillips Bradley (New York: Knopf, 1945, volume 2, page 124). Mary Jo Peppler asks the question I use in the title, "Can sports make a woman of a girl?" in her interview with Pat Jordan (Jordan, 1977).

2. In 1870, one doctor argued against women entering his profession in this way. "More especially is medicine disgusting to women, accustomed to softnesses and the downy side of life. They are sedulously screened from the observation of the horrors and disgusts of life. Fightings and tumults, the blood and mire, bad smells and bad words, and foul men and more intolerable women she but rarely encounters." (Barker Benfield, 1976: 87) Medical practice is described in battlefield terms.

3. The National Amateur Athletic Federation was founded early in the 1920s, with Mrs. Herbert Hoover initially having leadership of the girls' and women's side of things. She felt that "there were such fundamentally different factors underlying the athletics of men and boys and of girls and women that the athletics of the two groups should be under different direction" (Sefton, 1941: 2). The group was active until after World War II, and the philosophy was influential enough to shape most physical education programs for women.

4. "The A. I. A. W. announced in June that it would cease operations this year, charging that the N. C. A. A. had illegally lured its members away with cash and resources from its well-established men's sports programs. The women's association has filed an antitrust suit against the N. C. A. A. If the A. I. A. W. is victorious, it could resume sponsoring women's championships in 1983-84" (The Chronicle of Higher Education, Oct. 6, 1982, p. 19).

An illustration of the A.I.A.W.'s philosophy that women's sports should be different in important ways from men's is provided by the fact that, until it was forced to change its policies in 1973 under the Education Amendments of 1972, the A.I.A.W. did not allow teams having players on athletic scholarship to enter its tournaments.

5. See Becker, "Notes on the Concept of Commitment," in Becker, 1970. It may turn out by this understanding of career athlete that some sports are career sports. For example, many of us are runners and some of us are very fast, but being a sprinter seems to require being a member of a team and thus ranked, and taking part in matches in which one is ranked.

6. It took a very long time (and the development of genetic theory) to understand Darwin's evolutionary theory, based on the theory of natural selection. Until the turn of the century, Americans who thought about it understood evolutionary theory in a more Lamarckian way--that socially acquired characteristics were passed on to one's children. That is, they didn't make as sharp a distinction as we do now between genetics and socialization.

7. At the end of the nineteenth century, people also believed these "winners" should have more children so as to insure that the "race" would progress through their fitter children.

8. The quote goes on, "... women's 'dependence' is, I am sure, only an awkward name for less resentment at a mastery. The actual nursing of the young seems likewise to involve equally unreasoning tenderness to pet, coddle, and 'do for' others." (E. E. Thorndike, Educational Psychology, Columbia University, 1914, pp. 350-351, quoted in Bowles, 1976: 198). Thorndike was extremely influential. His views recommend different sorts of education for boys and girls to prepare the one for active mastery of the world and the other to "do for" others.

9. Patsy Neal gives the athlete's view of this; when she says, "possibly only an athlete can comprehend the obscenity of having a spectator or group of spectators be critical of the worth of years of effort.... For a spectator to feel he or she has the right to make a judgement concerning the quality of play on the court or the field, or to be the judge who can lessen a man's achievement through catcalls and boos, is to me one of the most depressing facets of our society today.

Probably the least qualified individual to judge excellence is the spectator" (quoted in Miller, 1974: 175).

10. Mitochondria are among the organisms which developed very early on earth, and thus they are among the winners in the "longest survival" contest. They exist in the cytoplasm of all cells, including human ones, and we couldn't live without them--nor for that matter could they live without the other organisms in whose cells they make their own life cycles. Cooperation is what's important here. On the other hand, it has recently been discovered that those unlikely warriors, the sea anemones, do battle with each other over the scarce territory in tide pools, but here members of groups of cloned individuals fight with members of other groups of cloned individuals of the same species. Obviously this can't be a battle to overtop and kill because any species incorporating that kind of activity would be suicidal. The battle serves to keep the groups of individuals separate by keeping bare trails between them, so that each group keeps on living as peacefully as the environment permits.

11. In sports, the battle sometimes has results that are contradictory to sound mind and body, e.g., the use of drugs and anabolic steroids. Even if we took Goldberg seriously, surely it makes no sense to say that the more aggressive (the ones who win) are the fitter when they win by using such means.

12. Cases from the early 1970s are cited in Neal and Tutko, 1975: 118.

13. See Haragan, 1978.

14. Special thanks to Richard Ullman Addelson and Howard Becker for their advice, comments, and criticism.

REFERENCES

Ainsworth, Dorothy S., et al. Individual Sports for Women. 2nd ed. Philadelphia: W. B. Saunders, 1949.

American Association for Health, Physical Education, and Recreation. Division for Girls and Women's Sports. Committee on Standards. Philosophy and Standards for Girls and Women's Sports. Washington, D.C.: AAHPER, 1969.

_____. National Section of Women's Athletics. Committee on Standards. Standards in Athletics for Girls and Women:

Guiding Principles in the Organization and Administration of Athletic Programs. Washington, D.C.: AAHPER, 1948.

Barker-Benfield, G. J. The Horrors of the Half Known Life. New York: Harper & Row, 1976.

Becker, Howard S. Sociological Work. Chicago: Aldine, 1970.

Beisser, Arnold R. The Madness in Sports. Bowie, Md.: The Charles Press, 1977.

Bowles, Samuel, and Herbert Gintes. Schooling in Capitalist America. New York: Basic Books, 1976.

Darwin, Charles. On the Origin of Species by Means of Natural Selection. London: Watts, 1950.

Davison, Fred C. "Intercollegiate Athletics and Title IX," USA Today, vol. 108, no. 2410 (July 1979).

Deatherage, Dorothy, and Patricia C. Reid. Administration of Women's Competitive Sports. Dubuque, Iowa: Wm. C. Brown, 1977.

Doran, Barbara L. "Armchair Symposium," The Sportswoman, vol. 3, no. 1 (Jan/Feb 1975).

Dulles, Foster Rhea. A History of Recreation: America Learns to Play. 2nd ed. New York: Appleton-Century-Crofts, 1965.

Eitzen, D. Stanley. Sport in Contemporary Society. New York: St. Martin's Press, 1979.

Felshin, Jan. "Status of Women and Sport" in Eitzen, 1979, pages 412-420.

Flexner, Eleanor. Century of Struggle. New York: Atheneum, 1976.

Haragan, Betty L. Games Mother Never Taught You: Corporate Gamesmanship for Women. New York: Warner Books, 1978.

Hogan, Candace Lyle. "Title IX from Here to Equality" in Eitzen, 1979, pages 420-424.

Jordan, Pat. Broken Patterns. New York: Dodd, Mead, 1977.

LaNoue, George R. "Athletics and Equality" in Eitzen, 1979, pages 424-432.

Lever, Janet. "Sex Differences in the Complexity of Children's Play and Games," American Sociological Review, vol. 43 (August 1978): 471-483.

_____. "Sex Differences in the Games Children Play," Social Problems, vol. 23, 4 (April 1976).

Meyer, Margaret H., and Marguerite M. Schwarz. Team Sports for Girls and Women. 4th ed. Philadelphia: W. B. Saunders, 1965.

Miller, Donna Mae. Coaching the Female Athlete. Philadelphia: Lea and Febiger, 1974.

National Amateur Federation. Women's Division. Women and Athletics. New York: A. S. Barnes, 1930.

Neal, Patsy E., and Thomas A. Tutko. Coaching Girls and Women: Psychological Perspectives. Boston: Allyn and Bacon, 1975.

Parkhouse, Bonnie, and Jack Lapin. Women Who Win. Englewood Cliffs, N.J.: Prentice-Hall, 1980.

Poindexter, Hally B. W., and Carole L. Mushier. Coaching Competitive Sports for Girls and Women. Philadelphia: W. B. Saunders, 1973.

Sage, George H. "Women in Sport: Cooptation or Liberation?" in Eitzen, 1979, pages 432-436.

Sefton, Alice Allene. The Women's Division, National Amateur Federation; Sixteen Years of Progress for Girls and Women, 1923-1939. Stanford, Calif.: Stanford University Press, 1941.

Twin, Stephanie L. Out of the Bleachers: Writings on Women and Sport. Old Westbury, N.Y.: The Feminist Press, 1979.

QUESTIONS

(1) a) What does Addelson mean by the phrase "competition as cooperative challenge"?

b) List all the factors you can which make it desirable that sports competition should be competition as cooperative challenge.

c) List all the factors you can which make it undesirable that sports competition should be competition as cooperative challenge.

(2) a) What does Addelson mean by the phrase "competition in a ranking"?

b) In your view, does the theory of evolution hold that there is a competition in a ranking among different species? Why or why not?

c) List all the factors you can which make it desirable that sports competition should be competition in a ranking.

d) List all the factors you can which make it undesirable that sports competition should be competition in a ranking.

(3) a) What does Addelson mean by the phrase "competition as combat"?

b) List all the factors you can which make it desirable that sports competition should be competition as combat.

c) List all the factors you can which make it undesirable that sports competition should be competition as combat.

(4) Can you think of any additional sense of the word "competition" which is relevant to sport? If so, what is it? What factors make it desirable that sports competition should be competition in this sense of the word? What factors make it undesirable that sports competition should be competition in this sense of the word?

(5) a) Which of the different types of competition discussed above are found in sports at your school? Explain.

b) How, if at all, do the different types of competition reinforce each other in sports at your school? How, if at all, do they hamper each other?

(6) a) What is the sexual division of labor?

b) How does the sexual division of labor interfere with girls' and women's access to character-building sports according to Addelson?

c) Do you agree or disagree with Addelson? Why?

(7) In your view, what must sports competition become "to build the kind of society in which the citizens of a democracy make their home"? Why?

(8) What else would you like to discuss from Addelson's essay?

10. COMPETITION, FRIENDSHIP, AND HUMAN NATURE

Drew A. Hyland

A few years ago in Connecticut, a female high school track athlete, obviously exceptionally talented at her sport, sought to compete on the boys' cross-country team, presumably because the competition she would meet there would be more at her own level. Her request was refused, and she took the matter to the state courts. She was turned down there, too. The judge explained his negative ruling with the following instructive remark:

> Athletic competition builds character in our boys. We do not need that kind of character in our girls. [1]

We may react with derisive laughter or perhaps with righteous indignation to this monumentally chauvinistic remark. Let us do so; but let us not dismiss it. For it hides a tissue of ambiguities and a number of important philosophic issues which it may be worthwhile to draw out and discuss.

Consider the first clause: "Athletic competition builds character in our boys." Given the context, we can presume that the judge is referring to the desirable character traits for which athletic competition is so often praised: discipline, teamwork, courage, perhaps the development of a high pain threshold. But there are numerous critics of athletic competition who, although they would certainly agree that such competition builds character, insist that it is a set of altogether undesirable character traits that is built: authoritarianism, mindless conformity, insensitivity to violence, and the "winning isn't everything, it's the only thing" attitude which inevitably breeds alienation from one's competitors. So the first clause generates the following questions for consideration: Does athletic competition build character at all? If so,

are desirable or undesirable character traits developed for
the most part? Is there a connection between either competition and friendship or competition and alienation, and if so,
what is the nature of that connection? Is it causal, that is,
does competition cause alienation, as is often claimed by its
critics, or does it cause friendship, as is (curiously) less
often claimed by its friends? If the relation is not causal,
what is its nature? Since I have already developed a response to these questions in print elsewhere, I shall in this
essay simply review my position and its basic defense.

   Consider now the second clause of the judge's remark:
"we do not need that kind of character in our girls." What
is implied by this remark? At least this: the judge assumes
that there is a fundamental difference in character between
girls and boys (hereafter, women and men), which differences
are such that competition enhances male character but is at
least unnecessary if not indeed detrimental to female character. But to evaluate this thesis adequately we must ask at
least the following: are there important differences between
women and men? The physiological answer to this question
may be easy, though the details undoubtedly complex. But
are there also "spiritual" differences or differences "in character" between women and men? If so, what are they? Specifically for our topic, if there are differences in character
(or perhaps even physiological), how are they related to the
desirability or undesirability of athletic competition? How do
we decide this question? After a review of my position on
the first set of questions, I shall turn to a consideration of
these latter issues.

   In an article entitled "Competition and Friendship"
(Journal of the Philosophy of Sport, Volume V, 1978, pages
27-37), I developed a position on the first set of questions
which I shall here review.[2] The first and essential point
would be so obvious as hardly to be worth mentioning were it
not so often overlooked. Sometimes athletic competition is
informed by alienation, and sometimes it is informed by
friendship. I daresay that anyone whose competitive experience has always been one of alienation and never of friendship
has had an unfortunately perverse athletic experience. Conversely, anyone whose competitive experience has always been
friendly and has never had a game develop into alienation has
had a peculiarly fortunate and probably overprotected sporting
experience. Most of us, surely, have experienced both friendship and alienation in our sport competition, and that simple
fact alone is sufficient to reject the two general claims that

athletic competition (or competition altogether) necessarily causes alienation or that it necessarily causes friendship. The relationship is evidently more complex.

Could we not say that although the relation is not a necessary one, sometimes, under certain conditions, competition causes alienation, and sometimes under other conditions it causes friendship? Only, in my judgment, if we expand our understanding of "cause" to include the Aristotelian notion of "final cause," or what we today often refer to as teleology. Athletic competition causes friendship in the sense that friendship is a telos, an end or perfection of that activity. Insofar as athletic competition attains the best that it can be, its highest possibility, it does so as a mode of friendship. In short, our very best experiences of competition are informed by friendship. Many of us have begun friendships on the playing field (both with teammates and with opponents), and have continued to nurture those friendships in that context. Still, like any loyal teleologist, I appreciate, however reluctantly, that things often fail to reach their telos. To use an old Aristotelian example, the telos, again the end or perfection, of an acorn is to become an oak tree. That is what the highest possibility, the final cause, of an acorn is, notwithstanding the empirical fact that a minuscule percentage of all acorns actually attain that telos. In this case, the final cause of an acorn is indeed a cause, but one enacted or fulfilled relatively infrequently. We can make the analogous point with sport competition. It is perfectly compatible with the recognition that such competition often--perhaps even for the most part--devolves into alienation to say that friendship is nevertheless the telos of competition and so the cause in this sense. It is important to note that on this view the actual causal relation gets reversed; if friendship is a telos of competition, then teleologically at least, friendship is a cause of competition rather than the converse.

What then is the status of the relation of alienation and competition? Alienation on this view is a defective mode of competition. When competition fails to be the best that it can be, alienation may ensue. This position thus enables us to found a most important claim: whenever athletic competition becomes infused with alienation, that represents a failure of that competition. If in a given game I become angry at my opponent and want to hurt him or her, my competitive situation is not attaining its highest possibility.

But, we now need to ask, how is all this so? What is it about human character that makes our competition sometimes a mode of friendship, sometimes of alienation? Indeed, what is it about human being that impels us to compete at all? To respond to these questions I need to adumbrate three different but compatible ways of characterizing the human situation.

The first depends on two conceptions of the individual which are often perceived as in tension. I call these conceptions the monadic individual and the relational individual. Briefly, the spokesmen for the monadic conception argue that human being is, or at least ought to be, an autonomous, self-reliant monad, whose essence (literally, whose being) is intrinsic. This does not mean that monadic individuals must be disciples of Henry David Thoreau, spending as much time as possible alone in the wilderness (although Thoreau is an excellent example of one who espoused and lived the ideal of the monadic individual). Monadic individuals can and will enter into relations with others. It is just that those relations are not essential to their natures; such relations do not make them who they are. Decisively, monadic individuals do not need relations with others. Being autonomous, they do not enter into "dependency relationships." It is important to appreciate that this conception of the individual is often (though not always) presented as an ideal, as something to be achieved. Most of us desire to feel independent, to "be our own woman (or man)."

This model of the individual has a long and esteemed history in our tradition, but no more so than the second conception of which I earlier spoke, that of the relational individual. According to the adherents to this conception, we are relational by nature. We do not, as with the monadic view, just happen to involve ourselves with others; such relations constitute what we are in our being. Sister, mother, artist, teacher, lover--these names of who we are all name modes of relationality. Adherents to this view usually (but again not always) recommend it as desirable, as the natural and best way for humans to be. Indeed, the appeal of participatory involvements, from team sports to nationalism, would hardly be understandable if the conception of the individual as relational did not contain some truth.

The study of the histories of these two viewpoints, the ebb and flow of their dominance, and the efforts to reconcile them would shed considerable light on the development of our tradition. Our purpose here is a more limited one for which the sketch above will suffice. We ought now at least to be able to suggest initially a relation between the monadic and relational conceptions of the individual on the one hand, and the central themes of competition, friendship, and alienation on the other. There is a certain prima facie congruity between the relational conception of the individual and that mode of competition that generates friendship, and conversely, between the monadic view and competition that leads to alienation. The relational view invites us to think positively of our relations with others and to hold them in high esteem, whereas the monadic view, with its emphasis on autonomy, independence, and not needing others, easily makes room for alienation. To be sure, these are not necessary connections but rather tendencies. As such, they nevertheless suggest a fairly strong though perhaps not exclusive opposition. Alienated competition typically arises when we are in monadic moods, friendship when we are in relational frames of mind, and those two conceptions of the individual seem in fundamental opposition.

There are, to be sure, thinkers who have argued exclusively in behalf of one of these standpoints and criticized the other. But to many a thinker, the appeal of both positions leads to the desire to reconcile them and hold them together in a unity, to say that we are, or can be, both monadic, with its connotations of autonomony and authenticity, and relational, with its connotations of community and participation, a position whose attractiveness is mitigated only by the recognition that it is easier said than justified. But suppose, as I believe, that they are reconcilable. What will this imply about the apparent opposition between that propensity for alienated competition presumably founded in the monadic view, and the propensity for friendly competition supposedly derivative of relationality? Evidently their connection is both closer and more complex. In order to take some steps toward understanding this, we must turn to a consideration of the second understanding of human being to which I earlier alluded.

Many a thinker has argued that there is in human being a "natural" urge to dominance or mastery. Indeed, in doctrines such as Nietzsche's famous teaching regarding will to power, this propensity is not limited to humans. All things strive naturally to enhance their power, which inevitably includes power over other things. In the case of humans, this tendency has often enough been recommended to us as a stance to take toward the world. "And thou shalt have dominion over the earth"; with this famous line, the Bible would seem to teach mastery over nature as literally a God-given right. More secularly, we need only point to the development of modern science, wherein from its seventeenth-century beginnings to the present, its development and achievements have been articulated in the vocabulary of dominance and even of war. The seventeenth-century clarion call of science was that we should become "the masters and possessors of nature," and to this day scientific achievements are described in such terms as the "mastery of nature," the "conquest of outer space," and the "control of our environment."

This attitude or stance of dominance toward nature was understandably transferable to relations among humans, with results that were not always so appealing. Thomas Hobbes' famous claim that the "state of nature" for humans was "a war of all against all" articulates well the problematic consequences of the stance of dominance when it is applied to the relations among humans. The "natural urge to dominance" has been used in accounts of everything from war and slavery to the relations between men and women. In these spheres, obviously, the stance of dominance, though it may preserve its appeal for the "masters," carries with it the bitter necessity for a second and concomitant stance, that of submission.

Initially, as is obvious from these examples, the stance of submission is looked upon as undesirable, as something to be avoided, as an "admission of defeat." But it has also been transformed into a stance that is portrayed as desirable and as something to be recommended, and with some very good reasons. Once one sees that the stance of dominance, precisely for those who succeed at it, often comes into conflict with one's conception of justice, the stance of submission becomes appealing as a way to avoid injustice, or as a way to escape "imposing one's own values" on others. The stance of submission is thus an antidote to "cultural imperialism," not to mention other forms of imperialism. Moreover, the stance can be seen as an honest effort to allow all things, and especially other people, to be what they can be without external imposition. It also becomes an articulation of a certain view of history; we are, or so we are told, "products" of our historical time and of the historical forces that determine that time. Rather than fight this, it is best to accept it, to accept one's place in the coursing of things, to affirm without contention "an idea whose time has come."

As we often hear in popular culture, "It's what's happening" --offered usually as an implicit argument for accepting what is happening. So we have the same situation here as with the monadic/relational dichotomy. Both stances of dominance and of submission can be presented as desirable, though both also can be criticized by friends of the contrary stance. But once again, because they both seem at least to have some appealing aspects, the inclination of many has been to try to reconcile them, to hold them together in a non-contradictory unity. As is obvious, such a reconciliation is not easy.

The third understanding of human being necessary to understanding the competitive urge has its origins in the thought of Plato, and especially in his dialogue The Symposium. It is the conception of human being as erotic. According to the Platonic Socrates, eros, or love, has two origins or "parents," Poros (Plenty, Resourcefulness), and Penia (Poverty, Lack). Insofar as human beings are erotic, then, we are characterized by an apparent tension between our incompleteness or partiality (our Penia heritage) and our capacity for overflowing or overfullness (our Poros genes). On the one hand, we are incomplete beings, incomplete in myriad ways, from wealth and political power, to our need for other people, to our lack of knowledge. Every way in which we are incomplete, recognize that incompleteness, and strive to overcome it, is a manifestation of our erotic natures. Are you an athlete, artist, senator, and wife? These, then, are some of the ways you have experienced your incompleteness and strived for wholeness, some of the ways in which you manifest your eros. But eros is at once overfullness, a capacity for overflowing, or as we sometimes say, for "giving of ourselves." We give ourselves in love, and the giving of that gift makes us in good measure who we are. Likewise, we express ourselves (literally, "press ourselves out") in a variety of ways, and those expressions also contribute to who we are. Our erotic natures, then, are constituted at once by our lacks and the ways we strive to overcome them, as well as by our fullness and the ways that we literally express that fullness. Together, these "moments" of eros make us who we are.

Our task now is to put these three understandings of the human situation together in such a way as to illuminate the origins of competition in human being, as well as the dual propensity of competition to become either alienated or friendship-enhancing. Let us begin with the monadic/relational duality. I have already suggested how easily the mo-

nadic conception of human being can found a view of competitive play which is accompanied by alienation, and how the
relational view can found a view of competitive play as fundamentally a mode of friendship. If this duality is joined
with the second duality of dominance/submission, however,
we see the situation from a different standpoint. To the extent that we are motivated by an urge to dominance, and
concomitantly, to the extent that the stance of submission
is fundamentally a stance of defeat, we could say that the
competition that arises from that stance will in all likelihood
be alienated. Does not our vocabulary of competition bear
this out? I submit that the closer the vocabulary of competition comes to the vocabulary of war (the extreme form of
dominance/submission), the more alienated our competitive
play is likely to be. The more our coaches exhort us to
"kill" the opposition, "bury them," or "humiliate them," the
more certain it is that alienation will ensue. Will taking the
stance of submission then be conducive to that form of competition which generates friendship? I think not. Indeed, it
is dubious whether the stance of submission will be the source
of any competitive urge at all (with the interesting exception
of passive resistance, often a politically astute strategy, but
rarely an athletic one). Rather, in this case, the significant
alternative to the stance of dominance will emerge if we see
dominance and submission as polar opposites whose alternative is a balance in the middle.

Suppose we consider the stance of dominance in its
"pure" form. One of its central characteristics would be an
extreme form of aggressive responsiveness or assertiveness.
"Pure" submission, on the other hand, might be characterized
by an excessive openness in which, as it were, we were open
to everything (here in the sense of passive acceptance) but
responsive to nothing. If we put the two together, we would
have a stance which might be called "responsive openness,"
in which our responsiveness is moderated by openness, and
our otherwise passive openness activated by responsiveness.
We would have a stance, if it could be lived, which would
then be open but not passive or submissive, responsive without being domineering. Elsewhere, I have suggested that this
stance of responsive openness is precisely the stance of play
("The Stance of Play," Journal of the Philosophy of Sport,
vol. VII, 1980, pages 87-99). Here the point that needs to
be made is that with responsive openness we have a stance
which can be seen as a source of the competitive urge through
its active responsiveness and its openness, among other things,
to test ourselves, yet which also would have as its highest

form of competition that of friendship. But as yet, that connection is still tenuous, and needs to be grounded in the third
understanding of human being, our natures as erotic.

We are incomplete and we strive for completeness.
In order to enhance that possibility, we obviously need to be
open to possibilities that might lead to our fulfillment. In a
word, we need other people for fulfillment, and this erotic
need is surely a source of our relationality. It invites an
openness to relations with others, to a striving together for
fulfillment, which is at the etymological root of the word
"competition," literally "to question or strive together."
Our overfullness, moreover, makes that openness at once
responsive and the gift of ourselves to others. Together,
they offer what we might call an ontological foundation for
our competitive urge, and one which makes the highest fulfillment of that urge one of friendship. We have thus set
out, at least in outline, that structure of human being which
would enable us to understand both the source of the competitive urge and how and why its highest achievement, its telos,
is friendship, while alienation is in every case a defective
mode.

We now need to ask after the set of questions raised
by the second sentence of the judge's comment discussed earlier, that set centering on the question of the difference between women and men and what difference the difference
makes in competition. Let us begin with the characterization of human being as erotic. The first and decisive remark to be made is that Socrates offers this as an account
of human eros, not of "male eros" or "female eros." The
clear implication of the Socratic/Platonic account of eros is
that it is characteristic of human being altogether. Not just
women, or not just men, but all humans are characterized
by this duality of incompleteness and overfullness, and so by
the strivings and expressions that it entails. If so, then to
the extent that I have shown that the competitive urge itself
is founded in our natures as erotic, it would follow that competition was literally natural for both women and men. It is
important to understand the conceptual situation here. The
Platonic point seems to be that although there may indeed be
important differences between male and female nature, either
physiological or, in the literal sense, psychological (having
to do with the soul), there is a deeper unity to human being
which is prior to the distinction between male and female nature. That unity is our eros. As human, we are erotic but
asexual. Sexual differentiation is subordinate to our natures

as erotic. In assessing any given activity, therefore, we must ask whether that activity is grounded in our "subordinate" natures as sexually differentiated, or in our more fundamental natures as human. If a given activity is founded in our subordinately sexual natures (to take an easy example, the activity of child-bearing), then its understanding must be accomplished at that level. If, on the other hand, we discover that a given activity is founded not in our sexually differentiated natures but in our unified natures as human, then this activity must be natural to, appropriate for, women and men. So it is with the competitive urge, and so it is, derivatively, with athletic competition. Grounded in our natures as erotic, it is an appropriate activity for us as human, whatever our sex.

If we turn now to the stances of dominance and submission on the one hand and responsive openness as the alternative on the other, we can see at once how a powerful sexual prejudice has become pervasive, and how the stance of play undercuts it. For the stances of dominance and submission will immediately be recognized as the source of a standard stereotyping of masculine and feminine nature. Men, we have long been told, are and even should be aggressive, responsive, dominating. Women, conversely, are and should be passive, submissive, receptively open. In short, those stereotypes are clearly founded in the affirmation of the primacy of the stances of dominance and submission as having their sexual locus in men and women respectively. But I have argued that the stance of play, and so of competitive play, undercuts that dichotomy and holds them together in a unity, a unity which I have called responsive openness. The stance of play is therefore androgynous, sexually undifferentiated. Once again, competitive play is seen as natural to women as much as men.

Finally, what of the significance for this issue of the monadic/relational duality? In order to make it sexually relevant, one would have to argue either that females were fundamentally monadic and males relational or vice-versa. It is true that some have claimed that women do not flourish in team sports but prefer individual sports (and so presumably are naturally monadic), but the empirical counter-evidence is so overwhelming as to make this claim ludicrous. It is obvious that some women are monadic, some relational, most fluctuating depending on mood and circumstance, and the same with men. No sexual differentiation can be grounded here. And so, insofar as the monadic/relational duality tends, as

I have argued, to be the source of alienated and friendly competition respectively, it is obvious that both possibilities are as natural to women as to men. On all three issues, then, the clear force of the argument is that athletic competition, in both its highest and its defective modes, is as natural a possibility for women as for men.

What follows from all this? Let me close by applying the results of these reflections to a few specific issues. Again, I shall begin with some questions about the issue of competition in general, then turn to some specific issues regarding women and athletic competition.

In his well-known book, Sport: A Philosophic Inquiry, Paul Weiss argues persuasively that one of the central aspects of the competitive urge is that it is a striving for excellence. 3   As he plausibly argues, young men (sic), long before they are capable of distinguishing themselves in ethical judgment, in political prudence, in intellectual facility, or in business acumen, are able to stand forth as excellent in athletics.   This makes athletic competition an especially attractive activity for young men, who can in that sphere strive for and perhaps achieve a level of excellence not yet possible for them in other fields.   For those of us who are older, the appeal of sport, especially the phenomenon of spectating at sport contests, remains founded in our continuing desire to witness excellence, an excellence which, again, can be clearly exhibited on the playing field.   If we now put this plausible thesis together with my earlier considerations regarding the etymological significance of competition ("to strive or question together"), we would arrive at the thesis, which I would defend, that competition at its best is a striving together for excellence.   As I have already argued, the "together" dimension of this enterprise means that that competition which most adequately fulfills its highest possibilities does so in the mode of friendship among the participants.   I have long regarded the traditional handshake at the end of a game as symbolic of this recognition.   "Thanks, friend, I couldn't have done that without you. "

Someone might object that this is all very well in theory, but the hard empirical truth is that in most instances of athletic competition the competitors are much less interested in excellence than in winning.   "Winning isn't everything, it's the only thing" may be an aphorism that we deplore, but as a description of most athletic contests it is the

truth. Moreover, it is precisely this primacy of the desire
to win which makes it all too rare that friendship can accompany competition. To desire to win is necessarily to desire
that the other team (or person) lose; to desire that the other
person lose is hardly conducive to friendship. To this there
are several responses. First, I have insisted all along that
friendship was the telos of competition, that the noble combination of striving for excellence and friendship occurs only
in the highest instances of competition. It is therefore neither
surprising nor destructive of my view that often this happy
combination is not attained. Most of the time acorns do not
become oak trees either. That does not deny that becoming
an oak tree is the telos of an acorn. What does follow, however, is that we should be very interested in what conditions
do bring it about that athletic competition so often fails to be
what it can be. Is it societal conditions, psychological phenomena, cultural aberrations? The point is, the cause, on
my teleological view, is not competition per se. To blame
alienation on competition itself, to insist that competition
causes alienation (a view often enough espoused, and especially by Marxists), is to misunderstand the teleological
character of athletic competition, to confuse a defective
mode of the phenomenon with the phenomenon in itself.

Second, the belief that most of the time competitors
are more interested in winning than in excellence is less
true than it seems, and probably derives from taking professional and quasi-professional sports teams as the paradigm. But there are far more "sand-lot" games of all sorts
played than there are professional or quasi-professional contests, and in those sand-lot games there is simple but powerful evidence that what is really at stake is the challenge
of a close contest, which will push the participants to excel
or even to surpass themselves. I refer to the phenomenon
of making up fair teams. I remember noting with enjoyment
the important stage of development in my own children when
they caught on to the significance of competition. When they
were very young, perhaps at the age of five or so, they would
come home and report with delight that they had beaten the
other team "sixty-six to nothing," or some similarly outra-
geous score. For them, at that time, "winning wasn't everything, it was the only thing." Slowly but surely, however,
they began to see that the real point, the real fun, or the
real challenge was to choose teams so that the sides would
be as close as possible, so that the outcome of the game
would be genuinely open to question, and thus that the challenge to each player's excellence would be more powerful.

The clear significance of this transition in their development is that it testified to their recognition that the deepest significance of competition is not the issue of winning, but of striving to win, and so of pursuing excellence.

But does it not remain the case that in striving to win, in striving for excellence, we in fact also desire that the opposing team or person lose, and doesn't that alienating element remain? No, although I understand that the logic of most games would seem to suggest it (if one team wins, the other must lose; if I desire to win, I must therefore desire for the other team to lose). In this case, conceptual logic must be superseded by phenomenological evidence. What our experience tells us, I submit, is that the only times that our fundamental desire is that the other team lose are those times when we want to "humiliate" the opposition, "rub their noses in it," in short, times when the situation is already shot through with alienation. What we want, most of the time, is a good game, and one of the central ingredients to a good game is a strong challenge to our ability.

Finally, should our responses to these questions be modified if we think primarily of competition between women athletes? As will be obvious from my previous remarks, I think the answer is clearly no. My own experience coaching women's basketball teams at Trinity College suggests that women athletes are women athletes, not women athletes. They are, in the context of competitive sport, athletes first, who run the same risks as their male counterparts, physical risks of injury, psychological risks of losing, the risk of alienation, but who also strive for the same rewards, rewards which certainly include the achievement of a level of excellence not possible without the challenge of strong competition, and most of all, the sheer fun of a good game.

NOTES

1. Sports Illustrated, May 28, 1973, page 95.
2. This material is used here with the kind permission of the Philosophic Society for the Study of Sport and the Journal of the Philosophy of Sport.
3. Paul Weiss, Sport: A Philosophic Inquiry (Carbondale: Southern Illinois Press, 1971); see especially chapter 1.

SUGGESTIONS FOR FURTHER READING

Harper, William. "Man Alone," in Sport and the Body: A Philosophical Symposium, edited by Ellen Gerber and William Morgan. 2nd ed. Philadelphia: Lea & Febiger, 1979, pages 125-128.

Hoch, Paul. Rip Off the Big Game. New York: Anchor Books, 1972.

Hyland, Drew. "Competition and Friendship," in Sport and the Body: A Philosophical Symposium. 2nd ed., pages 133-140.

Meier, Klaus V. "The Kinship of the Rope and the Loving Struggle," Journal of the Philosophy of Sport, volume III (September 1976), pages 52-61.

Weiss, Paul. Sport: A Philosophical Inquiry. Carbondale: Southern Illinois University Press, 1971.

QUESTIONS

(1) How could one go about confirming or disconfirming the picture of human nature which Hyland presents?

(2) a) On behalf of Hyland, construct the best argument you can in support of the position that alienation is a defective mode of competition. (If necessary, review the sections of the General Introduction entitled "Background on Arguments" and "Formulating Arguments on Our Own.")

   b) Construct the best objection you can to the argument which you have just constructed.

   c) In your view, does the objection which you have just constructed succeed in refuting the argument against which it is directed? Why or why not?

(3) For each of the following types of sport, give your opinion on whether competition as friendship can occur in this type of sport and explain why you hold this opinion. (The categories correspond to Raymond A. Belliotti's classification in his essay in Part I of this volume.)

   a) professional sports
   b) quasi-professional sports
   c) competitive recreational sports
   d) purely recreational sports

(4) Do you agree with Hyland that the same sort of competition which is ideal for men is ideal for women? Why or why not?

(5) Hyland holds that children's preference for evenly matched teams over lopsided victories shows that the children are beginning to value the pursuit of excellence more than winning. Do you agree with him? Why or why not?

(6) a) Do you agree with Hyland that we sometimes desire to win a game and yet do not desire that our opponents lose that game?

 b) In your opinion, would it be irrational to desire to win a game and yet not desire that one's opponent lose that game? Why or why not?

(7) What else would you like to discuss from Hyland's essay?

11. THE OVEREMPHASIS ON WINNING: A PHILOSOPHICAL LOOK

Joan Hundley

An overemphasis on winning is presently quite visible within athletic arenas. The "winning is the only thing" attitude pervades professional and intercollegiate athletics, and even youth and recreational athletic programs. The overemphasis on winning is often held responsible for much of the corruption and problems that exist within modern sport. It is believed that the corruption within modern sport occurs because winning is overemphasized to the extent that the major objectives of the games themselves (performance, enjoyment, health, and the like) are deemphasized or neglected. When these important objectives of sport are deemphasized, winning by any means may become an acceptable practice. Thus cheating, brutality, and the like may even be encouraged for the sake of winning. When a win-loss record is the only gauge for athletic success, attitudes toward athletic competition may easily shift from "It is not whether you win or lose, it is how you play the game" to "It is not how you play the game, just that you win!"

Because of the overemphasis on winning many of the traditional benefits of athletic competition, such as sportsmanship, seem to have disappeared. Also, great performances, efforts, and special feelings of personal and team achievements are often not acknowledged after a defeat. Therefore, it is not how you play the game, just that you win. The purpose of this essay is to suggest reasons for this overemphasis on winning, and to suggest steps which may be taken to put the fun and games back into fun and games.

This chapter is divided into five sections. Section I

presents sociological evidence indicating a deterioration of the play spirit and humanistic nature of modern sport. Section II attempts to explain the deterioration of modern sport from a neo-Marxist perspective. Section III attempts to explain the deterioration of modern sport from a play theorist point of view. Section IV gives a feminist explanation for this deterioration. Section V summarizes and draws conclusions.

I. The Misuse of Modern Sport:
The Overemphasis on Winning

Traditionally, sport has been regarded as an activity in which individuals strive for human physical excellence through sportsmanship and fair play. Such locker-room sayings as "sport builds character" and "it is how you play the game" clearly illustrate these attitudes toward sportsmanship and excellence.

Sport is sometimes even perceived as being an entity which stands outside of our everyday life experiences. Bernard Suits, along with several other sport theorists, regard sport, by definition, as being a rule bound activity. According to Suits, the rules make the game a game. Thus, activities that are not bound by rules or in which the rules are not followed are not games. Therefore, because players play games by following a set of rules, they are no longer playing the game when they break the rules. Hence Suits argues that because the act of playing a game starts with the players agreeing to follow a set of rules, cheating or the intentional breaking of those rules undermines the game itself.[1]

Also, according to Suits, because the act of cheating indicates the termination of the game, it is impossible to have a game in which the victors have cheated. Suits argues that the cheater is the ultimate loser, because not only does the cheater fail to win the game, the cheater fails to compete. Therefore Suits does not regard success as merely a win-loss record. Suits would argue that it is not just that you win, it is how you play the game.

Paul Weiss regards sport as an area in which young people are given the opportunity to attain physical excellence. According to Weiss it is the striving for and the performance of physical excellence which makes sport a unique experience. Weiss therefore argues that the major objective of sport ought not be the mere quest for victory, but the attainment of ex-

cellence.[2]   Hence, Weiss would argue that it is not just that
you win, it is that you attain excellence.

Competition is often perceived as an antagonistic act
of aggression in which opponents attempt to dominate one
another.   However, many sport theorists, such as Drew Hyland, regard competition as an act of cooperation in which
participants strive toward physical excellence.   Hyland clearly
illustrates this aspect of competition, as he states: "Consider ... the original meaning of the word.   Com-petitio
means 'to question together, to strive together.'   Immediately
we see that according to the original meaning of the word,
competition is in no way necessarily connected to alienation;
instead, it is easily tied to the possibility of friendship."[3]
Competition can therefore be regarded as something more
than the will to dominate an opponent or to win at any cost.
Rather, competition may be more correctly regarded as an
activity in which competitors aid each other in the act of
striving for excellence.   Even within a highly competitive situation, it is how you play the game.

So far, I have attempted to demonstrate that sport
cannot be reduced to the numbers on a score board, and that
the winning-is-everything perception of sport undermines the
meaning and objectives of sport.   Sport ought to be regarded
as an activity in which the will to win is a means to the end
of attaining physical excellence, not one in which human excellence is regarded as a means to the end of winning.   The
latter idea undermines sport because you can "win" without
physical excellence, e.g., by "psyching out" opponents.

This improper emphasis on winning (the notion that
winning is the only thing) is responsible for much of the corruption in modern sport.   In our modern society, people have
the attitude that winning is everything; consequently everybody
loves a winner.   Sport sociologists Stanley Eitzen and George
Sage elaborate on this point, stating: "Americans want winners, whether it be in school, or business, or politics, or
sport.   In sports, we demand winners.   Coaches are fired
if they are not successful.   Teams are booed for ties."
Therefore, although winning ought not be the only thing,
within modern sport, winning is everything.[4]

The overemphasis on winning is further reflected in
the following quotations popularly credited to several very
"successful" football coaches.

> "Winning is not everything. It is the only thing."
> --Vince Lombardi (legendary coach of the Green
> Bay Packers)

> "Everytime you win, you're reborn; when you lose,
> you die a little."--George Allen (coach of the Wash-
> ington Redskins)

> "No one ever learns anything by losing."--Don
> Shula (coach of the Miami Dolphins)[5]

The notion that winning is everything corrupts sport
because it reduces the game itself to its outcome (the numbers on the sports page). Eitzen and Sage reflect on our
attraction to the outcome of events as they write: "In learning the culture (through the socialization process), most
Americans have internalized values that predispose them to
be interested in the outcome of competitive situations--com-
petition is the sine qua non of sports."[6] The act of overemphasizing the outcome of a performance and ignoring the
performance itself is the key to the corruption in modern
sport. This overemphasis on the outcome of an athletic
event is quite visible in the sports pages, in which you will
find pages and pages of scores or outcomes accompanied by
little or no commentary regarding the performances. Consequently, as we have seen, winning is everything within
modern sport; however, this overemphasis on winning corrupts sport because it undermines the game itself.

The notion of winning being not everything but the only
thing is embedded in the fiber of modern sport. However,
we must keep in mind that for every winner there is a loser.
If winning is everything, is losing nothing? Are losers nothing? What about the game? Winning ought not be the only
thing, because when it is everybody loses. The dynamics of
athletic struggle cannot be reduced to a win-loss record.
As the improper emphasis on winning increases, modern
sport departs more and more from the ideal of an activity
which is mainly concerned with human physical expression
and excellence.

I shall center the discussion immediately following
around youth sport programs, because I believe youth sport
ought to be purer than intercollegiate and professional sports,
which are subject to corruption by the large sums of money
at stake.

No more than ten years ago the concept of the pick-up game was quite common. These usually unscored, untimed, unsupervised games, which ended either at dinner time or at nightfall, epitomized the notion of playing for fun, for the sake of playing. With the onset of organized youth sport, each year the concept of the pick-up game seems to die a little--and with it the notion of play, fun and games. The pick-up game has been replaced with youth Olympic and professional training camps in which each coach aspires to develop future professional and/or Olympic athletes. Youth sport is often regarded not as fun or games, but as serious business.

Youth sport leagues, often run by aggressive parents, place children into highly competitive situations. And although we often criticize Eastern bloc countries for their exploitation of young athletes, four- and five-year-olds are often placed on gymnastic and/or swim teams in this country. As members of these teams, they are required to practice hours daily. Further, these young athletes are taught to play with the attitude that winning is the only thing. What happened to playing for play's sake?

Another problem with organized youth sport programs is the supervision or coaching. Because the coaches of many Little League teams are volunteer parent/coaches and not professional physical educators, many youth sport teams are coached by enthusiastic parents who may possess little knowledge of physiology of exercise, motor development, or child psychology. Therefore, these weekend coaches may push a child beyond his/her physical or mental limit without knowing it. Youth sport teams are also often coached and supervised by weekend "Vince Lombardis," who may be frustrated ex-athletes pursuing their fantasies of NFL or major league success. Lacking adequate knowledge among other things, these imitation Vince Lombardis cleverly disguised as Little League coaches harm their athletes both physically ("Little League elbow" and the like) and psychologically--subjecting young athletes to pain and trauma, and instilling in them a sense of false values. Young athletes are taught that losing is nothing and losers are nobodies. Hence, no matter how hard they work or try, uncoordinated or less athletic children are made to feel inferior. Also, no matter how well these young athletes perform, they may be made to feel sad or guilty if or when they lose. Young athletes quickly learn that success means winning.

An overemphasis on winning also causes fun to become a secondary factor which can be appreciated only after victory. Great plays are remembered only in the context of winning. Hence, without victory great performances are reduced to nothing; great athletes are defined as the ones who score the most points. It clearly follows that high point scoring individuals are often idolized, while defensive players, individuals who assist and/or set up the big plays, are overlooked.

Further, when winning is a prime objective for participating in sport, cheating (without being discovered, of course) may be viewed as an acceptable practice. Why not? All the numbers say is that you won, not how. As a matter of fact, coaches often teach players tricks which enable them to cheat without being detected. These tactics are often considered more strategic than dishonest. In basketball, e.g., players are often taught how to foul without being detected.

Finally, as a consequence of the contest being regarded as a means to an end (winning) it follows that the opponent may also assume the status of a means to an end, rather than a person. Athletes are often taught to regard their opponents as being objects which must be overcome in the pursuit of victory, rather than the friends which Hyland discusses. Moreover, athletes are also taught to believe that physical aggression and brutality are part of the game. Most athletes feel little or no remorse after inflicting injury upon their opponents. In sports such as football, boxing, and hockey, athletes are praised for their ability to dehumanize and brutalize their opponents.

We have seen that there is a clear contrast between how sport ought to be played (emphasizing rules, enjoyment, performance, and excellence) and how it is being played (overemphasizing winning). It is clear that an overemphasis on winning presently undermines the objectives of athletic competition.

II. The Overemphasis on Winning: A Neo-Marxist Perspective

Ideologically, sport has been regarded as an autonomous institution, characterized by fair play, sportsmanship, courage, excellence, and a host of additional social and individual virtues. Modern sport, however, can be more accurately char-

acterized as a dog-eat-dog, win-at-any-cost, extremely competitive activity in which individuals go to great lengths to
win. The athlete's primary objective is no longer the quest
to achieve excellence through the physical. Rather, competitors strive to dominate one another. Also, the "good guys
finish last" attitude, now present throughout sport, has acted
to undermine the notion of sportsmanship, fair play, and the
like.

Neo-Marxists argue that sport is not really an autonomous institution, but rather a mere function of an alienated
capitalistic society.[7] The attitudes, norms, and values present within sport are the same attitudes, norms, and values
present within society. Neo-Marxists further argue that it
would be illogical to assume that anything other than dog-eat-
dog, highly competitive sport could exist within a dog-eat-dog,
highly competitive society. Sport would be unintelligible if
its values contradicted those of society. They conclude that
the only way to change sport is to change society.

In Rip Off the Big Game, a controversial critical analysis of the sport establishment, sport sociologist Paul Hock
illustrates this connection between sport and society, stating:

> There is nothing natural or inevitable about the
> sports we play or the way we play them. Sports
> would be completely idiotic without a common ac-
> ceptance of the rules of the game by the athletes
> and a common social appreciation of the game by
> large sections of society.... The sports most ap-
> preciated in a particular society, and the way in
> which they are played, in turn reflect the past and
> present development of that society; they are, in
> fact, a mirror reflection of the society. Thus, as
> the Vietnam war heated up, the more militaristic
> game of professional football rapidly surpassed
> baseball as America's favorite spectator sport.[8]

Hock further illustrates the interrelation between sport
and culture, stating: "To 'attack' sports would be like the
old witch's attacking the mirror that showed her how ugly
she is, for sport is nothing else but a mirror, a socializing
agent, and an opiate of the society it serves. To 'reform'
the mirror while leaving the society untouched would change
nothing at all. We will have humane, creative sports when
we have built a humane and creative society--and not until
then."[9]

Neo-Marxists argue not only that sport's values mirror or reflect the competitive values of modern society, but also that competitive athletics enhance the competitive nature of society. Critics Bero Rigauer and Jean-Marie Brohm both argue that modern sport has been reduced to an activity which perpetuates the same achievement principles found within alienated labor. Rigauer clearly expresses this point in his book, Sport and Work, where he states: "Within the context of this interpretation of human activity the connection between sport and work is clear: both systems of behavior enhance the status and prestige of the concept of achievement."[10] It is therefore argued that capitalism reduces sport to another form of production or achievement.

The neo-Marxists argue that modern sport is not based on lofty ideals such as sportsmanship, cooperation, excellence, and the like. They explain that these ideals are ideologies which disguise the true dehumanizing nature of sport. It is further argued that sport's true ideals are based on the ideals of production and achievement which are found within alienated labor. Therefore athletic success is reduced to the production of records and the accumulation of victories. Neo-Marxists thus conclude that capitalism transforms sport into a dehumanizing activity in which participants will do just about anything to themselves and/or their opponents to win.

Neo-Marxists further argue that capitalism also reduces sport to a commodity. Rigauer explains what is meant by a commodity: "By 'commodity' we mean an external 'object, a thing that by nature of its attributes satisfies some sort of human need.' An object becomes a commodity or an article of exchange only when it is something produced not to satisfy the producer's needs but to be exchanged in the marketplace for other values (money)."[11]

Taking a cue from the neo-Marxist line of thought, we may suggest here that modern sport overemphasizes winning because winning or success is the article which is exchanged within the athletic arena. Winning is a rare, valuable commodity because within our capitalistic society the sensation of being a winner or successful is rarely if ever experienced. Neo-Marxists give two broad reasons to explain why these sensations are rarely directly experienced. First, dehumanizing factors such as alienated labor, high achievement drives and/or a constant obsession to increase production, deny workers an opportunity to experience a sense of success through their work. Secondly, upward mobility is in fact extremely difficult under capitalism. These two reasons are elaborated in the next three paragraphs.

Alienated labor denies workers the opportunity to experience success because when workers sell their capacity to labor, they also relinquish their rights, ownership, and control of the product they produce. Therefore, workers often do not feel a responsibility for and/or a sense of pride in what they produce. Neo-Marxists further explain that division of labor also acts to undermine an individual's direct experience of success. They argue that when a task is broken down it becomes more difficult for a worker to identify his or her labor with the finished product. Thus the worker is unable to experience a sense of pride or success for his or her labor.

Further, because of high achievement drives and an obsession to constantly increase production, a worker's work is never done; thus workers never experience the sense of success that results from the completion of a difficult task. Within high production-oriented societies each goal achieved is reduced or perceived as a small step toward a higher unattainable goal. Success, therefore, becomes an unattainable entity. Athletic competition tends to act as a release valve at this point, because each game ends, thus providing spectators with a sense of completion. This gives rise to the neo-Marxist complaint that by providing workers with this sense of completion, which is otherwise unattainable, sport acts to perpetuate capitalism.

The second reason suggested for winning being a rare commodity is the conflict between capitalistic ideology and fact. Neo-Marxists argue here that because of the massive labor forces necessary to sustain capitalism it is extremely difficult, if not impossible, for an individual or group to gain significant social or economic mobility. But if workers knew this fact they would no longer work as hard. Therefore ideologies suggesting that work equals success are perpetuated. Because these ideologies maintain high levels of effort and/or production, individuals are socialized into believing them. Individuals are taught that hard work is the root of all success, and that failure to achieve status indicates a lack of work. Unsuccessful individuals often find few if any flaws in the system itself, and they tend to perceive themselves as inferior or losers. Sport is often blamed for perpetuating this ideology. This is because sport is one of the few areas within society in which hard work still counts and the better competitor still wins. Sport keeps alive the dream of working hard and attaining success.

Neo-Marxists argue that winning in sports is a commodity. Individuals, groups, businesses, cities, and countries exchange money and/or other valuables for winning. The fact that winning teams or individuals do receive large sums of money and support, while their losing counterparts are almost unheard of, strengthens the notion that winning is the article that is exchanged in the athletic marketplace. It is suggested that individuals support athletics because through the supporting of athletics individuals obtain the opportunity to experience vicariously the success that is denied them in their place of work.

It might be objected that individuals do not support athletics financially because most people do not go to the arena, field, or stadium to support their favorite team; they simply turn on the television. However, we must understand that large sums of money are exchanged in sports broadcasting. When games are viewed on television, individuals do not have to pay the price of a ticket because corporations foot the bill, after purchasing the right to attempt to sell spectators their products during intermissions. When an individual and/or business supports an athletic team it purchases the right to share vicariously in that team's success. The more a team wins, the more individuals will wish to support that team. Also as opportunities of directly experiencing success are reduced, the demand for vicarious winning increases, causing winning to be a more valuable commodity.

According to neo-Marxist arguments, then, winning is overemphasized in the athletic arena because individuals are denied the opportunity to experience winning within their everyday lives. This allows winning to become a valuable commodity, which is then pursued to the neglect of other aspects of sports.

III. The Overemphasis on Winning: A Play Theorist Perspective

> ... [M]an, as we said before, has been constructed as a toy for God, and this is, in fact, the finest thing about him. All of us, then, men and women alike, must fall in our role and spend life in making

our play as perfect as possible--to the complete
inversion of current theory. [Plato, Laws VII,
803C][12]

Johan Huizinga, play theorist and author of the classic
work Homo Ludens, [13] employs this Platonic metaphor to illustrate his notion of play. Huizinga's notions of modern
sport have been selected to represent the play theorist point
of view because much of modern play theory is a result of
Huizinga's work.

Huizinga's theory of play suggests that play is the ideal
form of human expression and the basis of human civilization.
In Homo Ludens (which translated means "Man the Player")
Huizinga argues that individuals, cultures, and civilizations
best express their creativity and humanity through their play.
He further argues that human civilizations have been built
from a concept of play rather than a work ethic, and that
play is the single element which separates humans from other
beings. Homo Ludens attempts to demonstrate that art, music, games, rituals, and the like are all fundamental expressions of the human play spirit, and that the deterioration of
modern culture is a result of a loss in this play spirit. The
purpose of this section is to present the play theorist point
of view regarding the overemphasis on winning in modern
sport.

Huizinga argues that because play allows individuals
to express themselves in a uniquely human manner, the deterioration of play has resulted in the deterioration of humanity. He concludes that the inhuman, violent nature of modern
society is due to a lack of a play spirit. Hence, it may be
further concluded that the inhuman, violent nature of sport is
also a result of this lack of a play-like attitude.

The play theorist's explanation of the overemphasis on
winning is fundamentally different from that of the neo-Marxist.
The differences rest in each type of theorist's perception of
the ideal form of human expression. Work theorists such as
neo-Marxists suggest that the ideal form of human expression
is work. Work is argued to be ideal because individuals are
said to objectify themselves and/or relate to their world
through their labor. Work theorists suggest that because
human beings have built and rebuilt their world in their attempts to fulfill basic needs, human civilizations were built
on the concept of work. Play theorists, on the other hand,
argue that work is merely an instrument of survival and/or

an act of fulfilling basic needs. They argue that play, rather than work, is the ideal form of human expression because it is a result of an individual's free will, while work is fettered to the fulfillment of needs. It is further suggested that because play transcends needs, it allows human beings to reach beyond the mundanities of everyday life to create things of beauty and spirit which transcend basic need. Play theorists suggest that this beauty and spirit are readily visible in art, music, games, culture, and other play forms which are uniquely human.

Play theorists argue that play is the factor that separates humans from other beings, because only humans possess the ability to play or to act outside of biological or psychological need. They suggest that while other beings' existences are limited to the obtaining of food and shelter, procreation, and other survival-related activities, human beings possess the ability to search for beauty, truth, and other things which transcend mere survival. They infer that when individuals ignore their ability to play, the quality of their lives is decreased to a subhuman level of existence which is fettered to the fulfillment of needs. Extending this line of reasoning, one may conclude that the lack of a play spirit within modern society is responsible for a decrease in the search for beauty and truth and an increase in violence, brutality, inhumanity, and alienation.

According to Huizinga the deterioration of play is the result of an overemphasis on work and/or utility values. He suggests that because work and play are contradictory concepts they cannot exist at the same time. Thus the greater the emphasis that is placed on work, the more play is de-emphasized. Play theorists argue that the extremely high value that modern technical society places on work, success, progress and the like, causes play and/or nonproductive activities to be perceived as nonsense. It is therefore suggested that in an attempt to fulfill the productive standards of modern society, traditional play activities such as games have assumed work-like natures. Hence more and more individuals are no longer participating in play-like activities for the sake of play or enjoyment; rather they are playing to obtain fitness, money, education, psychological relaxation, and/or records or other manufactured needs. Play is then perceived as a means of fulfilling some other need; hence play is reduced to another form of work. And, humans are reduced to other forms of beings.

Play theorists argue that play is the only logical form of human existence and that it would be irrational to conduct life in any other manner. They offer three arguments. The first is that play is the function of each participant's creativity and/or intrinsic motivation; thus play is a demonstration of who an individual is rather than what his/her needs are. They conclude that individuals best relate to their world through play. Need forces individuals to work; freedom allows individuals to play.

In The Grasshopper, Bernard Suits gives a second argument explaining why the life of a player is a more logical existence than one of a worker.[14] Suits argues that a playful existence is more logical because play is a self-justifying activity while work is not. Work is not regarded as a self-justifying activity because during work the ends, or the fulfilling of needs resulting from work, are separate from the means of obtaining those ends. If an individual could obtain a need (e.g., money) without working, then working would be avoided. In other words, individuals do not work to work--they work to fulfill needs; thus work is not self-justifying. Play, on the other hand, is considered self-justifying because individuals do play for the sake of playing.

In a further, related argument, Suits reasons that it is illogical to regard work as self-justifying activity because during work individuals attempt to eliminate the need to work. Thus if work were the fundamental basis of existence, through work individuals would attempt to eliminate their purpose of existence. Suits illustrates this idea when he compares work to preventive medicine, stating: "The ideal of prudence [work], therefore, like the ideal of preventive medicine, is its own extinction. For if it were the case that no sacrifice of goods [play time] needed ever be made, the prudential actions [work] would be pointless, indeed impossible ... the true grasshopper [player] sees that work is not self-justifying, and that his way of life is the final justification of any work whatsoever."[15] Play theorists conclude that play is a logical foundation of existence. It is logical for individuals to work to play, or to play to play, but illogical to work for the sake of working.

Play theorists conclude that the winning-is-the-only-thing attitude which pervades modern sport is a result of the illogical nature of a society based on a work ethic. They suggest that the importance placed on work within our present society has resulted in a loss of the play spirit. Hence, even sport has lost its play-like nature. Huizinga explains that modern sport is no longer play, stating: "In the case of sport we have an activity nominally known as play but raised to such a pitch of technical organization and scientific thoroughness that the real play spirit is threatened with extinction."[16] Play theorists therefore suggest that the violent, inhuman nature of modern society and modern sport can be successfully eradicated through a revitalization of the play spirit, which would result from a deemphasis on the present work ethic. If individuals realized that they were God's playthings, and spent their lives making their play as perfect as possible, they would experience the peace and fulfillment necessary to restore humanity to modern society.

IV. The Overemphasis on Winning: A Radical Feminist Perspective

Like the neo-Marxists and the play theorists, feminists[17] tie the degraded state of modern sport to the degraded state of society. Radical feminists, however, argue that the degradation of society is due to the patriarchal foundation on which it is based. They hold that the downfall of sport is ultimately a result of patriarchy, rather than of alienated labor or an overemphasis on work.

Radical feminists argue that sport, like education, family, economics, and other social institutions, has been manipulated and employed to maintain the power of men over women. They conclude that the violent nature of modern sport and the overemphasis on winning within modern sport are side effects of patriarchal manipulation. In his essay, "The Super-Bowl Culture of Male Violence," sport sociologist Eugene Bianchi supports this feminist argument, stating: "The sexism in football [is] symbolically fundamental to the other evils of our culture. It is also worth noting that in a culture that encourages people to admire and revel in aggressiveness, sports of intended brutality gain the highest appeal both at the box office and on television."[18] Lucy Komisar further explains the connection between violence and masculinity, stating: "Violence and male supremacy have been companions in the course of civilization. The domination of women by men has been the prototype of the control men have tried to exercise over other men--in slavery, in war and in the marketplace."[19]

Male-dominated sports are regarded as instruments which are employed to perpetuate male supremacy because they reinforce what I will refer to as the ideal of physical dominance, aggression, and violence. By this I mean quite simply the ideal that supports the antiquated notion that stronger and more aggressive individuals or nations have the right to dominate weaker, less aggressive individuals or nations. Bianchi explains that athletic contests are struggles for dominance, rather than tests of skill, stating: "It is not just a rivalry that helps a person enjoy the contest for the pleasure and skill involved in it; rather it's a confrontation with others in which a man's self-identity, self-respect and public acceptance is [sic] at stake.... Winning is all even if it means trampling on one's fellows. Hostility and violence are instruments for removing obstacles on the road to the top...."[20] The overemphasis on winning may therefore be explained as the result of a masculine obsession to dominate.

Aside from its other flaws, the ideal of physical dominance is extremely oppressive to women because women as a group are inferior to men in their ability to dominate physically. It may therefore be concluded that support for the ideal of physical dominance is an attempt to sustain women's inferior status. Sport further acts to sustain the idea of feminine inferiority by placing women on the sideline. Bianchi suggests that sport attempts to demonstrate feminine inferiority and women's place by emphasizing masculine ideals such as toughness and insensitivity, and placing women on the outside: "The weekend trek to the arena is not an escape from the world of corporate America; rather it is a weekly pilgrimage to the national shrines where the virtues of toughness and insensitivity can be renewed. This is especially true in the man/woman relationships. In the football spectacle the role of woman in our society is clearly defined against the masculine criteria of value. The important action is male-dominated; women can share only at a distance in man's world. They can shout and squeal from afar, but their roles are accessory to the male event."[21]

From this perspective, the overemphasis on winning in modern sport seems to be the result of an attempt to maintain and perpetuate this ideal of physical dominance. In present industrialized society the ideal of physical dominance is obsolete; using physical strength as a basis of status is as arbitrary as using physical characteristics such as eye color, height, or weight. Males, therefore, in an attempt to retain this masculine ideal, have overemphasized physical dominance within the athletic arena, and then made athletics a model for the remainder of society.

In "The American Seasonal Masculinity Rites," sport sociologist Arnold Beisser explains that sport is a social "safety valve," because it emphasizes masculine physical superiority: "In sports, males and females are placed in their historical biological roles. In sports, strength and speed do count, for they determine the winner. As in pre-mechanized combat, women can never be more than second place to men in sports. They can cheer their men on, but a quick review of the record books comparing achievements in sports of men and women confirms the distinctness of the sexes here."22

Beisser further demonstrates how athletics perpetuate this ideal of physical dominance: "It is a small wonder that the American male has a strong affinity for sports. He has learned that this is one area where there is no doubt about sexual differences and where his biology is not obsolete. Athletics help assure his difference from women in a world where his functions have come to resemble theirs."23

Because of its ability to demonstrate an individual's physical strength and violent nature, sport is often considered a means of determining masculinity. The notion of an athletic contest being used to determine the better man and the statement "may the best man win" clearly illustrate how athletics have been employed to maintain this antiquated ideal. Sport determines who is the better man; therefore all that is considered masculine is overemphasized in the athletic arena. Violence, aggression, physical dominance, and an exaggerated will to win are concentrated to the point that athletic contests have become brutal displays of "masculinity," rather than artful displays of skill. Radical feminists conclude that the overemphasis on winning within modern sport is the result of a patriarchal attempt to oppress or suppress women.

V. Conclusion

Each of the theorists discussed in this essay suggests that the overemphasis on winning within modern sport is the result of some flaw in modern culture. Neo-Marxists blame the deteriorated state of modern sport on alienated labor, capitalistic production, and the achievement principle. Play theorists argue that the overly competitive nature of modern sport is the result of a loss of the play spirit. They suggest that the problems that pervade sport are the result of the irrational respect and admiration which modern society has placed on the work ethic and technology. Radical feminists conclude that the overemphasis on winning is a result of a patriarchal struggle to maintain the ideal of masculine superiority within a society which is becoming increasingly androgynous.

The notion that the deterioration of modern sport is the result of a capitalistic, work-oriented and/or patriarchal society appears to lead sport reformers and sociologists to a dead end. This occurs because it would make little sense to attempt to change a reflection of the brutal, competitive nature of modern society. Therefore, if sport is a mere reflection, the only way to change sport would be to reform the society in which it exists. If the cultural influence on sport were as pervasive as suggested, to participate in a sport while employing countercultural values would be an unintelligible or nonsensical act. It makes no sense, for example, to attempt to lose a contest in a culture where winning and achieving is revered.

Sport, however, does not merely reflect the values of the culture in which it exists. It also perpetuates them. Sport reform is necessary because sport perpetuates the alienated, oppressive, brutal, violent nature of modern society. Furthermore, if sport can be employed to perpetuate capitalistic ideologies, irrational work priorities, and patriarchy, sport may also be used to undermine them. Reforms within the athletic arena may thus result in social changes and reformations. It must be kept in mind, however, that to maintain intelligibility, influence, and viability, athletic reform must be slow and deliberate.

Neo-Marxists, play theorists, and feminists all suggest that the attitudes and structures accompanying modern athletic participation ought to be changed. New game enthusiasts argue that this change can be best implemented by creating less competitive games. They suggest that new cooperative games would aid in the elimination of brutality and violence in sport by deemphasizing winning in the structure of the game itself. In the game of rotational volleyball, for example, players rotate to the opposite team after relinquishing service.[24] I believe, however, that because the structure of games is not solely responsible for the overemphasis on

winning, and its violent, brutal nature, the mere creation of
new games will not by itself be an effective measure in athletic reform.

Neo-Marxists and play theorists would more than likely
agree on similar athletic reforms. Changes would be similar
because both groups suggest that the work-like nature of
modern sport is responsible for its deterioration. Neo-
Marxists accuse modern sport of perpetuating capitalistic
values such as alienated labor, production, and the achievement principle. Play theorists argue that modern sport overemphasizes the significance of work. In any case, both argue that sport, games, and other playful activities ought to
be participated in with a humanistic, creative, play-like attitude.

Both groups would more than likely suggest that rigid
time periods allotted for play be less structured. Neo-
Marxists would be opposed to rigid playing periods because
they resemble the rigid working hours found within capitalistic alienated labor. Neo-Marxists could argue that rigid time
periods perpetuate and reflect the irrational attitudes toward
time found within capitalistic society. Because all things
connected with production are perceived as sacred commodi-
ties within capitalism, time is viewed as sacred. Time's
sacred nature is alienating because individuals often rush
through lives in their effort to save the precious commodity,
time. In an effort to produce as much as possible, most
people in capitalistic society never take the time to relax,
to find out the meaning of their existences, or to enjoy life.

Neo-Marxists would object to the rigid time periods
found within modern sports because the rigid periods allow
time to be a significant factor in the outcome of a contest,
thus perpetuating an irrational capitalistic attitude toward
time. These rigid time periods are also accused of paral-
leling the rigid working hours found within capitalistic labor.[25] It is suggested here that a 9:00 to 5:00 working day
with an hour off for lunch and coffee breaks is extremely
similar to a football game with its half time and time outs.

Because play theorists define play as an activity that
is engaged in freely, and sport as play, they would attempt
to remove rigid playing times which restrict the choice of
when to begin and end playing. The notion of an athletic
contest without structured playing times may sound nonsensical at first; however, the pick-up game is not bound by time

and it makes sense. Therefore, less structured sport could be easily implemented through a reemphasis on the concept of the pick-up game and a deemphasis on organized youth sport programs, intercollegiate athletics, and professional sport.

Work theorists and play theorists would also agree that records and statistics detract from modern sport. The keeping of statistical records is unique to modern sport. Even the Greeks, founders of the first Olympic games, never bothered to calculate exact times and distances.[26] Neo-Marxists argue that the keeping of statistical records perpetuates capitalistic production and the achievement principle, because it stresses attainment and production.[27] Play theorists argue that statistics, records, and extrinsic awards distract from the game, because participants often place more value on the attainment of records than the enjoyment of the game. Record keeping pervades modern sport. Most teams employ at least one statistician who, disguised as a "sports information director" keeps every record from yardage gained on a rainy day to the number of substitutions within a five-minute period. Record keeping also pervades the sports media; presently most athletic contests are reported in terms of game statistics rather than athletic performance.

Our earlier discussion of the radical feminist perspective suggests that equal participation by women in athletics on all levels, including youth sport programs as well as professional athletics, would be significant in the undermining of the patriarchal nature of modern society. It stands to reason that if women are considered equals within the athletic arena, men could no longer use sport as a proving ground for masculinity; this would also undermine the notion of sport being a safety valve for masculine expression.

A further argument, suggested by Jane English, is that if women had an equal place of honor within the athletic arena, especially professional and Olympic programs, they would have the opportunity to enhance the self-respect of all women and to negate the idea of female physical inferiority.[28] English elaborates: "It contributes to a woman's self-respect to see or read about the best women golfers. But this pride is tempered by the knowledge that they are 'only' the best women. The very need for a protected competition class suggests inferiority. The pride and self-respect gained from witnessing a woman athlete who is not only the best woman but the very

best athlete is much greater."[29] Thus, although women
would benefit[30] as individuals from mere equality of opportunity to participate in sport, the image of feminine inferiority can be undermined only by equality of honor in sport.
English thinks this feasible: "Before we conclude that women
are permanently relegated to inferiority, however, let us note
that what is a physiological disadvantage in one activity may
be an advantage in others: weight is an asset to a Sumo
wrestler and a drawback for marathon running.... The hip
structure that slows running gives a lower center of gravity.
Fat provides insulation and an energy source for running fifty-
mile races. The hormones that hinder development of heavy
muscles promote flexibility."[31] English suggests that new
women's sports ought to be developed from these physiological advantages to allow women to achieve this place of honor
within the athletic arena.

Bonnie Beck argues that female equality within the athletic area would be impossible without attitude changes. She
argues that violence, aggression, and dominance enhance and
perpetuate the notion of male-dominated athletics. She further
argues that this model of athletic participation is oppressive
and ought to be discarded and replaced with a more humanistic model, stating: "NowSport/ManSport oppresses all, even
those to whom it gave birth. With life risking conviction we
must demand new life-energizing com-test, play days, sport
days, JoySport activities for AllSelves in every activity."[32]
Play days are suggested as alternative sport models because
the whole atmosphere of a play day promotes an emphasis on
enjoyment and participation rather than on victory. Brutality
is not encouraged, and is almost unheard of. Prizes are
nominal, and everyone receives a ribbon. School rivalries
are obviated by drawing each team from various schools.
Beck would probably agree, however, that play days must
not try to abolish competitive drive and the will to achieve
athletic excellence. Otherwise they would turn athletics into
the frustrating farce described by the dissatisfied player
quoted by Mary Vetterling-Braggin in Chapter 8 of this volume.

Feminists would conclude that to lessen the overemphasis on winning in sport, we must 1) allow more women to
participate on all levels (thereby lessening sport's attractiveness as a male proving ground and escape valve); 2) change
the emphasis on male physiology (thereby fighting the image
of women's physical inferiority which supports the masculine
identity that men express in sport); and 3) substitute a human-

istic model of sport for the old violent attitudes. Changing the attitudes with which sports are played is just as important as changing the participants of the game and the games themselves. As Beck points out in her essay, if women participate in athletics without changing its violent, brutal, dominant nature they will merely be perpetuating their own oppression. [33]

In considering measures for athletic reform, we must keep it in mind that because sport is influenced by society, these reforms must be slow, deliberate and introduced in social institutions outside of sport as well as within sport. Education, through youth sports and physical education programs, is the most logical institution to initiate athletic reform. Because sport acts as a socializing agent, humanism and athletic appreciation (rather than capitalistic, work-like, or patriarchal values) can be taught in educational institutions through athletic participation. A reemphasis on pick-up games, creative free play and other forms of less organized youth sport could allow children to learn to appreciate the joy of participation for the sake of participation, rather than the importance of winning.

Sport reform can undermine the oppressive nature of modern society by demonstrating that the ideologies perpetuated in the athletic arena are false. I believe that no matter what the underlying cause of sport's deterioration, a change in the attitudes and the model of athletic participation can change social attitudes by redefining "success" and demonstrating that success can be attained through humanistic rather than violent means. [34]

NOTES

1. Bernard Suits. The Grasshopper, Games, Life and Utopia (Toronto: University of Toronto Press, 1980), chapter 4.
2. Paul Weiss. Sport: A Philosophic Inquiry (Carbondale: Southern Illinois University Press, 1979). The major argument presented in Weiss's work is that through sport individuals seek excellence.
3. Drew Hyland. "Athletics and Angst: Reflections on the Philosophical Relevance of Play," Sport and the Body: A Philosophical Symposium, ed. Ellen Gerber and William Morgan (Philadelphia: Lea & Febiger, 1979), p. 137.

198 / The Overemphasis on Winning

4. Stanley Eitzen and George Sage. Sociology of American Sport (Dubuque, Iowa: Wm. C. Brown, 1978), p. 67.
5. Ibid., p. 66.
6. Ibid.
7. Most neo-Marxists do not discuss sport explicitly. The positions I present are either implicitly present in their views and/or explicitly advocated by particular authors whom I credit.
8. Paul Hock. Rip Off the Big Game (Garden City, N.Y.: Doubleday, 1972), p. 7.
9. Ibid., p. 10.
10. Bero Rigauer. Sport and Work (New York: Columbia University Press, 1981), p. 13. Jean-Marie Brohm's book is Sport: A Prison of Measured Time (London: Villiers Publications, 1978).
11. Rigauer, p. 67. Rigauer is quoting F. W. Taylor.
12. Translated by A. E. Taylor in Edith Hamilton & Huntington Cairns (eds.), Plato: The Collected Dialogues (Princeton, N.J.: Bollingen, 1980).
13. Johan Huizinga. Homo Ludens (Boston: Beacon Press, 1955).
14. Suits, chapter 1.
15. Ibid., p. 8.
16. Huizinga, p. 199.
17. All feminists believe that women suffer systematic injustice. Radical feminists believe, in addition, that the oppression of women is the most fundamental of all sorts of oppression. Most feminists do not discuss sport explicitly. The positions I present here are either implicitly presented in their views and/or explicitly advocated by particular authors whom I credit.
18. Eugene Bianchi. "The Super-Bowl Culture of Male Violence," Jock: Sport and the Male Identity, ed. Donald Sabo Jr. & Ross Runfola (Englewood Cliffs, N.J.: Prentice-Hall, 1980), p. 122.
19. Lucy Komisar. "Violence and the Masculine Mystique," Jock: Sport and the Male Identity, p. 140.
20. Bianchi, p. 121.
21. Ibid., p. 123.
22. Arnold Beisser. "The American Seasonal Masculinity Rite," The Madness in Sport (New York: Appleton-Century-Crofts, 1967. Chapter 16, pp. 214-225). Reprinted in Sport Sociology: Contemporary Themes, Yiannakis, et al. (Dubuque, Iowa: Kendall/Hunt, 1976), p. 196.
23. Ibid.

24. Terry Orlick. Winning Through Cooperation (Washington, D.C.: Hawkins, 1978), p. 166. The number of players on each team remains constant because the team switching occurs only after a player from each side has relinquished service and is thus ready to switch to the other team.
25. Rigauer discusses this parallelism in the work cited in note #10.
26. Rigauer, p. 58.
27. Both Brohm and Rigauer argue that sport perpetuates the achievement principle.
28. There is presently no participation by women at the youth levels of some sports. There is also no professional level at all in women's sports with a few exceptions, such as tennis and golf.
29. Jane English, "Sex Equality in Sports," Philosophy & Public Affairs, 7, no. 3 (Spring 1978), p. 5.
30. English's basic benefits are health, self-respect to be gained by doing one's best, the cooperation to be gained from working with teammates and the incentive gained from facing opponents, the "character" of learning to be a good loser and good winner, the chance to improve one's skills and learn to accept criticism, and just plain fun.
31. English, p. 5.
32. Bonnie Beck, "The Future of Women's Sport: Issues, Insights, and Struggles," Jock: Sports and Male Identity, p. 301.
33. Ibid.
34. I would like to thank Betsy Postow for her very helpful comments and suggestions.

QUESTIONS

(1) a) List all the bad effects which Hundley attributes to the attitude that winning is all important.

b) In your opinion, does this list leave out any important bad effects? Does it include any effects which are not bad? Does it include any effects which should not be attributed to the attitude that winning is all important?

(2) a) What, if anything, do you agree with in the neo-Marxist explanation of the overemphasis on winning in modern sport? Why?

b) What, if anything, do you disagree with in the neo-Marxist explanation of the overemphasis on winning in modern sport? Why?

(3) a) What, if anything, do you agree with in the play theorist explanation of the overemphasis on winning in modern sport? Why?

b) What, if anything, do you disagree with in the play theorist explanation of the overemphasis on winning in modern sport? Why?

(4) a) What, if anything, do you agree with in the radical feminist explanation of the overemphasis on winning in modern sport? Why?

b) What, if anything, do you disagree with in the radical feminist explanation of the overemphasis on winning in modern sport? Why?

(5) a) Present an explanation of the overemphasis on winning in modern sport which you think Addelson would accept. Why do you think she would accept it?

b) What, if anything, do you agree with in the explanation which you have just presented? Why?

c) What, if anything, do you disagree with in the explanation which you have just presented? Why?

(6) Drawing on your answers to part (a) of questions 2-4 and to question 5 (b), present your own explanation or partial explanation of the overemphasis on winning in modern sport.

(7) a) List all the sport reform measures described by Hundley.

b) Add any other measures which you can think of that might reasonably be expected to help counteract the overemphasis on winning in modern sport. (Include measures which are actually practiced in some sports but are not common in sport generally, e.g., the beer bash with the opposing team traditionally hosted by the home team after a rugby game.)

c) For each of the sport reform measures which you have listed in answer to parts (a) and (b) above, do the following: List all the reasons for instituting this reform measure and all the reasons against instituting this reform measure in each of the following types of sports: professional, quasi-professional, competitive recreational, purely recreational. (The categories correspond to Raymond A. Belliotti's classification in Chapter 7 of this volume.)

(8) What else would you like to discuss from Hundley's essay?

PART III:

WHAT CAN THE THEORY OF EDUCATION
TEACH US ABOUT PHYSICAL
EDUCATION FOR WOMEN?

INTRODUCTION

The topic question of Part III is "What can the theory of education teach us about physical education for women?" The term "theory of education" is meant to include both the philosophy of education and educational psychology. The first four authors look primarily to the philosophy of education to determine what reforms are desirable in physical education. The last author adds the explicit perspective of an educational psychologist and provides empirical findings that can be used to evaluate the feasibility of various suggestions for reform.

A systematic philosophy of education can be generated from an ideal of a good or just society. If we have a picture of such an ideal society, we can determine what place education would have in it, and we can deduce the ideal features of a program of education. In Chapter 12 J. Theodore Klein presents three philosophies of education which are based on three different ideals of society: Plato's ideal (which grounds a classical philosophy of education), the assimilationist ideal, and the modified pluralist ideal. On Plato's ideal, society is divided into classes in which individuals are placed according to their natural abilities and propensities. Those in the ruling class require an education that will develop their intellects, emotions, and desires in proper balance to enable them to rule wisely. The other two ideals are more democratic and do not envision a special ruling class. The assimilationist ideal places a very high value on individual autonomy. Thus, it abolishes all sex roles on the ground that they limit people's autonomy. The assimilationist ideal calls for the abolition or restructuring of activities in which differences between men and women are important, since these activities support the idea of sex roles. According to an assimilationist philosophy of education, physical education should be purged of all activities in which either sex naturally excels.

The ideal of modified pluralism, which Klein supports, also places a high value on individual autonomy and hence on the abolition of sex roles. Unlike the assimilationist ideal, however, the modified pluralist ideal does not require us to ensure that sex-based differences are irrelevant. Sex-based differences, such as different athletic abilities, do not necessarily harden into sex roles, Klein holds. Furthermore, abolishing activities in which sex-based differences are important limits people's options and interferes with their autonomy. Therefore, physical education should not be purged of activities in which sex-based differences are important. But care must be taken to combat sex roles and the greater prestige of males. Klein suggests a variety of measures for this purpose, including the introduction of activities at which females excel, sex-integrated physical education activities, and the allocation of resources and staff positions equally to males and females.

In the next chapter Margaret Atherton expresses doubts about the usefulness of introducing "separate but equal" activities at which females excel. The idea has failed in the past, and we cannot know in advance that athletic activities at which women excel will be valued equally with those at which men excel. More importantly, Atherton argues that Klein misconceives the inspiration of the assimilationist ideal. The main reason this ideal seeks to abolish sex roles is not that sex roles limit individual autonomy. Instead, the importance of abolishing sex roles lies in the moral necessity of combatting the attitude (which can be held either consciously or unconsciously) that labels human virtues "manly" and regards women as less than fully human. It is worth the sacrifice of some individual autonomy to combat this attitude, she holds. Thus we can justify the limitation of options that would occur when we restructure physical education to eliminate all activities in which there are important sex-based differences of ability. It is especially important that we eliminate these activities because physical education is linked to the development of certain virtues of character. Thus, if the activities that constitute physical education include ones at which females are inferior, this will feed the notion that women are less than fully human. If, at some future time, we change our conception of what it is to do well at a physical activity so that we regard consistent losing as compatible with doing well, then we will be able to restore to the physical education curriculum those activities at which females consistently lose to males.

Ann Diller and Barbara Houston explain in Chapter 14 that the total educational experience is shaped not only by the intentional actions and decisions of educators, but also by the "hidden curriculum," i.e., messages that are not openly intended yet are conveyed by the setting and the social context. They give examples of the hidden curriculum and show that it is sexist, containing messages such as the one that the physical activities of females should be more restricted than those of males. It is therefore important that physical educators become aware of the hidden curriculum and deal with it. When the hidden curriculum is amenable to direct educational intervention and control, appropriate measures include the reform of organizational structures (to alter the hidden curriculum) and the reform of the deliberate curriculum (to counterbalance the undesirable effects of the hidden curriculum). An example of an organizational change is the equalization of the number of male and female physical educators at all levels. An example of a change in the deliberate curriculum is the introduction of different sports or other activities. By direct intervention, such as correcting students' sexist remarks or behavior, teachers can also counter sexist presumptions which are a result of the prevailing culture. It is also important to make students aware of the hidden curriculum and to teach them how to defend themselves against it. Which measures are most useful is largely determined by the level of education involved--e.g., elementary or university.

In Chapter 15 Linda J. Nicholson defends and elaborates on the position taken by Diller and Houston that sex differences must be taken into account in devising a program of physical education if that program is to avoid perpetuating sexism. For example, boys and girls in our society develop differently with regard to their attitude towards rules. Thus physical education programs that emphasize rule-governed sports rather than other physical activities might discriminate against females by discouraging their participation. More generally, being male and being female carry with them different social meanings which should be recognized, evaluated, and challenged where appropriate. Being male in our society means, among other things, being a member of the group which dominates the public (i.e., non-domestic) sphere. Some feminists find this a desirable group to be in, and so their goal is for "women to be able to occupy the same positions of power and public responsibility traditionally limited to men." Insofar as physical education helps fit young people

for the public world, e.g., through competitive sports, the
aim of these feminists would be to institute those reforms
in physical education which give females equal access to it
and its benefits. Other feminists, however, find various aspects of the public world as defined in our society to be undesirable. Insofar as physical education perpetuates these
undesirable aspects, they would say that physical education
should be radically reformed--not merely made more accessible to females. One suggestion along these lines is to reject the segmentation inherent in limiting physical activity to
special times.

In the last chapter Linda Nielsen adds the insights of an
educational psychologist to our consideration of physical education for females. Nielsen uses empirical studies to demonstrate the sometimes surprising educational benefits for females of participation in physical activity, and she suggests
tested methods for motivating females to participate. The
findings reported by Nielsen also allow us to make more confident predictions about the usefulness of some of the measures for reforming physical education which are suggested by
the other authors. For example, she reports that female
role models in athletics (which would be provided by one of
the reorganization measures suggested both by Klein and by
Diller and Houston) are extremely important in motivating females to participate. She also confirms that the baneful influence of sexism and sex roles can be significantly counter-
acted by explicit discussions which, in Diller and Houston's
terms, would amount to teaching about the hidden curriculum.

It should be noted that much of what has gone before
in this book is also relevant to the topic of physical education. In Part I, for example, we reached certain conclusions
concerning fairness to female students in school sports programs. These conclusions are relevant to any program of
physical education which includes a school sports program.
Our conclusions about fairness to women in athletics-related
employment must also be considered in any recommendations
for reforming physical education. Finally, the discussion in
Part II of desirable and undesirable types of competition is
extremely relevant to the topic of physical education. It
would certainly be undesirable to include in any program of
physical education competitive activities that injured the characters of the participants. On the other hand, it would serve
the goals of physical education to include the sort of competition that can provide participants with an avenue to a fuller
life.

12.   PHILOSOPHY OF EDUCATION, PHYSICAL EDUCATION, AND THE SEXES

J. Theodore Klein

What can philosophy of education teach us about physical education and the sexes? I will respond to this question by examining three philosophical approaches, each of which addresses key issues involved with physical education for women and men.   The examination of these approaches will provide examples of how philosophies of education can be related to physical education.

The three approaches I will examine are the philosophy of education in Plato's Republic, a contemporary philosophy of assimilationism which can be the basis for a philosophy of education, and a philosophy of education that I will identify as modified pluralism and develop as an alternative to assimilationism.   These approaches have something very important in common, because each one involves outlining some concept of an "ideal," "good," or "just" society and considering what physical education would be like in such a society. If one has a concept of what physical education would be like in a "good" or "just" society, this concept can be compared with physical education as it exists in our present society. From this kind of comparison, proposals can be made about structuring physical education in a "better" or "more just" way.

The best starting point for relating philosophy of education to physical education and the sexes may be certain key questions about physical education and the sexes.   One such question is to what extent, if any, there should be separate physical education for females and males.   There is a considerable degree of separation in physical education, and this separation needs to be examined.   One example of separation is in school athletics where certain activities are identified as boys' sports and other activities are identified as girls' sports, each set of activities being limited to members of one sex. Should this kind of separation be continued as it is, expanded, reduced, or eliminated? In other areas separation sometimes occurs, as in separate "gym" classes for females and males. Should such classes be continued as they are, expanded, reduced, or eliminated?

It might be argued that maintaining a considerable degree of separation by sex in physical education reinforces sexist practices and attitudes. Is separation itself an important contributor to sexism or is sexism due to other factors which happen to accompany separation? Would a non-sexist approach require total integration of women and men in all areas of physical education? Or would a non-sexist approach be compatible with some degree of separation?

Central to applying a philosophy of education to physical education is answering questions involved with sexual equality as it relates to sex differences. Physical education raises a particularly interesting set of questions for sexual equality, because it may call for an approach to "equal educational opportunity" that is quite different from what would be appropriate in all other areas of education. If there happen to be average differences in mathematics achievement between men and women, it can be reasonably said that such differences are due not to any "innate" differences in ability between women and men but to "environmental" influences. The same could be said, for example, about any average differences in achievement in philosophy or the arts. It can be reasonably argued that since there are no innate differences in ability between females and males in such areas as mathematics, philosophy, and the arts, education in these areas should be carefully structured to provide equality of opportunity for females and males.

The idea of equality of educational opportunity can be seen as permitting differences of treatment only in the presence of "educationally relevant" attributes.[1] Because of this, sex, race and class can be excluded as a basis for any difference in treatment. However, would this exclusion apply to sex in relation to physical education? There are certain average physical differences between males and females that cannot be explained as a result of "environmental influences" or "socialization." What do such differences mean for sexual equality and equality of educational opportunity for females and males?

Still another set of crucial questions relates to the topic of competition. School athletics involve competition between teams, and less formal sports and various physical activities involve competition between groups or among individuals. Certain ideals of competition have dominated athletics and physical education. Is the idea of competitiveness in any form acceptable? Can there be a distinction between positive and destructive approaches to competition? Are there some kinds of competition that should be encouraged through physical education and others that should be discouraged? Should the approach to competition involving females be any different from the approach involving males?

These questions illustrate key issues involving physical education and the sexes. These questions relate to policy issues concerned with how physical education should be structured in schools. They also relate to individual teachers of physical education by leading naturally to questions about what the goals of their teaching should be. Each philosophy I will examine suggests some systematic answers to the questions. In examining these philosophies, I will concentrate on the following interrelated areas:

1) The idea of a "good" or "just" society. This will include the idea of a society that is just in its treatment of the sexes.

2) The role of physical education in a society that is "good" or "just," with particular emphasis on treatment of the sexes.

3) Goals and values of physical education.

4) Positive and negative features of how sports, athletics, and physical education are approached in our present society.

5) Discussions of separation and integration in physical education, sexual equality and sex differences as related to physical education, and competition in relation to physical education.

A philosophical examination of these areas can suggest specific proposals for needed directions in physical education.

I will begin my examination of philosophies of education by considering Plato's Republic. Plato develops a very systematic philosophy of education and applies it explicitly to physical education and the sexes. His approach illustrates much of what a philosophy of education can do, regardless of how much one would agree or disagree with it.

Plato's Republic outlines a picture of an ideal or just society. The question of how a person is to live justly is answered through an examination of justice as a characteristic of an entire society. Plato stated that justice in the individual will correspond with justice in the society as a whole.

Plato viewed each person as by nature fit to do certain things, to perform a certain function in society. The goal of education, in his view, would be to prepare the individual to perform his or her function in society. Plato spoke of three types of persons corresponding with three faculties that are present within each individual person. There is a reasoning faculty, a spirited faculty, and a desiring faculty. With some persons the reasoning faculty naturally dominates, with others the spirited faculty, and with still others the desiring faculty. Plato seemed to believe that each person is born with one quality dominant, but that education is needed to develop this dominance in a proper harmony.

In a just society, according to Plato, there would be three classes, each class corresponding with one of the three features of individual persons. Justice would involve each class performing its proper function without disrupting the functions of the other classes. According to Plato, those who through contemplation have insight into what is good should make the ultimate decisions in society. These "rulers" would be assisted by a group which Plato called "auxiliaries," who would be entrusted with defending the society and carrying out policies developed by the rulers. Plato sometimes identified these two groups together as "guardians," and a large part of the Republic involves a detailed description of the education potential "guardians" should receive.

Plato saw physical education as an integral part of the education needed for potential "guardians." The goal of physical training, for him, was a harmony between mind and body. Plato saw a sound body as an aid to a sound mind, although he did not think having a sound and healthy body was enough to produce a sound mind. He stated that a sound mind has the power to make one's bodily condition as perfect as it can be. [2]

Physical training, according to Plato, should be simple, flexible, and unified. He contrasted this training, aimed at a special kind of harmony in a person, with, for example, training aimed at developing physical strength. In contrast to the development of sheer physical prowess, physical education for Plato was actually aimed at developing the "spirited" faculty within the "mind" or "soul."[3]

Plato saw the need for an integration between two branches of education, one aimed at the "spirited" part of the person and one aimed at a person's "philosophic" disposition. A life-long devotion to one branch at the exclusion of the other would lead either to uncivilized hardness or to over-civilized softness.[4] According to Plato, the right training would produce a needed balance between gentleness and strength.[5] The spirited and philosophic elements, according to Plato, need to be brought into tune and the tensions of each adjusted to the right pitch.[6]

Plato's philosophy of education clearly relates physical education to a concept of a just society. Physical education, according to Plato, contributes an essential part in educating a certain kind of person, the guardian, for certain places in society. Its value is in the harmony, both between soul and body and between spirited and philosophic dispositions, to which it contributes. Plato did not appear to see participation in athletics or other physical activities as good in itself. Such participation would seem to be good as a means for developing the qualities Plato saw as needed.

Very striking in Plato's Republic is his treatment of sexual equality, and this clearly relates to physical education. Plato stated that if women are to share in the same tasks in society with men, they need to be taught the same things. Women must receive the same mental and physical training as men.[7]

Plato thought that there are certain natural differences among people which cause them to be unequally qualified for certain things. These innate differences he saw as a basis for education and for determining what tasks in society a person should perform. However, Plato did not in any way correlate these natural differences with sex differences.

Plato stated that no occupation concerned with the management of social affairs belongs exclusively to either men or women. A woman, just like a man, may or may not have a particular talent for medicine, music, warfare, athletics, love of knowledge, or being high spirited. Since these qualities are essential for being a guardian, a woman, equally with a man, could have the talent to be a guardian. Men and women being trained to be guardians should have the same education since the "nature" to be educated is the same.[8]

Plato does refer to biological differences between women and men, but he did not see these as grounds for denying women access to occupational or educational opportunities. He does, however, describe women as physically "the weaker" sex, and suggests that women have "the lighter" duties among guardians.[9] Despite this modification of sexual equality, Plato did not see a need for any kind of separate physical education for women and men. As indicated earlier, he proposed one physical education for men and women together.

Plato's philosophy of education provides a strong statement on sexual equality. He did not see talents or abilities as differentially distributed according to sex. A particular man and a particular woman may have the same talent or ability. In this situation, the woman equally with the man should have access to the appropriate positions in society and the appropriate education or training needed for these positions. Physical education would involve sexual equality as a literal sameness of treatment, unless perhaps there would be some "lightening" of women's tasks and activities. Plato's great emphasis on integration of the sexes in physical education indicates either that this "lightening" would not occur in physical education activities or would not be significant when it did occur.

Objections can be raised against Plato's overall philosophy of education. One can question such aspects of his philosophy as the analogy between classes in society and parts of the individual, the apparent definition of an individual's worth by function in society, the authoritarian and undemocratic implications of some of his proposals, and the idea of innate "natures" as he develops it. However, in the discussions of sexual equality and the discussions of physical education, Plato's philosophy of education anticipates contemporary issues in many ways.

In response to the question of what a philosophy of education can teach us about physical education, Plato's philosophy presents a statement of goals for physical education and an outline of a "good" or "just" physical education in a "good" or "just" society. The value of physical education is not in the physical activities and training themselves, but in what such activities and training, if properly structured, can contribute to the personal development of "guardians." Plato's views suggest that he does not see competition as good or bad in itself; a form of competition would be good if supportive of the needed personal development, bad if destructive of this development.

Despite its concept of sexual equality, Plato's philosophy involves a kind of elitism. He suggests that there should be a highly developed program of education, including physical education, available only to certain members of society (potential guardians). The remaining members of society would not have access to this program. Could the values Plato finds in physical education be extended to all individuals? Plato's emphasis on the "whole person," his suggestion of balance between elements, and his concept of physical education as reaching the "mind" could all be appealing ideals today, although each ideal would need to be clarified and given specific content. One often hears references to the importance of the "mental aspect" of sports or other physical activities. Physical education does not seem to develop merely _physical_ skills.

Someone might object to Plato's approach by saying that athletics and other physical activities are "good" in themselves. This basic goodness would then have to be distinguished from abuses in athletics and physical education. Plato's approach suggests that whether or not certain physical activities are "good" depends on how they are structured and their impact on individuals.

Plato's views relating to sexual equality are quite interesting. One can object to his reliance on "innate natures" and his linking of individual identity to one's place in society. However, as indicated earlier, he does not tie "innate" differences to sex. Also, he does not identify any kind of sex-role division in society, except possibly in the "lightening" of women's tasks.

Plato's emphasis on men and women receiving the _same_ education and having the _same_ opportunities is extremely important. In physical education, Plato's philosophy goes against excluding individuals from opportunities to participate because of their sex. Plato's idea of a physical education which integrates the sexes provides a challenge to anyone defending any degree of separation by sex in physical education.

Although it may not create a major problem for Plato's concept of integrated physical education, his idea of women as the "physically weaker" sex can be questioned. On the average men may have certain physical "advantages" compared with women. However, there also seem to be certain physical "advantages" that women have, on the average, compared with men. If women and men each, on the average, have some distinctive physical talents and "advantages," how are these talents to be developed? Would an integrated physical education be the best avenue for their development or would some degree of separation of the sexes be better? This question will be considered more fully later.

Plato's overall approach to the sexes suggests a kind of "sexual blindness." In considering, for example, fitness for a certain activity, one should consider only how each person might "do" in the activity without thinking of anyone's sex. The idea of sexual blindness is an important part of the assimilationist philosophy of education, which I will now examine.

The point of departure for the assimilationist philosophy of education I will examine is Richard Wasserstrom's concept of an assimilationist society.[10] Although Wasserstrom does not develop a detailed philosophy of education, his views could be the basis for a philosophy of education applied to physical education and the sexes. This assimilationist philosophy of education would involve concepts of a "just" society and sexual equality. These concepts would have implications about the role of physical education in a just society and goals of physical education. Whether or not such a philosophy is accepted, it can teach us about several important issues involved with physical education for women and men.

The kind of assimilationism I will discuss needs to be distinguished from other kinds of assimilationism which have been involved in discussions of cultural differences.[11] One of these forms of assimilationism might be called conformism. This view suggests that individuals from all cultures should come into conformity with a dominant culture. One would need to conform to the values of the dominant culture in order to significantly "make it" in society. Both Wasserstrom's

assimilationist view and the pluralist view I will develop later
are opposed to the ideas of one culture being dominant and it
being desirable for persons to come into conformity with this
culture.

Another kind of assimilationism can be called the
"melting pot" view and suggests a process of amalgamation. [12]
This view suggests a merging or blending in which various
cultures give way to a new culture. In contrast to this view,
Wasserstrom's concept is closer to what might be called an
"open society" concept, [13] which pictures a society in which
cultural differences either cease to exist or are no longer
significant. Cultural identity and identification (i. e., considering oneself part of a culture) would seem to be important in an "amalgamated" society but not in an "open society."

Wasserstrom contrasts racism and sexism with the
way race and sex would be confronted in a just society. A
just society, for him, would exemplify what he identifies as
the assimilationist ideal. In such a society race or sex
would be no more significant than eye color is in today's
society. Sex and race would be irrelevant to any political
or social institution, practice, or arrangement. [14]

In contrast to defined male and female roles, an assimilationist society would remove all sex-role differentiation. In such a society there would not be qualities identified as inevitably masculine or feminine. There would not
be special virtues or disabilities associated with being a man
or a woman. [15]

How might an assimilationist society approach activities in which people of one sex, on the average, seem to excel, or at least do significantly better, compared with people
of the other sex? These sorts of activities would seem to
make sexual differences appear to be significant and not simply like differences in eye color. Thus sexual blindness
would be undermined. Wasserstrom confronts this problem
by proposing that activities be arranged so that women and
men can succeed and excel equally at each activity. For example, if the kind of physical strength now required for life-
guarding gives men an advantage over women, the way life-
guarding is practiced would be changed to remove this advantage. [16]

The life-guarding example leads naturally into the
question of what an assimilationist philosophy of education

would teach us about physical education. What role would
physical education have in an assimilationist version of a
just society? What kind of physical education for females
and males is suggested?

Quite clearly an assimilationist philosophy of education would require an integrated physical education for males
and females. There would not be distinct "needs" of females
and males that would call for separate physical education
classes or activities. Any separation of the sexes in physical education would go against sexual blindness, since it would
use sex as a basis for differentiating people and treating them
differently.

In applying his assimilationist ideal, Wasserstrom
makes some very significant remarks about sports that would
have radical implications for athletics and physical education.
Some activities, such as life-guarding, Wasserstrom views
as significant because of the services they perform. Such
activities would be retained but restructured in an assimilationist society. These activities Wasserstrom contrasts with
certain sports, such as boxing and weightlifting, which he
thinks do not perform a service and are not significant. In
these sports men have advantages over women, and the sports
function in existing patriarchal societies to help maintain male
dominance.[17]

What an assimilationist approach recommends would be
the elimination of some, perhaps many, sports on the grounds
that they do not perform any significant services and they perpetuate male dominance. The sports that are retained would
be structured in a "sexually blind" way with neither males
nor females having advantages. Physical education and school
athletics would be changed through the elimination of some,
perhaps many, physical activities and the restructuring of
others.

The activities retained as part of physical education
would be activities in which neither sex dominates. Ability
groupings might be used so that persons could find a level of
participation which would correspond with their degree of
skill. For example, there could be at least beginning, in-
termediate and advanced classes in such activities as movement, jogging, and swimming. Basic physical health and opportunities for recreation could be emphasized. Athletic activities would have a greatly reduced role compared to their
place in physical education today.

One important implication of the assimilationist view would seem to be that there should be something close to numerical equality between females and males in teaching, coaching, and administration. An imbalance would go against sexual blindness and could suggest domination by one sex over the other. This distribution of positions could provide role models for both girls and boys, although role modeling would not involve sex-roles.

Applications of the assimilationist view might not eliminate all forms of competition, but this view would require elimination of the kind of competitiveness that is now characteristic of many professional sports and physical education activities. This competitiveness correlates with "macho" ideals of male dominance and would have no place in an assimilationist concept of a just society. Emphasis on physical dominance, excessive aggressiveness, violence, and winning as "the only thing" would be morally objectionable from an assimilationist point of view.

The assimilationist view is different from Plato's view in some fundamental ways. Its emphasis is on individual autonomy rather than a person's function in society. There is no reliance on the idea of fixed "natures" as the basis for social or educational opportunities. Women are not seen as "the weaker" sex in any significant sense. There is no proposal for a separate system of education and physical education for one group (potential guardians).

There are basic similarities between Plato's view and the assimilationist view in their approaches to physical education and the sexes. Equality for females and males in physical education would involve sameness of treatment. Males and females would receive the same physical education. Sex would be irrelevant in the structuring of physical education activities and opportunities.

The assimilationist philosophy of education presents an ideal for a non-sexist society that is appealing in many ways. There are strong arguments to support elimination of sex roles and the restrictions on autonomy they impose, identifying certain qualities as inevitably masculine or feminine, and tying special virtues and disabilities to being male or female. Sex should not be a barrier to opportunities in society and education. The assimilationist view seems to eliminate any basis for discrimination and prejudice.

The assimilationist view also presents some very strong recommendations for restructuring physical education. The idea of an integrated physical education is very appealing, as is the idea of eliminating the present male dominance and undesirable competitive qualities. The idea of a balance between females and males in teaching, coaching and administration is just and positive.

Despite having many strengths, the assimilationist philosophy of education is open to several objections. One objection is that an assimilationist society would either eliminate cultural differences or make them insignificant. Cultural communities can be an important basis for the identity of individuals, and a variety of cultural communities may be crucial for a viable democracy.[18] Many authors have spoken, for example, of the need for blacks to identify with a specific "black" culture. Similarly, many authors have spoken of the need for a "female" or "woman's" culture with which women can identify. The assimilationist might respond by saying that in a truly non-sexist and non-racist society, there would not be a need for this kind of cultural identification. I am inclined to think that some forms of cultural identification would continue in a non-sexist and non-racist society. In any case this issue, in itself, poses no direct difficulties for the assimilationist approach to physical education. Still the issue of cultural differences may relate to the "solidarity" issue, which does directly affect physical education.

It has sometimes been said that certain sports provide a needed avenue for the development of male identification and solidarity. The importance of male solidarity could be given as a reason for limiting participation in certain sports and physical activities to males. The assimilationist can respond that this would perpetuate male dominance and negative kinds of competitiveness, and would go against the autonomy and liberty of females. It can be argued both that there are other avenues to male solidarity available in society and that exclusion of women from the sports in question is unfair and harmful to women.[19] Yet "feminist" arguments can be given for maintaining some separate sports and physical activities for females as avenues for developing female solidarity. However, if it is unfair to exclude women from "male" activities, it would also be unfair to exclude males from "female" activities. There may be a conflict in values between liberty and autonomy on the one hand and solidarity on the other if solidarity requires activities limited to one sex. At this point the solidarity issue does not provide a decisive objection against assimilationism, although I will consider it further in developing a pluralist philosophy of education applied to physical education.

A more decisive objection to assimilationism is based on the existence of certain physical differences between the sexes which have an impact on physical education. The assimilationist philosophy suggests that these differences be made insignificant. This would require eliminating some activities and restructuring others; many of the sports and physical activities that now exist would cease to exist or exist in a very different form. Since the activities to be eliminated are important and significant to a number of people, it can be argued against assimilationism that it would be wrong to eliminate them. The assimilationist might respond by saying that the sports and physical activities proposed for elimination function in our present society to maintain male dominance and perpetuate sexual inequality. However, it does not follow from this that these activities would have the same role in a non-sexist society.[20] A better approach might be to maintain many, if not all, of these activities, and seek to eliminate their undesirable and morally objectionable features.

Sex differences need not be inconsistent with sexual equality. Average differences in physical abilities between females and males need not indicate that either sex is physically disadvantaged. It may be true that in terms of certain kinds of physical strength females are disadvantaged compared to males. However, females also have certain physical advantages, such as the kind of flexibility necessary for ballet or the balance beam. Physical disadvantages in some activities can be advantages in other activities.[21] Eliminating sports and physical activities in which either males or females would be, on the average, advantaged could destroy opportunities to develop talents and build self-esteem for many people. A better approach would seem to be a reorganizing of athletics and physical education so that activities in which females have an advantage are equally important with activities in which males have an advantage.

The assimilationist philosophy rightly objects to sex-roles, but what can be called "sex activity correlations" need not develop into sex-roles.[22] That more males than females, or vice versa, engage in an activity does not mean that this activity is part of a "male" or "female" role. Suppose that almost all, or even all, of the people who choose to participate in a certain physical activity happen to be of one sex.

This in itself would not go against sexual equality. One would need to consider a physical education program as a whole. An overall balance without injustices in particular areas would seem consistent with sexual equality and would contrast with the present male dominance in much of athletics and physical education.

Sports and other physical activities can satisfy important human needs by providing opportunities for self-expression and excellence.[23] Many of these activities are to some extent art forms and involve great skill and intricacy.[24] These qualities of many physical activities indicate how they are important avenues for developing self-respect. Eliminating a significant number of these activities, as the assimilationist view seems to require, would result in great losses. The assimilationist might respond that new activities could be found to "make up" these losses. However, it is not clear what these new activities would be or that the losses could be "made up."

Wasserstrom argues that the assimilationist ideal provides for a kind of individual autonomy that a non-assimilationist society cannot attain. He claims that any non-assimilationist society will have sex roles and institutions which distinguish between individuals by virtue of their gender. He suggests that if one's sexual identity is important in a society, this would cause there to be substantial psychological, role, and status differences between males and females. These characteristics would limit and impair the abilities of individuals to develop their own characteristics to the fullest extent.[25]

It does seem true that sex-roles, status differences, distinctions based on gender, and other characteristics described by Wasserstrom are destructive of individual autonomy. But would these characteristics have to be present in any non-assimilationist society (such as a pluralist society)? A society could accept, for example, certain average differences between females and males without these hardening into the negative differentiations Wasserstrom describes. Sports and other physical education activities can be approached in a way which allows for average physical differences while supporting individual autonomy. The assimilationist approach supports individual autonomy by proposing the elimination of negative differentiations based on sex. However, the assimilationist approach restricts and limits individual autonomy by proposing that a variety of physical activities be eliminated.

The assimilationist approach to physical education would rightly remove male dominance and features of athletics and other physical activities that correlate with this dominance. However, what would be left in a physical education program after the elimination of activities in which members of one sex are, on the average, better? The losses would be great, and it is not clear that they could be "made up" in any way.

Despite many very important strengths, the assimilationist philosophy of education is not satisfactory either in defining a social ideal or in applying that ideal to physical education. What I will undertake in the remainder of this essay is the development of an alternative approach which will share the strengths of assimilationism and avoid its weaknesses. I will identify this approach as modified pluralism. The applications of modified pluralism should teach us much about physical education and its relation to the sexes.

Pluralism involves the acceptance of certain diversities as necessary and good.[26] A pluralist point of view involves respect for differences, and differences are not viewed as justifying any kind of discrimination or favoring of one group or individual over others. I speak of modified pluralism to emphasize that all diversities, or diversity in general, should not be blindly identified as good. Some diversities, such as those found in sex roles, are destructive. Positive differences and kinds of differentiations need to be distinguished from negative ones.

In relation to ideals of a just society, the assimilationist and modified pluralist views would be in agreement on many issues. Modified pluralism would oppose the negative differentiations based on sex which assimilationism opposes. Both views see sex as irrelevant to occupational choices and opportunities. Both views, in contrast to Plato, heavily emphasize the value of individual autonomy.

In relation to physical education, modified pluralism would also be in agreement with assimilationism on several points. Modified pluralism, like assimilationism, would support ending male dominance in sports and physical education and eliminating undesirable competitiveness. Modified pluralism would support the idea of having something close to numerical equality between females and males in teaching, coaching and administrative positions in physical education.

A variety of role models for both boys and girls would be seen as very desirable from a pluralist point of view.

The major difference between assimilationism and pluralism is in approaching differences, including those sex differences which are relevant to physical education. While assimilationism would attempt to make sex differences insignificant, modified pluralism would see these differences as acceptable and significant. Very helpful to a pluralist view is a distinction between sex and gender. Sex relates to physical or biological characteristics, while gender, including concepts of what is "masculine" and "feminine," relates to psychological characteristics.[27] The connection between sex and gender needs to be broken so that one's sex does not imply a set of rigidly defined "masculine" or "feminine" qualities. This would open the way for various ways of "being a woman" and "being a man," which would enhance individual autonomy.[28]

How would a just society approach activities that require a kind of strength at which men, on the average, are better than women? A pluralist approach would not support suppressing opportunities in these areas, but multiplying and diversifying opportunities overall.[29] There might continue to be far fewer women than men involved in these activities. However, there could also be a whole range of activities emphasizing fineness of movement and dexterity in which women, on the average, are "better" than men. Far fewer men than women would be involved in these activities. The range of activities as a whole would provide a variety of opportunities for both males and females.

A pluralist philosophy applied to physical education in schools would not suggest one single plan for structuring physical education in all schools. The best solution for each school would depend greatly on the needs and interests of the students. However, certain general guidelines would seem to be necessary, and these can be summarized as follows:

1) Most physical education activities would be integrated. Activities limited to one sex would be considered as an option only in situations where there are great average differences in skill level between the sexes.

2) Ability grouping would be widely used. The sexes would be integrated in activities using ability grouping.

3) Activities in which females have natural advantages would be equally emphasized along with activities in which males have natural advantages.

4) Allocation of resources and staff positions (teaching, coaching, administration) would be close to numerically equal between the sexes.

5) There would be a variety of physical activities · structured so that basic benefits of physical education would be available to each student.

6) The negative aspects of competition would be discouraged, but competition would continue in positive forms.

I will now explore these guidelines in more detail.

As a general principle, the pluralist view I suggest does support integration of the sexes. Excluding interested persons from participation in a particular activity at a particular skill level is wrong unless there are very strong overriding reasons for making an exception. The distinction between sex and gender supports the idea that males and females do not have distinct sets of needs which require separate physical activities. Also, as indicated earlier, providing solidarity for males or females does not seem to be a sufficient reason for segregating the sexes in physical activities, and it is not clear that solidarity would require exclusion of persons of the "other" sex from an activity.

There is only one kind of situation that strikes me as sufficient for justifying a physical activity which excludes one sex. This would be situations in which an activity involves average physical differences that are great and with which there is no other way to adequately provide for participation. Once an exception is allowed, it is difficult to "draw lines." Suppose, for example, that a school provides separate programs for boys' basketball and girls' basketball. Should a girl who is "good enough" to make the boys' varsity team be allowed to join it? If so, does this mean that a boy who cannot "make" the boys' varsity team should be allowed to join the girls' varsity team? If the girl is allowed to join the boys' team, should the boy be allowed to join the girls' team? It seems unfair to allow one but not the other. Yet, given the average physical differences between the sexes that may affect performance in basketball, allowing boys to participate in the girls' activity could result in it being "taken over" by boys.

The moral and legal implications of some alternative schemes should be investigated. One approach could be to have a varsity team open to both sexes with at least two remaining teams that would be separated by sex. [30] Another approach would be to have different teams for different ability levels with membership determined by lottery. [31] Still another approach would be to have enough teams available at different ability levels to accommodate all students who wish to participate (with resources being spread very thin). [32] I am inclined to say that no scheme is clearly best for all situations. Simply eliminating activities separated by sex in situations where there are great average differences in skill levels between the sexes could exclude most or all of the people of one sex from participating. Thus, unless an alternative scheme can be implemented, there should be separate physical activities for those persons who are at a great physical "disadvantage" due to sex.

Many of the problems involved with separation based on sex can be avoided through the use of ability grouping. A pluralist approach would recommend that ability grouping be used in many physical education activities. Ability grouping can provide activities for people with a wide range of skill levels. Sex would not be a relevant consideration, since inclusion in a particular activity would be based solely on one's skill level. People would have opportunities to benefit from activities even if they do not "do them well."

A danger in ability grouping is that there may be disrespect for those in lower ability groups. [33] An important part of physical education would be recognizing a distinction between appraisal of skill and performance level in a particular activity and respect for oneself or another as a person. That a person is not highly skilled, or even very unskilled, in a physical activity should not lessen that person's self-respect nor respect for that person from others.

Neither the provision of "girls' teams" nor the use of ability groups adequately addresses the situation of females in physical education. Segregated activities and teams for females in areas where males are physically advantaged can easily be perceived as "second class." When ability groups are used for these activities, females would tend to be in groups with "lower abilities."

What needs to be provided is a greater variety of physical activities, including more physical activities at which women can excel. [34] Some of these activities, such as ballet, synchronized swimming and forms of gymnastics, already are included in some school programs. The role of these activities would need to be greatly expanded.

If no females participate on a school's varsity football team, this is not in itself unjust. What is unjust would be the existence of several activities dominated by males, with few or no females participating, and no corresponding group of activities dominated by females. There should be an equal emphasis, along with a balance of resources, so that females and males can have equal opportunities to participate and excel.

Corresponding to equal opportunities for females and males there would be a need for something close to numerical equality between the sexes in staff positions. As indicated earlier, this would provide a needed variety of role models for males and females. It would also strengthen the availability of equal opportunities and reinforce the equal importance of females and males in physical education.

The provision of female role models, along with the provision of activities in which females have natural advantages, could help to promote solidarity among females. This would not require exclusion of males from activities, but the provision of positive opportunities for females. Similarly males could have opportunities for solidarity through male role models and the existence of activities in which males are naturally advantaged. This would not require exclusion of females and could be freed from the negative features of "macho" competitiveness.

Modified pluralism would emphasize certain values or benefits of physical education. Jane English distinguished basic benefits, to which everyone has an equal right, and scarce benefits, which are available to relatively few people. [35] The kinds of scarce benefits discussed by English, such as fame, financial gain and prizes, apply to professional sports. However, appropriate to school physical education programs would be such scarce benefits as the self-respect and the respect and recognition that can come from excellence in performance. Such benefits could not be available to all students, but students who achieve excellence can be said to deserve respect and recognition (although not nec-

essarily external rewards). Quality of performance could be
recognized without students who excel becoming "sports celebrities." Along with equality of opportunity to develop excellence in physical activities, women are entitled to an
equality of recognition for the excellence they achieve in
these activities.

While providing respect for excellent performances
by both females and males, without falling into a heavy emphasis on external rewards, schools would need to provide
for all students access to the basic benefits of physical education. Basic benefits of sports described by English[36]
would apply to all physical education activities, although all
of the benefits might not apply to each activity.

1) Physical education can help a person learn how to
take care of his or her health.

2) Physical education can help a person learn how to
enjoy recreational activities.

3) Persons can learn self-respect through experiences
of "doing their best" in physical activities.

4) Persons can learn to cooperate with others through
involvement with teams or group activities.

5) Physical education can contribute to "character
building." In athletics experiences of both "winning" and "losing" can contribute to "character development."

6) Persons can improve their skills by making efforts
and learning from criticisms.

These benefits should be available to all students.

With a greater variety of physical activities drawing
more on "female" skills, and an equalizing of opportunities
and resources, the physical differences between males and
females are compatible with sexual equality in physical education. This is what a pluralist approach suggests. The
male dominance in sports and physical education would be
ended, and each person, regardless of sex, would have a
variety of opportunities for developing his or her talents.

As suggested earlier, a pluralist approach would elim-

inate much of what goes into competitiveness as it exists today. This would not mean the elimination of all competition
in the sense of teams or individuals competing and "winning"
or "losing." However, it would mean the encouragement of
attitudes and behaviors quite different from those involved
with sports and athletics today.

Winning should not be an "end in itself"; the end of a
competitive activity should be the benefits of the activity for
all of the participants. A person may "lose" and yet "do
one's best" in performing. Lip service is sometimes given
to such ideals as "building character" through sports, and a
person being a "good winner" and a "good loser." These
ideals need to become more the reality, and school athletics
need to be restructured to avoid the pitfalls of "big business
sports" with its emphasis on "winning as all."[37]

Sexual equality and the greater valuing of "female" excellence in certain activities would go with a movement away
from "macho" competitiveness. Along with these changes
should come a curbing of the degree of violence present in
some "masculine" sports. School physical education programs would include kinds of competition oriented toward
basic benefits and opportunities to develop excellence in performance.

A pluralist philosophy of education can thus teach us
much about a possible restructuring of physical education.
The social ideals, the goals of physical education suggested,
and the various proposals for restructuring deserve attention.
If a person does not accept the pluralist view, still there
could be much for that person to consider in the recommendations about physical education.

I have attempted to develop a philosophy of education
related to physical education for females and males. The
consideration of Plato's Republic provided a clear example
of how a philosophy of education can teach us about physical
education by identifying what its goals should be. The consideration of assimilationism shows how an important contemporary social philosophy suggests a philosophy of education with important and controversial suggestions about physical education. Building on critical discussion of Plato's
view and assimilationism, I develop a pluralist philosophy of
education applied to physical education and include recommendations about how physical education should be restructured.

NOTES

1. Cf. Thomas F. Green, "Response to Burbules and Sherman," Philosophy of Education 1979: Proceedings of the Thirty-Fifth Annual Meeting of the Philosophy of Education Society (Normal, Ill.: Philosophy of Education Society, 1980), p. 118.

2. Republic, iii. 403. All references to the Republic are taken from The Republic of Plato. Translated with Introduction and Notes by Francis MacDonald Cornford (New York and London: Oxford University Press, 1964).

3. Republic, iii. 410.

4. Ibid.

5. Cf. Republic, iii. 410-411.

6. Republic, iii. 411-412.

7. Republic, v. 542.

8. Republic, v. 455.

9. Republic, v. 455, 457.

10. See Richard Wasserstrom, "Racism, Sexism and Preferential Treatment: An Approach to the Topics," UCLA Law Review, 24 (February 1977), pp. 581-622; Richard Wasserstrom, "On Racism and Sexism," in Richard Wasserstrom (ed.), Today's Moral Problems, 2nd ed. (New York: Macmillan, 1979), pp. 75-105. The latter is a somewhat revised version of Parts I and II of the former.

11. For distinctions somewhat similar to the ones I make see Michael Novak, "Ethnicity for Individuals: What to Do and Why," in Michael Belok and Ralph Shoub (eds.), Sex, Race, Ethnicity, and Education (India: anu prakashan, 1976), pp. 67-89; Richard Pratte, "Five Ideologies of Cultural Diversity and Their Curricular Ramifications," Philosophy of Education 1979: Proceedings of the Thirty-Fifth Annual Meeting of the Philosophy of Education Society (Normal, Ill.: Philosophy of Education Society, 1980), pp. 264-278. I have also explored similar distinctions in an unpublished ms. entitled "Assimilation, Separatism and Pluralism."

12. This process might be better described as amalgamation than assimilation. Cf. Pratte, "Five Ideologies of Cultural Diversity," pp. 265-266.

13. Pratte, "Five Ideologies of Cultural Diversity," pp. 268-269.

14. Wasserstrom, "On Racism and Sexism," p. 96.

15. Wasserstrom, "On Racism and Sexism," p. 97.

16. Wasserstrom, "Racism, Sexism and Preferential Treatment," p. 611, n. 59.
17. Ibid.
18. I have developed detailed concepts of a culturally pluralistic democracy elsewhere. See J. Theodore Klein, "Cultural Pluralism and Moral Education," The Monist, 58 (October 1974), pp. 683-693; J. Theodore Klein, "A Pluralistic Model for Educational Policy Making," Educational Theory, 28 (Spring 1978), pp. 85-89; J. Theodore Klein, "A Model for a Pluralistic Democracy," Contemporary Philosophy: Philosophic Research and Analysis, VIII (Early Spring 1980), pp. 16-18.
19. Cf. B. C. Postow, "Women and Masculine Sports," Journal of the Philosophy of Sport, VII (1980), p. 54.
20. Cf. Bernard Boxill, "Sexual Blindness and Sexual Equality," Social Theory and Practice, 6 (Fall 1980), p. 283.
21. Jane English, "Sex Equality in Sports," Philosophy & Public Affairs, 7 (Spring 1978), p. 275.
22. Boxill, "Sexual Blindness and Sexual Equality," p. 290.
23. Boxill, "Sexual Blindness and Sexual Equality," pp. 285-286.
24. Boxill, "Sexual Blindness and Sexual Equality," p. 286.
25. Wasserstrom, "On Racism and Sexism," p. 104.
26. For elaborations on various aspects of pluralism see the articles listed in note 18 above.
27. Joyce Trebilcot, "Two Forms of Androgynism," Journal of Social Philosophy, 8 (January 1977), p. 4.
28. Cf. Klein, "A Pluralistic Model for Educational Policy Making," p. 89. My pluralistic view is close to the P form of androgynism advocated by Trebilcot. See Trebilcot, "Two Forms of Androgynism," pp. 4-9.
29. Cf. Boxill, "Sexual Blindness and Sexual Equality," p. 295.
30. Richard Alan Rubin, "Sex Discrimination in Interscholastic High School Athletics," Syracuse Law Review, 25 (1974), p. 566.
31. Postow, "Women and Masculine Sports," p. 56.
32. Cf. Postow, "Women and Masculine Sports," pp. 55-56.
33. Cf. English, "Sex Equality in Sports," p. 274.
34. Cf. English, "Sex Equality in Sports," p. 275.
35. English, "Sex Equality in Sports," pp. 270-271.
36. Cf. English, "Sex Equality in Sports," p. 270.
37. Very important, although beyond the scope of this paper, is the need to critically examine competition and competitiveness in our society as a whole, not simply in

sports. The competitiveness characteristic of our
"capitalist" society presents serious obstacles to de-
veloping a viable approach to "equality of opportunity."
Cf. Nicholas Burbules and Ann L. Sherman, "Equal
Educational Opportunity: Ideal or Ideology?" Philoso-
phy of Education 1979: Proceedings of the Thirty-Fifth
Annual Meeting of the Philosophy of Education Society
(Normal, Ill.: Philosophy of Education Society, 1980),
pp. 111-112; William E. Brownson, "The Structure of
Competition in School and Its Consequences," Philoso-
phy of Education 1974: Proceedings of the Thirtieth
Annual Meeting of the Philosophy of Education Society
(Edwardsville, Ill.: Philosophy of Education Society,
1974), p. 239.

SUGGESTIONS FOR FURTHER READING

Boxill, Bernard. "Sexual Blindness and Sexual Equality,"
Social Theory and Practice, 6 (Fall 1980), pp. 291-299.

Brownson, William E. "The Structure of Competition in the
School and Its Consequences," Philosophy of Education
1974: Proceedings of the Thirtieth Annual Meeting of the
Philosophy of Education Society (Edwardsville, Ill.: Philosophy of Education Society, 1974), pp. 227-240.

Burbules, Nicholas C., and Sherman, Ann L. "Equal Edu-
cational Opportunity: Ideal or Ideology?," Philosophy of
Education 1979: Proceedings of the Thirty-Fifth Annual
Meeting of the Philosophy of Education Society (Normal,
Ill.: Philosophy of Education Society, 1980), pp. 105-114.

English, Jane. "Sex Equality in Sports," Philosophy & Public Affairs, 7 (Spring 1978), pp. 269-277.

Green, Thomas F. "Response to Burbules and Sherman,"
Philosophy of Education 1979: Proceedings of the Thirty-
Fifth Annual Meeting of the Philosophy of Education Society (Normal, Ill.: Philosophy of Education Society,
1980), pp. 115-120.

Klein, J. Theodore. "A Pluralistic Model for Educational
Policy Making," Educational Theory, 28 (Spring 1978),
pp. 85-89.

Plato. The Republic. Translated with Introduction and Notes

by Francis MacDonald Cornford. New York and London: Oxford University Press, 1964.

Postow, B. C. "Women and Masculine Sports," Journal of the Philosophy of Sport, VII (1980), pp. 51-58.

Rubin, Richard Alan. "Sex Discrimination in Interscholastic High School Athletics," Syracuse Law Review, 25 (1974), pp. 535-574.

Trebilcot, Joyce. "Two Forms of Androgynism," Journal of Social Philosophy, 8 (January 1977), pp. 4-9.

Wasserstrom, Richard. "Racism, Sexism and Preferential Treatment: An Approach to the Topics," UCLA Law Review, 24 (January 1977), pp. 581-622.

Wasserstrom, Richard (ed.). Today's Moral Problems. 2nd ed. New York: Macmillan, 1979. Chapter Two.

QUESTIONS

(1) Plato held that physical education should contribute to a harmony between mind and body.

    a) In your view, what is the proper harmony between mind and body?

    b) In your view, should it be a goal of physical education to contribute to this harmony? Why or why not?

    c) How might a program of physical education be designed to contribute to a proper harmony between mind and body?

(2) Plato held that physical education should contribute to a proper development of the spirited part of the soul or mind. (For the purpose of this question, assume that the spirited part of the soul or mind includes a person's attitudes towards competition.)

    a) In your view, what would count as a proper development of the spirited part of the soul or mind and what would count as an improper development? (Your conclusions from Part II of this book are relevant.)

    b) In your view, should it be a goal of physical education to contribute to a proper development of the spirited part of the soul or mind?

    c) How might a program of physical education be designed to serve that goal?

(3) According to Wasserstrom, the author whom Klein cites as an advocate of the assimilationist ideal, the autonomy of individuals is decreased if society assigns different roles to the members of the two sexes. Do you agree or disagree with Wasserstrom? Why?

(4) On the basis of a modified pluralist philosophy of education, Klein lists six guidelines for physical education.

a) For each guideline, answer the following: Does this guideline promote a just society according to the pluralist ideal? Why or why not?

b) Can you think of any additional guidelines for physical education which would promote the pluralist ideal of a just society?

(5) In your opinion, should the promotion of a just society be a goal of physical education? If so, how important a goal should it be compared with other goals? Support your opinion.

(6) What else would you like to discuss from Klein's essay?

13. EDUCATION FOR EQUALITY

Margaret Atherton

Physical education and the issue of sports generally pose
special problems for attempts to design an educational system in which the sexes are treated equally. For, at least
as sports are presently conceived, it seems likely that differences in ability are not entirely the product of social ar-
rangements to be dissolved by some form of tinkering, but
rather are the result of inevitable physical differences between the sexes.[1] So it seems that there is at least one
area of education and of human endeavor generally in which
perfect equality between the sexes is a pipe dream. Some
might be inclined to dismiss this fact of inequality as unimportant in the general scheme of things. There are, it might
be supposed, far more significant inequities to deal with at
present, and if we can successfully provide for an otherwise
equal society, the issue of sports can be ignored without loss.
I hope to provide some reasons later to show that sports cannot be dismissed quite so easily. But, be that as it may, it
is undoubtedly helpful in clarifying the notion of equality between the sexes in general to consider the particular problems
that arise in thinking about what a sexually equal physical education would look like. Working through the proposals and
arguments that Theodore Klein has offered is very useful for
coming to a deeper understanding of what we ought to be looking for when a goal of education is sexual equality.

It is noncontroversial and indeed downright obvious to
point out that as things now stand in our society, in common
with most others, men and women are not treated equally.
It is a much harder task to say exactly what their inequality
consists in, and yet, without a proper account of this inequality, it becomes difficult to say what an ideal society would be
like in which men and women are treated equally. Klein's

discussion is predicated on a particular assumption about the
nature of the inequality women suffer from. Though his account contains much that rings true, I think further scrutiny
reveals complications.

Many analyses of women's inequality, like Klein's,
point out that what's missing for women are options. Women
are shunted into a small number of roles, overwhelmingly
the private role of looking after a house and family, and
even those few positions available to them in the public world
tend to be those like that of secretary, nurse or waitress,
which mimic the caretaking functions that traditionally are
thought to belong to women. If women's lack of options is
singled out for criticism, then the wrong being done them is
presumably that of curtailing their opportunities to make decisions and choices about what they will do. The wrong that
is being done to women, on this account, is that they are
being deprived of the freedom to make important choices
about what their lives will be like. Their autonomy is not
being appropriately respected. If women's inequality is
rooted, as this analysis suggests, in limitations on their
ability to make choices, then the correct way to go about
righting this wrong is obviously to increase the options available to women. We want women to be able to choose to do
things other than what has been traditionally reserved for
them to do. But so long as other choices are genuinely
available, the ideal society will nevertheless be one in which
some people will choose for themselves those roles which
women used to perform exclusively. It might even be, of
course, that some of these people will be men. But it will
not be necessary, for example, in order to achieve an equal
society, to insist that all men and all women take on an
equally significant public and a private role. Indeed, so
long as the inequality that needs correcting is identified with
the ability to make choices, then to make such "assimilationist" demands would make no sense. Instead, a full plurality
of roles should be available to everyone.

If we ask what part a good education ought to play in
bringing about an ideal society so characterized, the answer
to this question seems obvious. Boys and girls, regardless
of gender, should be trained to make and carry out informed
decisions about what to make of themselves. Their education
should be directed to preparing them to take on any role that
seems good to them. It is important that no one be restricted to one kind of training or another because of their
sex, although it is not recommended that any sort of training

now available be abandoned. When the problem is described in this way, it doesn't seem, right off, that physical education presents any theoretical difficulties, even though the existing structure of physical education provides a good example of the way women's options are reduced. For, at present, the division into "boys' sports" and "girls' sports" itself receives a good deal more institutional support than any corresponding division into "boys' subjects" and "girls' subjects," and since this division seems unavoidable because of what appear to be inevitable physiological differences between the sexes, simply allowing girls to try out for boys' teams will not significantly increase the things they will be able to do. And, as well, there is the additional factor that boys' participation in their sports is considered to be more valuable to them and to the outside world than is girls' participation in their sports. In consequence, more funding is made available, for example, and more attention paid to what the boys do than is the case for the girls. It is much more rewarding for a boy to choose to excel at sports than it is for a girl. This imbalance, it would seem, can be easily corrected. Girls will have the same sorts of opportunities to choose to excel at sports as boys so long as the nature of what it is to be a sport is not limited to a male-centered picture. There must be sports in existence which capitalize on what is special to women's bodies, so that women can excel in some sports in the way men can now, and what women can do must be valued and rewarded in the way that male capacities are valued and rewarded. In this way, without decreasing men's options to learn to take part in sports, similar sorts of options will be available to women. This is the picture Klein supports, and there is a great deal that sounds attractive about it. Nevertheless, the kinds of revisions necessary to bring about this equality of options with respect to physical education are more problematic than they at first appear to be, and for reasons that cast some doubts on the analysis of inequality between the sexes as an inequality with respect to the freedom to choose.

There are two kinds of revisions that Klein recommends which have to be made in our current conception of sports if women are to be able to have the kind of options that men have now. The first is that there should be more sporting events designed for the female body, at which women but not men can excel (gymnastics is often cited as an example of such a sport). The kinds of sports that are now most important to us are designed with the male body-type in mind. Thus it is possible for a man, for example, to come to feel good about himself because of his success at playing football, but there are fewer similar choices available to women. This imbalance is held to be correctable if more sports are designed for the female body. Secondly, of course, success at such sports must come to be seen as just as valuable and as rewarding as success at football is now thought to be. In this way, women will come to feel good about themselves for excelling at those skills which only they possess. These will be circumstances under which both men and women will have equal opportunities to participate in sports and to excel, each at their own special endeavors.

Two kinds of consideration cast doubt on this sort of suggestion. The first is the obvious one that separate has never meant equal. The pluralist solution seems to suppose that so long as women are given opportunities to excel, their excellence will be recognized and rewarded, even when, as is the case with sports, this excellence will be in an activity restricted to women. But, of course, women have been provided throughout history with opportunities to excel at activities restricted to women. Students of women's history point out that although there have always been avenues of accomplishment for women, nevertheless the woman's largely private sphere has been overlooked. Thus, one cannot assume that so long as women are doing worthwhile things, they will be valued and achieve self-esteem for doing them. It is, in fact, often the case that in discussing the kinds of sports designed for women, people emphasize the differences between male and female sports in such a way as to suggest that what women play are not "real" sports. Thus, Paul Weiss makes much of the fact that many women's sports, like gymnastics or figure skating, allow a woman to be graceful rather than strong or fast, whereas others, such as women's basketball or field hockey, treat a woman as a less able or "truncated" man.[2] The things that "count" as items to be valued and the standards of evaluation are frequently such as to have application to the male sphere only. The point I want to emphasize is that we cannot simply announce that excellence at a particular activity will henceforward be found to be valuable. Evaluating a particular kind of activity is more complicated, more culture-bound, and not quite so arbitrary as the search for equality through a plurality of options seems to suggest.

This leads to the second problem with Klein's pluralistic approach: it seems to require dubious assumptions about what's involved in feeling good about oneself. One complaint

which pluralism addresses seems to be that some men have
opportunities to feel good about themselves that are not available to women because men have skills women lack. Therefore, it is proposed that we equalize opportunities by praising
women for their own peculiar skills. Now it is perfectly
true that baseball, football, basketball, and soccer are not
laid down in heaven as the ideal forms of sport, and I do not
want to claim that it is impossible to invent others at which
women can excel. But it is not obvious that everything a
person can do is equally deserving of praise. I might discover in myself an unusual facility for reading texts that are
printed upside down and backwards or perhaps I can wiggle
my ears with remarkable ease. It is true that these talents
of mine go unrewarded while someone else's skill at throwing
a football or solving mathematical puzzles is singled out for
praise. But it is not clear to me that I can claim to have
been unfairly denied an opportunity to feel good about myself.
For there is no reason to assume that people ought to be
provided with opportunities to feel good about themselves because of anything they might be able to do. If skills are
found to be valuable not arbitrarily, but for good (or even
bad) reasons, then we cannot simply demand that women's
skills are to be valued. We have to show there are reasons
for finding them to be valuable. It therefore requires an argument and not just a hope or a demand to show that women
do have skills of their own that can contribute to success at
sports. More importantly, the success or failure of such an
argument would depend upon what we take success or failure
to be like and on the skills women actually possess. In order to claim to be able to provide people with opportunities
to succeed we must make reference to criteria of success.
Since these are non-arbitrary, complicated and culture-bound,
we cannot know in advance that there will be a plurality of
ways in which people can be successful at sports. And we
cannot identify equality with equality of options, because it
is not true that every option ought to be equally rewarded.

It is instructive to consider a theory which depends
heavily on differences in the natures of men and women, the
doctrine of separate spheres for men and women. An argument for separate spheres rests on the idea that there is a
range of virtues that men are to be praised for exhibiting,
such as being logical and analytical, being active, being sto-
ical and unemotional, being "sporting" and even perhaps, being competitive and aggressive, and that there is a different
and complementary range of virtues that women are to be
praised for exhibiting. As in the argument for pluralism in

sports, it is clearly possible to claim that people's options for virtuous behavior are reduced. Men will not be able to feel good about themselves for exhibiting any of the womanly virtues, nor will women feel good about being manly. So the recommendation ought to be that anyone should feel free to assume any personality type, from the most traditionally masculine to the most traditionally feminine or anything in between.[3] But, particularly as gets developed by this complementary theory of male and female nature, some of the virtues that women are to be praised for possessing can be quite peculiar, such as being passive or dependent, or being irrational and illogical (even when more flatteringly called being intuitive). It is not obvious that these are characteristics that we genuinely want anyone, male or female, to develop. Now modified pluralism deals with this by excluding undesirable characteristics. But I think this ad hoc maneuver does not get at the heart of the problem.

Since pluralism must be modified, the account of what is going wrong that appeared to justify pluralism must be modified also. It is not enough simply to point out that a person's options have been reduced. What I want to suggest is going wrong with the proposal that there are separate manly and womanly virtues is that it gives rise to the suggestion that women are less than fully human. This happens because human virtues are frequently labeled "manly." The list of alleged feminine virtues is drawn up in complement to the list of manly (i.e., human) virtues.[4] One indication that manly virtues frequently coincide with human virtues is this: when people attempt to explain why humans, as opposed to other animals, have distinctive rights and privileges, they tend to mention as distinctive of humans, facts that are often associated with lists of male virtues, such as a capacity for independent judgment or rational decision making. When we are talking about what humans owe and are owed by virtue of being human, it does not seem as though we actually think there are lots of different kinds of optional conduct that can be called really good or really virtuous. For these sorts of arguments make use of a single standard by which conduct, if it is to count as fully human, will be judged. And to the extent that fully human conduct tends to overlap with masculine conduct, the result of the doctrine of separate spheres is to give tacit support to the belief that women are not as good as men, are less than fully human. It would be possible to correct this situation by claiming that everyone ought to be able to do whatever he or she wants, but another possibility would be to locate the wrong elsewhere and to argue that a woman should be thought to be as good as a man, that is, should be judged and evaluated by the same standards.

I am proposing that so long as a major flaw with the doctrine of separate spheres is not that it cuts down on people's options, but that it denigrates women as less than human, this suggests the importance of using the same standards to evaluate men and women. If we want a society in which the same standards are thought to be applicable to men and women, and if we want a sexually equal society, in which men and women have an equal likelihood of being praised regardless of gender, then the assimilationist society recommends itself. Under such an arrangement, education should not be directed to providing different activities for boys and for girls, and physical education must therefore be drastically restructured so that there be no sports at which either men or women excel. But if we are to adopt a model of equality which is promoted by the assimilationist ideal, the reason for it cannot be that adopting this model of equality will bring about greater opportunities for autonomy to be exercised. It is true that adopting the assimilationist ideal may give the appearance of producing greater autonomy because it encourages the elimination of undervalued and undesirable roles to which more women than men have been confined. Thus, women would experience the opportunity to choose from among all and only roles in which men and women can excel equally as an increase in their ability to act on the basis of freely chosen, autonomous decisions. But as the example of physical education shows, this sort of consideration cuts both ways. Women will not be trained to work the balance beam, nor men to play football, so that men and women will not be judged to be good at sports for different reasons and according to different criteria. In an assimilationist society, women will be liberated from certain roles only to be confined, along with men, in certain others. Thus the assimilationist ideal places requirements for a just and equal society above freedom of choice. Both men and women are to be forced into molds for the good of society, so that they will be treated equally. Since it makes no sense to propose an assimilationist solution in order to overcome a lack of options, any justification of an assimilationist ideal must give some other account of the wrong being done to women in an unequal society--an account which does not appeal to the undesirability of limiting options.

In the light of these difficulties, it is instructive to go back and look again at Plato's reasons for recommending

an education in which there is no distinctive training for
men and for women. Plato thought that individual fulfillment comes about when people take on those social roles
for which their nature is best suited. In making this claim,
Plato uses assumptions that Klein finds objectionable, in particular, Plato's "reliance on 'innate natures' and his linking
of individual identity to one's place in society." Indeed,
many people today would share Klein's objections, for it is
often thought that there is no morally acceptable way of arguing from facts about people's nature or about what is natural to conclusions about what they ought to do or about
what society should expect of them. [5] But I think there is
a way of turning Plato's conception of the wrong that is being done to women into an argument that is not unfamiliar
and that deserves to be taken seriously.

Suppose we claim that women are naturally as rational
as men, but only receive an education and have available to
them opportunities which diminish the chances of their developing their rationality to the fullest. Then we can claim
that the wrong being done to women is that, in being encouraged to be, for example, passive and dependent in their judgments, they are being turned into something they are not.
Their nature as fully rational beings is not being respected.
The life--and hence the education--that a given society makes
available to its citizens ought to be one that allows them to
fulfill their natures, to make the best of themselves. Plato
also held that the life that a given society has an obligation
to provide its citizens is one that is socially valuable. He
thought that people should not be encouraged or taught to develop any exceptional talent, such as ear-wiggling. People
will be valued, on their account, not arbitrarily, but for the
contribution they can make to the overall good of the society.
Nevertheless, that contribution will be not only of general
value, but will be valuable to the individual, so long as the
roles by means of which each person contributes to the general good are constrained by considerations about what humans are like and about the kinds of activities that permit
all individuals to develop themselves to the fullest. Thus,
since Plato thinks that we are mutually dependent upon one
another for our welfare, it is in the interests of all of us
that each of us develops to the fullest.

Although a Platonic picture of the ideal society provides limitations on what people can do, these limitations
have built in, as part of their conditions, considerations of
human psychology. The charge that people are not being

allowed a full range of options to choose from is perfectly appropriate. But in Plato's eyes, something has gone wrong if you are asked to take on roles that are contrary to your own nature or to your human nature, and it is still wrong whether you choose them or someone else asks them of you. So the life that is available to women (the life of the house-wife, for example) will be wrong if it is stultifying, whether or not it is a life that has been chosen.

There are, no doubt, a number of different objections that could be raised with respect to this proposal, but if we restrict our attention to the issue of physical education, then one objection springs immediately to mind. The value of Plato's argument for an assimilationist society in which men and women are to be judged by similar standards depends upon the truth of his claim that men and women are talented by nature in the same sorts of ways. But even if people are prepared to grant him this claim for such characteristics as rationality, it can be argued that it is just not true with re-spect to those characteristics by virtue of which people excel at sports. We cannot argue that women are naturally as strong or as fast as men are. An argument such as this supposes, however, that we ought to praise people and judge them to be good at sports when they demonstrate extreme strength or speed, and here again it is interesting to con-sider what Plato would say, for with this claim Plato would certainly disagree. He is explicit that what is to be de-veloped in physical education and to be found valuable in sports is not strong muscles (Republic III, 410). Rather, physical education is to be directed towards developing men-tal abilities, in particular what Plato calls the "spirited" part of the soul. What he means by the spirited part of the soul is a matter of some controversy, and I am not going to try to settle it here. J. C. B. Gosling, [6] however, has made a suggestion that is interesting in this particular context. He proposes that someone with a lot of spirit is someone who has a tendency to govern action because of an admiration for and desire to emulate a particular kind of conduct that is thought to be honorable or manly. Spirit, for example, is at the root of the desire not to be ashamed of oneself for not living up to such standards of conduct, which desire gives people courage. If Plato is right, and the value of physical education within an education generally is the development of this sort of character trait, then there is no particular rea-son to assume that women as well as men are not equally suited to develop this kind of character, and no reason to assume that it can only be developed in situations that re-quire muscle power.

Though it is not necessary here to worry about particular details of Plato's analysis of the aims of physical education, I think it is important to pay attention to his conception of the connection between physical education and the development of virtues of character. To the extent that he is right about the function of physical education, this argues for an importance that physical education would not have if the main reason for its presence in schools were to have fun, or to release high spirits or to allow a few unusually strong or well-coordinated students a chance to develop their peculiar talents. And if physical education is important for the development of virtues of character, then the problem of providing a physical education that is sex blind is a serious one.

It is worth noticing that connections between being good at sports and being a particular kind of good person are often made, if only tacitly. For, even though relatively few adult males participate in or make a success at sports, succeeding at sports is nevertheless associated with the range of "manly" virtues like aggressiveness or competitiveness, which are often appealed to in order to account for male success generally, and in order to argue for women's necessary lack of success in the public world. And this means that the existence and attention paid to sports like football or basketball in which women cannot compete with men cause women greater harm than simply that of denying them opportunities to excel at a particular line of physical endeavor. The existence of such sports suggests that women are not as capable as men of developing the particular virtues of character that are associated with sports. Women, who cannot play games designed for a male body type as well as men can, will not be thought to be as aggressive, courageous, or competitive as men, but instead merely to be aggressive or courageous or competitive "for a woman."

Plato recommends that women receive the same training that men do because he supposes that they have the same nature that men do, and hence can be trained to develop the same virtues. He says they should be trained in the gymnasium along with men because he thinks that the purpose of physical education is to develop courage and women are just as suited to be courageous as men. The physical training is to develop women's ability to be courageous in the same sorts of circumstances that men will be expected to be courageous. No training is appropriate which does not respect women's equal ability to become and be valued for being courageous.

If the line of argument suggested by Plato is correct, it becomes a powerful argument in favor of assimilationist sports, for, by playing games which do not favor either body type, men and women will have exactly the same opportunities to develop and display the virtues associated with physical training. Neither sex will be thought to be less than fully courageous. Such a revision, of course, will require a sacrifice of activities now precious to us. I do not want to deny or overlook the nature of this sacrifice. For, as Plato's argument emphasizes, we cannot disentangle the goals of education from the goals of society generally. If we require an assimilationist education in order to encourage the development of identical virtues of character in men and women, then we will also require an assimilationist society in which those virtues are valued and rewarded. If this education cannot be accomplished except by abolishing baseball, then there can be no more baseball anywhere. And a world without baseball is undoubtedly a sadder and drabber world than this one. I can only hold out one ray of hope. So long as we understand our education to be directed towards instilling virtues of character, rather than, for example, inculcating some range of skills, then it might be that our notion of or the importance of ability groups might change. Making out a case for this would require saying a good deal more about what these virtues of character consist of. But perhaps, as an example, it could be that the virtues of character that we ought to be interested in will not require things like competition or winning. And then perhaps baseball, if not the World Series, would be restored to us.[7, 8]

NOTES

1. See Jane English, "Sex Equality in Sports," Philosophy and Public Affairs, 7 (Spring 1978), for an interesting discussion of the implications of physical inequalities for notions of sexual equality.
2. Paul Weiss, "Women Athletes," reprinted in Out of the Bleachers, edited by Stephanie L. Twin. Westbury, N.Y.: The Feminist Press; New York: McGraw-Hill, 1979.
3. See Joyce Trebilcot, "Two Forms of Androgynism," Journal of Social Philosophy, 8 (January 1977), for a discussion of this proposal which she calls poly-androgynism and its complement, monoandrogynism. Trebilcot, like Klein, excludes morally objectionable

traits from the plurality from which each individual may ideally choose.

4. A study of clinical judgments made by practicing clinical psychologists showed that "ideal concepts of health for a mature adult, sex unspecified, are meant primarily for men, less so for women." (Inge K. Broverman, et al., "Sex Role Stereotypes and Clinical Judgments of Mental Health," Journal of Consulting and Clinical Psychology, 34 (1970), 1-7, p. 1.) The psychologists tended to identify the same characteristics as belonging to the healthy adult and the healthy male, but mentioned a different set of characteristics as those of the healthy female.

5. See, for example, Christine Pierce, "Natural Law Language and Women" in Sex Equality, ed. by Jane English. Englewood Cliffs, N.J.: Prentice-Hall, 1977.

6. J. C. Gosling. Plato. Boston: Routledge and Kegan Paul, 1973.

7. It is also true that these conclusions all rest on the assumption that women are significantly weaker than men. But women are in many areas narrowing the gap. Perhaps an assimilationist and equal physical education would show that the existence of this gap is a myth and then again baseball could be restored.

8. I would like to thank Mark Kaplan, John Koethe, Robert Schwartz, and Joan Wiener for their help in writing this paper.

QUESTIONS

(1) Klein recommends that we encourage both physical activities at which men excel and physical activities at which women excel. Atherton casts doubt on the soundness of the recommendation.

a) What are the reasons which Klein gives in support of this recommendation in his essay?

b) What are Atherton's reasons for doubting that Klein's recommendation would work?

c) Answer the following for Klein's position as you described it in part (a) above and for Atherton's position as you described it in part (b) above: Which parts of this view, if any, do you agree with? Why? Which parts of this view, if any, do you disagree with? Why?

(2) a) On behalf of Atherton, construct the most plausible argument you can in support of the conclusion that we should

reject any ideal which distinguishes between manly virtues and womanly virtues. (If necessary, review the section of the General Introduction entitled "Background on Arguments.")

b) Present the most plausible objection which you can think of against the argument which you have just presented on behalf of Atherton.

c) On behalf of Atherton, reply as well as you can to the objection which you just raised.

d) In your view, is the reply which you made on behalf of Atherton a satisfactory reply to the objection? Why or why not?

(3) a) In your view, what are the proper goals of physical education? (Refer to your answers to the questions asked after Klein's essay.)

b) Which goals of physical education would be made more difficult or impossible to achieve if physical education were drastically restructured so as to exclude activities at which men excel and activities at which women excel?

c) Which goals of physical education would be made easier to achieve by a restructuring of the sort described in the previous part of this question?

(4) What else would you like to discuss from Atherton's essay?

14. WOMEN'S PHYSICAL EDUCATION:
A GENDER-SENSITIVE PERSPECTIVE

Ann Diller and Barbara Houston

> Active exercise was my delight.... No
> boy could be my friend till I had beaten
> him in a race, and no girl if she refused
> to climb a tree, leap fences, and be a
> tomboy.[1]
>
> --Louisa May Alcott

Why should one talk about <u>women's</u> physical education? Why
not talk about physical education for both women and men,
for children, for adolescents, for adults, for persons? Some
would argue that to raise the separate question of women's
physical education is to already affirm and perpetuate a detrimental distinction based on biological sex where such a distinction is neither required nor desirable.

There is no question that physical education has been
differentiated for the sexes for reasons having to do with both
perceived biological and social differences between them.[2]
Women have played an active role in the development of their
own formal physical education since its modern beginnings in
the mid-nineteenth century, and it has differed in character
from men's physical education in the following ways:[3]

    a) The philosophy of physical education for women has
       emphasized the importance of securing "the greatest
       good to the greatest number"[4] and has all along
       placed a greater emphasis on amateur as opposed
       to professional sport, on cooperation rather than
       competition, and on the basic benefits to be gained
       by everyone rather than pursuit of the scarce bene-
       fits affordable to the few.

b) Women and men have differed in their conceptions
   and administration of competitive athletics. In
   women's programs extramural sport has been developed within the educational context, with goals
   and staff allocations the same for general education, professional preparation and intramural and
   extramural programs. Men's physical education
   has been characterized by a severance between
   physical education and extramural competitive
   sport.

c) There have been different explicit curricula for
   women and men. Although sport has been a major ingredient of both programs, the selection of
   sports has been different; and when the sports were
   the same, women developed them differently "by
   way of such affectations as shortened matches, divided basketball courts and special rules and techniques."[5]

d) Curriculum development has borne a different emphasis in the two programs with dance and movement education developed primarily by women and
   given more attention within women's programs and
   colleges.[6]

A more significant observation to make, however, is
that in contemporary American society it is obvious that
equality has not been realized through gender-differentiated
physical education programs. Women's physical education
has received less money for programs and personnel, and
women have had unequal access to facilities. In general,
women's sports have been underfunded, less well coached
and equipped, and players have not had equal fringe benefits such as medical benefits, housing, food and travel allowances. Women have not had equivalent opportunities for
athletic scholarships. In schools and in society, women's
sports have been accorded much less status and attention
than men's.[7]

In short, it is fair to say that the gender-differentiated
programs have suffered from sexism; they have been different
and unequal. This has made many educators properly skeptical of proposals that we continue to take sex and gender
differences into account when designing physical education
programs.[8] But there is still fierce debate about the best
way to realize sex equality.

On a general level the disagreement about sex equality has a dual focus. In part it concerns our interpretation of the concept of sex equality.[9] Does sex equality entail the elimination of activities in which there might be significant sex differentiation by virtue of natural and ineradicable sex advantages? Or does it allow for significant sex differentiations and merely require the elimination of sexist attitudes and values now associated with these differences?[10] Additional disagreement arises over the best means to realizing the ideal of sex equality, however it is interpreted. Should we, need we, take account of gender in the methods we propose for the realization of our ideal?[11] In physical education this controversy takes the form of a debate over the extent to which physical education programs should be sex integrated or sex segregated.

In this chapter we assume the viewpoint of an educator who is already strongly committed to sex equality and to equal educational opportunity but recognizes that this still leaves a number of practical questions and policy problems undetermined. In Section I we examine the physical education debate over sex integration in an effort to identify central legitimate concerns on each side. In Section II we introduce the concept of a gender-sensitive perspective as one way of doing justice to the concerns of both sides. We then take this gender-sensitive perspective as our viewpoint on women's physical education for the rest of the chapter. In Section III we apply this perspective to our definition of physical education and discover the importance of the hidden curriculum. Section IV sketches some prominent features of the hidden physical education curriculum for girls and women. In Section V we address the question of the educator's responsibility for dealing with undesirable hidden curricula and suggest a number of alternative approaches. Section VI is a brief summary of our conclusions on what it means to take a gender-sensitive perspective toward women's physical education.

I. Sex Integrated Physical Education: For and Against

In this section we will examine some of the major arguments for and against sex-integrated physical education. We shall start with those that favor integration.

1.

In addition to the prima facie case against sex segretion in physical education[12] there are strong considerations that favor sex integration. Integrationists argue that we will never come to have an accurate knowledge of the abilities of girls and women until we have sex-integrated classes and similar expectations for the two sexes. Many constraints have been unfairly imposed on girls and women because of erroneous beliefs about physiological differences between the sexes. Specialized rules for girls have circumscribed their play and women are still kept from competing in certain events.[13] These sorts of constraints have led to serious confusion about the causes of the differential in female and male sports performance. Differences arising from unequal experience have been mistakenly attributed to natural or physiological differences.

A well-known example of this mistake is captured in the phrase "throwing like a girl." The implication is that girls throw badly by nature. Dr. Jack Wilmore of Arizona University devised an ingenious experiment which is easy to replicate:

> When he asked boys and girls to throw the ball, the boys did much better than the girls. Then he asked each of them to throw with their non-dominant arm (i.e. right-handers throw with their left hand and vice versa). On this occasion both boys and girls threw the same distances.[14]

The point this simple experiment makes is that physiological differences alone obviously do not account for performance differences. We cannot know what accounts for performance differences until we give equal training to girls and boys. The same point might also be made with respect to attitudinal differences. For example, women's attitudes toward competition may have been so thwarted or distorted by our continually being forced to compete in unfair circumstances that these attitudes may be more a testament to our imposed disadvantages than to our moral superiority.

The general failure to differentiate between performance discrepancies attributable to physiological differences and those resulting from training has also given us inaccurate estimates of the gap between the athletic potential of the two sexes. Very few women have ever had training equivalent to that of many men. Consequently, women are nowhere near exploring the limits of their potential. As more women become involved in sports and their training is taken seriously, we see amazing improvement in their world records.

For example, when Don Schollander won his Olympic medals
for men's swimming in 1964, no one would have predicted
that ten years later his times would not be good enough to
win the women's gold medal.[15]

The integrationist concludes that since we do not and
cannot know for some time what a realistic estimate of the
sex distinction in athletic potential might be, it is premature
to think of having anything other than coeducational physical
education.

A second argument posed by those favoring integration
is that the differences in athletic potential, once we do know
more about them, will deserve relatively little attention in
physical education. As with research on sex differences in
general, more attention has been paid to the differences than
to the relevant similarities. Even if we were to rely on our
presently available estimates of sex differences we should be-
ware of exaggerating their significance for physical education.

Granted that some physiological differences between
the sexes are relevant for the sports performance of equally
well trained world class competitors, there are several points
more salient for physical education. Whatever their differences, "neither sex has a structure that is unsuitable for
sports,"[16] and both sexes have physiological advantages dependent upon the choice of sport. A physical education program designed to include only or mostly activities favoring
one of the sexes would be a poor program. There are other
activities one should want to include for a variety of reasons
such as their appeal to student interest, their contribution to
physical fitness, their life-time playability, the facilities they
require, and their expense.

Further, females and males are similar physiologically
in such areas as coordination and the ability to learn particular skills. These similarities, along with other considerations, are more relevant to the design of physical education
programs than are the sex differences in the performances
of world class competitors. It is not the point of physical
education classes to train top level sports competitors.

Another argument in favor of sex integration is that it
offers girls a better opportunity to realize their potential.
This view is expressed rather clearly by two fifteen-year-old
girls who explain in a recent study why they prefer coeducational physical education:

> I feel I have to set higher goals when playing with the boys.... I do better, too, when I compete with them.

> When I was in an all girls class I knew I was the best and it was easy to slack off. Now I really have to work to stay near the top. It's better that way. [17]

It might be argued that integration provides a better opportunity only for the very best girls and not for the others. But this argument relies on assumptions about the overall ability of girls as a group in comparison with boys and this is the very point at issue. The expectations of performance for girls have generally been lower than for boys and this itself may account for most of the differences at a physical education class level. [18] Sex-integrated classes and ability groupings within these classes should reduce the chances that sex, rather than individual abilities and interests, will determine the performance expectations.

2.

Those who favor sex-segregated classes or a gender-differentiated physical education curriculum acknowledge many of the points raised by integrationists, but still remain unconvinced of the desirability of coeducational programs. They are concerned not only with the advantages any physiological differences might give boys and men but also with the social power advantages which males hold in our sexist culture. They call attention to the fact that males dominate coeducational interactions in ways that limit female participations, undermine women's values, and discount their concerns. [19] They argue that integration will, contrary to what has been claimed, bring about a greater loss of opportunity for girls.

Recent empirical research reported by Griffin legitimates this concern that sex-integrated physical education classes will not necessarily eliminate sex bias. Solomons' observations of game interactions among fifth grade integrated classes showed that

> girls tended to be left out of game interactions by the boys. This was true even when the girls had a higher skill level than the boys did. Additionally, both girls and boys regarded boys as better players even when the girls were more highly skilled. Boys

> preferred to pass the ball to an unskilled boy rather
> than to a skilled girl. Girls tended to give away
> scoring opportunities to boys. Unskilled girls were
> almost completely left out of game action. How-
> ever, both skilled and unskilled girls received fewer
> passes than boys did.[20]

A second argument against sex integration is a straightforward political argument about male dominance. There are
more men than women involved in physical education and athletics; they are better established in the hierarchy; and men
are and will continue to be regarded more favorably by the
general educational administration which is also male dominated. Therefore, whatever we think of it in principle, in
practice integration in physical education is a bad political
strategy if we are concerned to further women's interests
and increase their autonomy in this field.

Among women physical educators a further worry is
that women's distinctive interests and values will be sub-
merged in integration so that coeducational programs will be
shaped in a masculine mold. A frequently cited example is
the way in which cooperative participation may be devalued in
the face of a male preoccupation with competitive excellence.[21]

Another argument arising from concern about male
dominance is somewhat more complex. In its most sophisticated version the argument is a plea for diversity and pluralism. It rests on the contention that women and men have
distinctive cultures which need to be preserved. The strong
segregationists argue then that we can better realize equality
by opting for an organizational arrangement that recognizes
genuine differences and provides protection for them.[22]

II. A Gender-Sensitive Perspective

In philosophy of education this same tension, between the case
for sex integration and the apparent need for some gender
differentiation, finds its expression in the search for a just
and unbiased conception of the educated person. In her Presidential Address to the Philosophy of Education Society, Jane
Roland Martin speaks to this issue. She talks about the evolution of her own views on the "ideal of the educated person."
Martin concludes that at this time we need what she calls a
"gender-sensitive ideal." She summarizes her position as
follows:

For some time I assumed that the sole alternative
to a biased conception of the educated person was a
gender-free ideal, that is to say an ideal which did
not take sex or gender into account. I now realize
that gender may have to be taken into account if an
ideal of the educated person is not to be biased according to sex. Plato was wrong when, in Book V
of the Republic, he said that sex is a difference
which makes no difference. I do not mean by this
that there are inborn differences which suit males
and females for separate and unequal roles in society. Rather I mean that identical educational
treatment may not yield identical results so long
as that treatment contains a male bias. And supposing it were to yield identical results, so long
as those results themselves involve the imposition
of a masculine mold, sex bias will not be overcome.
To opt at this time for a gender-free ideal is to
beg the question. There are sex differences in the
way people are perceived and evaluated. There
may be sex differences in the way people think and
learn and view the world. A conception of the educated person must take these into account. What
is needed is a gender-sensitive ideal, one which
takes sex or gender into account when it makes a
difference and ignores it when it does not. Such
an ideal would truly be gender-just.[23]

Martin raises two separate questions: 1) should our
ideals of the educated person be different for the sexes? and
2) should our way of going about the realization of even a
common ideal be different for each sex? In this chapter we
shall concern ourselves with the second question and argue
in favor of a gender-sensitive perspective. We use the term
"perspective" to indicate a particular point of view, or standpoint, which is taken in order to give proportional importance
to the component parts, in this case those having to do with
gender.

We shall use the term "gender-sensitive" in the spirit
outlined by Martin, namely as an alternative both to a gender-
free perspective, which completely ignores gender, and to a
sex-differentiated approach, which chooses to perpetuate sex
differences. Thus, one should take gender into account when
doing so makes a difference by furthering sex equality or by
preventing sexist bias.

What would a gender-sensitive perspective mean for physical education, especially for women's physical education? The rest of our chapter will be an extended answer to this question.

III.   The Domain of Physical Education

Up to this point we have talked of "physical education" in an ordinary language sense without defining it precisely.   It is time now to look more closely at our concept of physical education.   How would a gender-sensitive perspective view the domain of physical education?   What is included?   What ought to be included?   This is an important question because the issue of which gender differences need to be taken into account will be determined, in part, by what one includes within the domain of physical education.

Definition 1:   Deliberate Physical Education or What Is Taught

What is "physical education"?   What are we talking about when we talk of anyone's physical education, whether woman or man, girl or boy?   A first, perhaps obvious, clearcut answer is to say that physical education consists of the formal instruction given in "physical education classes."

Since physical education classes are usually required of all high school students, these classes are the one instance of deliberate instructional efforts to attend to physical learning for all young persons.   But there are numerous other instances of deliberate physical education.   Within formal schooling itself, the "extracurricular" sports often include effective teaching.   Physical education in non-school settings is done in classes at summer camps and playgrounds, fitness classes, Y programs, Little League baseball, private and group lessons in tennis, swimming, etc.

What all of these instances share is a deliberate, intentional effort to do physical education; almost everything else about these classes varies.   The expectations, the participation levels, the facilities, and staffing all range from high quality levels to the barest minimum.

What is of more philosophical interest is the wide variety of educational aims and curricular emphases.   Physical fitness and physical health have been a more or less constant theme and concern of all physical educators. But the form these have taken and the additional emphases have varied considerably.[24] As noted above, some women's programs have developed movement education and have included dance, neither of which has been emphasized in male programs.

The role of sports has been varied and controversial. In some cases sports and physical education have been entirely separate, recognizing that physical education need not entail sports. On the other hand, many physical education programs consist almost entirely of a combination of intramural and extramural sports. But even where sports are dominant, different ideals are reflected in the emphases which vary from competitive sport to life-time sports to the non-competitive "new games."

Anyone addressing educational questions from a gender-sensitive perspective would want to consider how these different educational aims have affected each sex. This then requires us to ask a further question: What does each sex actually learn from their physical education?

Definition 2: What Is Learned

So far we have defined physical education from the point of view of the educator--i.e., in terms of what is taught. If we consider the student's point of view as well, then we must broaden our definition to include what is actually learned by the students.

For many students, especially those with able teachers or high motivation, their education includes a large amount of what is deliberately taught--the physical skills, the knowledge and information, as well as attendant values and attitudes. But this is not the sum total of any student's physical education. A more inclusive view must also ask what else students have learned about their physical selves, their physical abilities and capacities. What physical propensities have they acquired? What have they learned about their physical being-in-the-world? A gender-sensitive perspective needs to know whether these learning outcomes are different for girls and boys.

If we want to know what girls and women learn about themselves as physical beings in a physical world, especially from informal settings and situations, we must turn to the "hidden curriculum."

IV. The Hidden Curriculum

In Memoirs of an Ex-Prom Queen, Alix Kates Shulman describes, with wit, humor, and incisive accuracy, much of
the hidden and not-so-hidden curriculum for girls' physical
learning. Shulman's account of minimally supervised school
playground activities and their cumulative effect for girls and
boys provides us with an instructive microcosm of the informal, incidental, and exceedingly powerful lessons girls
learn about their physical being in the world. If we read
Shulman's description from an educational point of view, we
can see that it captures the major features of many girls'
informal physical education.

> Once I started school I learned I would have to
> choose between hair ribbons and trees, and that if
> I chose trees I'd have to fight for them. The trees,
> like the hills, belonged to the boys.
> Before and after school, the boys would fan out
> over the school grounds and take over the ball
> fields ... we played girls' games under the teach-
> ers' protective eyes. We could jump rope, throw
> rubber balls for a-meemy-a-claspy, practice tricks
> on the bars nestled in the ell of the building, play
> jacks or blow soap bubbles--all safe, dependable
> and sometimes joyous games which the boys dis-
> dained because we did them.... Though in my
> summers and on my street I had wandered freely,
> taking to the woods and the very tips of the trees,
> in my first weeks of first grade I learned to stay
> uncomplainingly in my place on the steps or in the
> shadow of the school. I learned masculine and
> feminine.
> "Go on to the Mountain, girls, it's a gorgeous
> day," Mrs. Hess would urge us as we stood on the
> steps at recess trading cards. Or, "Why don't you
> play some freeze tag? You need the exercise."
> But we knew better. We knew that going near the
> ball fields or behind the backstop or near the bas-
> ket hoop or in among the fruit trees or around the
> Mountain or near the skating pond were extremely
> dangerous expeditions, even if we went in a pack--
> for that was all boys' territory, acknowledged by
> everyone. Despite Mrs. Hess's prods and assur-
> ances, we knew that at any moment out there a pair
> or trio or more of boys might grow bored with their
> own game and descend on us with their bag of tricks.

If a girl was spotted on their territory the boys
felt perfectly free to: give her a pink belly, or
lock her in the shed or not to let her down from
a tree, or tie her to the flagpole or....
    We knew better than to tell Mrs. Hess. The
one time I ran crying to her with my dress ripped
after Bobby Barr had pulled me out of an apple
tree, she hugged and comforted me with a double
message: "I know, dear, those are rough boys.
Why don't you play with the girls?" ... from the
moment we got kicked out of the trees and sent
into the walk-in doll house back in kindergarten,
our movements and efforts had been so steadily
circumscribed, our permissible yearnings so confined, that the only imprint left for us to make
was on ourselves. By the third grade, with every
other girl in Baybury Heights, I came to realize
that there was only one thing worth bothering about:
becoming beautiful. [25]

One thing to notice in Shulman's account is the extent
to which these informal sex-segregated playground activities
mirror the standard forms of sex discrimination and the undesirable outcomes we have already discussed as part of our
historically sex-segregated formal physical education programs; the unequal distribution of resources, facilities, and
"territory"; the reification of gender differences; the stratifi-
cation with male dominance; and finally the attendant loss of
opportunities for girls. Shulman's passage illustrates how
the hidden curriculum for girls includes, indeed demands,
their acquiescence to these inequalities.

The girls learn to accept gender-differentiated constraints on their physical movements, while male-imposed
limits on their rights to physical space are established and
maintained by physical intimidation. The girls' physical being in the world is "circumscribed" and "confined" in direct
contrast to the physical freedom of the boys. And the girls
soon learn that their games are devalued while the one and
only physical priority for their own sex is physical beauty.

What is of further interest to us here is the way in
which the school setting both allows for and contributes to
a hidden curriculum which runs counter to the explicit values
and directives for physical education. So Mrs. Hess urges
the girls to go to the mountain, to play freeze tag because
they "need the exercise." Thus we have a deliberate physical

education directive for girls--exercise. But the situation,
the setting, and the girls' own experiences, as well as Mrs.
Hess's unguarded comments about "rough boys" teach the
girls that for them to engage in any interesting or strenuous
physical activity will be difficult, dangerous, and costly.

In most contemporary schools the hidden curriculum
is presumably less blatant and the deliberate physical education program is better organized. We nevertheless have reason to suspect not only that it still exists but also that the
essential content of the hidden curriculum for many, if not
most, girls remains substantially the same, whether from
school or non-school settings.[26] If we take a gender-sensitive
perspective we must address this problem: What should the
educator do about sexist hidden curricula?

Before we attempt to answer this question, there are
several remarks that need to be made about our use of the
term "hidden curriculum."[27] We use the term in a broad,
but nontrivial, sense to refer to learning that is not openly
intended. Our usage allows us to speak not just of the hidden curriculum of the school but also of the hidden curriculum in other settings, whether overtly educational or not.
But more importantly our usage allows us to focus on the
hidden curriculum there may be for an identifiable group of
learners. We are specifically interested in what women
learn, from a variety of settings, which can interfere with
the success of physical education programs designed for them.

One might well object to our use of the term "hidden
curriculum" to cover this informal learning. In particular,
in the case of the hidden curriculum of sexism, it could be
argued that it is no longer hidden, it has been found and articulated rather clearly. Thus, if we mean to discuss unin-
tended educational outcomes perhaps the term "informal curriculum" might seem preferable. But we shall purposely
keep the term "hidden" for two reasons: first, the existence
of a sexist curriculum may be clear to some but there are
many who are quite unaware of it still; second, and more
importantly, the term "hidden" indicates a concern for recognizing that we have not agreed upon or chosen to teach this
"curriculum" and students have neither been asked nor told
about these learning outcomes.

V. Confronting the Hidden Curriculum

Hidden curricula are, of course, not confined to physical education; and we can ask, in general, what educators should do when the content of their students' hidden curricula runs counter to the aims and values of the deliberate formal curriculum which they are trying to teach. Let's consider, for a moment, the general problem of hidden curricula and the possible alternatives open to the educator. We will then return to the particular problem of hidden curricula for women's physical education.

1.

Faced with an undesirable hidden curriculum, an educator or educational institution can make one or more of the following moves:

1) Give up. The educator can simply give up and change the deliberate curriculum to bring it in line with the hidden curriculum so as to eliminate any inconsistency.[28]

2) Do nothing. In this case one merely goes about one's business as usual, teaching the deliberate curriculum and ignoring what is not a direct part of it, assuming either that these other influences already get too much time and attention, or that they are not serious impediments.

3) Create a more desirable alternative. A more positive move is to alter the emphasis of the deliberate curriculum or create a new deliberate curriculum to counterbalance the undesirable effects of the hidden curriculum.

4) Reform the organizational structures. A more drastic move is to intervene directly in the educational setting, altering structures and organizations so as to eliminate as much as possible those practices and situations which contribute to or perpetuate the undesirable learning that arises from or occurs under the jurisdiction of the educational institution itself. This might involve changes in classroom formal instruction, teacher-student interactions, administrative organization, or changes within the institutional environment affecting rules, procedures or informal relationships.

5) Study the hidden curriculum. In this case one addresses the hidden curriculum directly by making

articulation and critical scrutiny of it an integral
part of the deliberate curriculum. In short, make
the hidden curriculum part of the subject matter to
study.

6) Take the offensive. Perhaps the most far reaching
move is to teach students self-defense skills "against
the onslaught of unasked for learning states"[29] i.e.,
teach students how to identify hidden curricula, how
to discover the sources, and how to avoid the learning outcomes one does not wish to acquire.

2.

These six alternatives sketch what the educator can do
in response to undesirable hidden curricula. But we have yet
to answer the question of what an educator should do. In
particular, what is the educational responsibility toward hidden curricula as seen from a gender-sensitive perspective?
In order to answer this question we shall distinguish three
types of cases. Our criterion is the extent to which the locus of control for an undesirable hidden curriculum lies within
the educational institution:

a) the hidden curriculum is a direct outcome of educational practices or in-school procedures;

b) the hidden curriculum comes from the larger society but manifests itself within the school in ways
which are amenable to direct educational intervention and control;

c) both the source and the control of the hidden curriculum lie outside the school, but the learning outcomes constitute a serious impediment to the
achievement of educational goals.

3.

Let us start with the first case. Whether one finds
sexism hidden in the explicit curriculum or in the institutional practices, the educator's responsibility for direct intervention is clear. This responsibility is generally acknowledged; and a number of appropriate reforms, which exemplify
our fourth alternative, have been proposed and undertaken;
for example, efforts to arrange a fairer allocation of resources and attempts to redress the blatant inequalities in

physical education expenditures and facilities for women. Re-allocation of resources is also necessary to prevent perpetuation of the assumption that men's programs are more important and valuable than women's.

Equalizing the numbers of women and men who teach physical education, coach, and carry administrative responsibilities is another example of organizational reform. But we still need to change the pattern in which males frequently coach females while females rarely coach males if we are to avoid the implicit message that sports is a male domain in which males have the expertise.

The proposal to integrate sport activities using ability groupings is often seen as an important way to counter the belief that biological sex is relevant to athletic participation. Heide makes this point:

> Girls and boys, women and men must participate together in sports with decisions about participation of individuals and groups to be based on current skill, agility, experience, strength, size, weight, interest, speed and/or other relevant criteria, not the irrelevant factor of biological sex. [30]

Our discussion so far indicates that the most obvious way of countering undesirable learning outcomes from in-school hidden curricula is to reform the organizational structures. But the third approach of curriculum change in order to create a more desirable alternative may also be necessary and useful. Suggestions that we introduce new sports for which women are naturally advantaged would be another way to counter beliefs that male biological sex determines general athletic prowess. [31]

The efforts of many women physical educators to preserve a sex-differentiated curriculum in order to avoid what they believe to be immoral or unhealthy attitudes toward competition and violence hidden in men's programs might plausibly be seen as examples either of the Do Nothing or of the Create a More Desirable Alternative approach.

4.

Let us turn now to case (b) in which the manifestations of the society's hidden curriculum are amenable to educational intervention. Patricia Griffin's examples of teacher-student interactions illustrate ways in which teachers can intervene to offset standard sexist stereotypes and to discourage sexist comments:

> (Male student to another male student who is crying): John, if you're going to act like a girl, get off the field.
>
> Teacher: Tom, anyone, boy or girl, who gets hit and knocked down that hard might cry.
>
> Student: Why do the girls have to play?
> Teacher: John, the girls want to play as much as you do. Everyone will have a fair turn to play.
>
> Student: Mark throws like a girl.
> Teacher: No, Jane, Mark throws like he needs practice throwing. Lots of girls throw well and lots of boys don't. [32]

Thus a gender-sensitive perspective would emphasize the important difference between saying that "Mark throws like he needs practice" and "Mark throws like a girl" even though both comments are criticisms of Mark's throwing.

Another pertinent example of behavior that manifests standard sexist presumptions is male students poaching from female students' territory in games, also cited by Griffin. Notice the difference between a teacher who encourages poaching: "Susan, if you can't catch it, back off and let Steve get it" and a gender-sensitive approach: "John, that was Susan's ball" or "Don't crowd her out, Dan."[33]

These are examples of a gender-sensitive perspective because they illustrate ways in which a teacher takes gender into account in order to further sex equality or to prevent sexist bias. But how does a teacher come to notice these numerous incidental cases of gender bias in the first place, especially when they are part of the prevailing culture? It seems likely that many teachers will neither notice nor intervene unless they themselves have studied the hidden curriculum.

Thus one might argue that the first students to study the hidden curriculum, and take the offensive, ought to be teachers themselves. If curricular and organizational changes are to succeed, teachers must know what the hidden curricula are, how to identify sources and how to make the necessary

interventions. Courses and workshops on "sexism in education" and on "sex roles" are needed for teacher education
and in-service teacher training.[34]

Once teachers are prepared to notice and intervene in
sexist interactions, the case for sex integration becomes
stronger. Since the interactions in sex-integrated programs
are more likely to reveal sexist hidden curricula, an atten-
tive teacher can then address this explicitly. Furthermore,
one of the findings on coeducational teaching in university
physical education is that both teachers and students are
challenging and correcting one another's biases.[35] Griffin
shows that similar corrections could also occur with younger
students:

> Student: I'm the third base person, not the third
> base man.
> Teacher: You're right, Sue. Thanks for correcting
> me.[36]

5.

We believe there is also a strong educational case to
be made for extending alternatives (5) and (6) above, i.e.,
the study of the hidden curriculum and teaching students to
defend against it, whenever we suspect that the hidden curriculum for a group of students is a direct impediment to
these students' learning. This brings us to case (c), our
final case for examination in this chapter. Here the issue
of responsibility is much less clear than in cases (a) and
(b); and our discussion must be somewhat speculative. Indeed it is important to emphasize at the outset that study of
the hidden curriculum cannot and should not take the place
of able teaching, sound training, regular practice, and equal
opportunities for participation, all of which have been historically unavailable to most girls and women.

But what if we do have good pedagogy and relatively
equal opportunities for women, can we then discount the hidden curriculum? Not if we believe the literature on female
physicality. In her book Body Politics, Nancy Henley quotes
and then verifies Marge Piercy's description of the different
ways women and men move and occupy space. Piercy describes Wanda teaching a theater group about movement:

> Wanda made them aware how they moved, how
> they rested, how they occupied space. She demon-

> strated how men sat and how women sat on the sub-
> way, on benches. Men expanded into available
> space. They sprawled, or they sat with spread
> legs. They put their arms on the arms of chairs.
> They crossed their legs by putting a foot on the
> other knee. They dominated space expansively.
> Women condensed. Women crossed their legs
> by putting one leg over the other and alongside.
> Women kept their elbows to their sides, taking up
> as little space as possible.... Women sat protec-
> tively using elbows not to dominate space, not to
> mark territory, but to protect their soft tissues.[37]

But what does this have to do with impediments to
women's physical education? Let's compare Piercy's description with Iris Young's phenomenological description of
the difference between the movements of untrained males and
untrained females when they engage in athletic activity.

> Now most men are by no means superior ath-
> letes, and their sporting efforts more often display
> bravado than genuine skill and coordination. The
> relatively untrained man nevertheless engages in
> sport generally with more free motion and open
> reach than does his female counterpart. Not only
> is there a typical style of throwing like a girl, but
> there is a more or less typical style of running
> like a girl, climbing like a girl, swinging like a
> girl, hitting like a girl. They have in common,
> first, that the whole body is not put into fluid and
> directed motion, but rather, in swinging and hitting,
> for example, the motion is concentrated in one body
> part; and second, that the women's motion tends not
> to reach, extend, lean, stretch, and follow through
> in the direction of her intention.
> For many women as they move in sport a space
> surrounds them in imagination which we are not
> free to move beyond; the space available to our
> movement is a constricted space. Thus, for ex-
> ample, in softball or volleyball women tend to re-
> main in one place more often than men, neither
> jumping to reach nor running to approach the ball.[38]

The point here is that the restrictions women have
learned to accept or to impose on their physical being in the
world may explain why many so-called "unathletic" women
seem unable to move freely in athletic activity. If this is

true, then it is hard to imagine how such deep-rooted physical inhibitions can be altered without direct attention to both their sources and their behavioral manifestations. In other words, one would need to study the society's gender differentiated physical norms and help students identify the ways in which these norms can interfere with physical self-determination on a basic level.

But the question of educational efficacy as well as educational responsibility remains problematic in these (c) cases, where both the source and the control of the hidden curriculum lie outside the scope of formal education. We can urge the importance of studying the impact of society's physical norms on women's physicality; and we can attend to the ways in which our norms may even prescribe physical vulnerability for women. But we must also recognize that educational efforts alone are bound to be limited when women's ability to protect themselves depends in large part upon social and political conditions. The prevalence of rape and physical violence against women is a case in point. Although it is difficult to determine the precise impact of such conditions, it is also unrealistic to ignore the complex connections between physical freedom and educational equality.[39]

6.

Our discussion of educational responsibility for hidden curricula leads us to conclude that alternatives (3), (4), (5), and (6) are all necessary for women's physical education. But different approaches need to be taken at different times.

In elementary school less reification of gender differences has occurred and the creation of a concrete alternative model of coeducational-physical activities should be relatively successful. Children's conceptions about what is and is not sex-role appropriate are still comparatively loose. However, because of their limited experience and less developed reasoning abilities, children are more dependent upon the examples in their immediate environment than are older students who have better abilities to imagine alternatives and to avoid over-generalizing from single cases. We also have a greater degree of control over the young child's environment.

Thus the emphasis in elementary school should perhaps rest on the energetic and thorough construction of a better alternative. We can, to a great extent, more systematically control the sexism in elementary school through this method

than we can later on. But a gender-sensitive perspective for
elementary schools would also require us to notice that between the ages of four and twelve, boys usually have a number of outside school advantages, including additional athletic
practice, coaching, advice, information about sports, many
male role models, and general encouragement for their physical feats. We would recommend, therefore, that in addition
to integrated physical education classes and sports there be
opportunities for extra activities for girls, such as additional
coaching and teaching. This is especially important in elementary school because most sports and physical activities
which one engages in as an adolescent or an adult require
early development of physical motor skills and build on these.

In the present situation, at the older ages this struc-
tural intervention is probably not adequate to deal with the
sexism that has become entrenched. At this level one must
both create an alternative and address the hidden curricula
from other settings. At adolescence whatever sex differences
there are emerge most obviously; and much social attention
is given to accentuating them. The socialization literature
on girls consistently reports that although there is some tol-
erance for "tomboys" and a greater latitude in expectations
of gender role conformity given to prepubescent girls, with
adolescence there is increasing pressure for girls to come
to terms with their physical femininity and to develop the
"properly feminine" beliefs, attitudes and behaviors.[40]

Gender roles are, however, interdependent; and as
Money noticed early on, one only learns what girls are supposed to do and be like by simultaneously learning what boys
are supposed to be like and vice versa.[41] This symbiotic
interplay of norms defining femininity and masculinity means
that we cannot hope to alter one without having the other
come under critical scrutiny as well. Although there may
be a greater need for girls to examine the hidden curriculum for themselves because of a greater incongruity between
the socialization message and the developmental objectives of
the physical education programs, we know that in general sex
roles can be limiting to educational achievement for both females and males.[42]

VI. Beyond Sexism in Physical Education

In essence we have tried to address the transitional problems
of moving from a sexist education in a sexist culture to a

non-sexist education that will nevertheless continue for some time to be influenced by a wider sexist culture.

We have argued that inasmuch as it will affect the success of educational practices, one cannot separate the sexism in the larger context of society from the educational setting. Hence, educators must, if they are to be responsible, adopt a gender-sensitive perspective. A gender-sensitive perspective on physical education requires that we be sensitive to what the larger society is teaching that is relevant to its subject matter, what girls and women are learning about their physical selves. It requires that we attend to this learning, recognize its influence upon our goals and find ways of dealing with it that are appropriate to each level of education.

A gender-sensitive perspective is not a blueprint for physical education that will answer all our questions about particular practices. Rather, it is a perspective which reminds us of conditions that must be met before we are entitled to hold our physical education theories up for admiration or even for adoption. We have contrasted a gender-sensitive perspective with a gender-differentiated ideal suggesting that the latter is often negligent with respect to sex equality. We are now in a position to indicate what the concept of gender-sensitivity might require of any women's physical education. It requires, among other things, that

a) theories or proposals for women's physical education should be formed in the knowledge of the sexism that has been associated with the history of women's physical education;

b) theories or program proposals can demonstrate that they are non-sexist;

c) theories or program proposals acknowledge some responsibility for foreseeable educational outcomes even when these are partially attributable to hidden sexist curricula from other settings.

Our gender-sensitive perspective is like the "Pushmi-Pullyu" in the Dr. Dolittle story. It has two heads that look in different directions, one ahead to our ideal of sex equality, one backwards to the social realities from which our ideal has emerged. It is useful to have two heads for the ideal of equality has been with us a long time, but there is an equally long history of its failure in practice. It is only by constantly exploring the tension between the views from both heads that physical education can help women achieve physical freedom as well as physical well-being.

NOTES

1. Quoted in Gerda Lerner, The Female Experience: An American Documentary (Indianapolis: Bobbs-Merrill, 1977), p. 7.
2. The historical documentation of attitudes towards women's physical education and, in particular, women's own views about what their physical education should be can be found in several articles. See: Roberta J. Park, "Concern for the Physical Education of the Female Sex from 1675 to 1800 in France, England, and Spain," Research Quarterly AAHPER (May 1974), pp. 104-119; Roberta J. Park, "'Embodied Selves': The Rise and Development of Concern for Physical Education, Active Games and Recreation for American Women, 1776-1865," Journal of Sport History, 5, no. 2 (1978), 5-41; Patricia Vertinsky, "Sexual Equality and the Legacy of Catherine Beecher," Journal of Sport History, 6, no. 1 (1979), 38-49.
3. This summary of characteristics is drawn from June A. Kennard, "The History of Physical Education," Review Essay in Signs: Journal of Women in Culture and Society, 2, no. 4 (1977), 835-843.
4. Betty Spears, "Prologue: The Myth," chapter one in Women and Sport: From Myth to Reality, ed. by Carole A. Oglesby (Philadelphia: Lea & Febiger, 1978), p. 11.
5. Kennard, p. 836.
6. For a more elaborate discussion of the history of these developments within physical education see Daryl Siedentop, Physical Education: Introductory Analysis (Dubuque, Iowa: Wm. C. Brown, 1972), especially chapter 6.
7. Documentation of the inequality of opportunity in physical education and sports may be found in: A. Fishel and S. J. Pottker, "Sex Bias in Secondary Schools: The Impact of Title IX," in A. Fishel and S. J. Pottker, eds., Sex Bias in the Schools (New Brunswick, N.J.: Rutgers University Press, 1977); T. Saario, C. Jacklin, and J. C. Tittle, "Sex Role Stereotyping in the Public Schools," Harvard Educational Review, 43, no.

3 (1973), 386-416; B. Gilbert and N. Williamson,
"Sport Is Unfair to Women," Sports Illustrated (May
1973); B. Gilbert and N. Williamson, "Are You Being
Two-Faced?" Sports Illustrated (June 1973); B. Gilbert
and N. Williamson, "Programmed to Be Losers,"
Sports Illustrated (June 1973). See also D. Stanley
Eitzen, Sport in Contemporary Society: An Anthology
(New York: St. Martin's Press, 1979), chapter eleven,
"Sexism in Sport."

8. One of the common distinctions employed in the literature
on sex roles is that between sex and gender. When
the distinction is drawn, "sex" refers to the biological
differences between females and males and "gender"
refers to the social differences between the sexes.
However, the matter is far from simple; usage of the
terms is often inconsistent and some have argued that
the distinction itself is unsuccessful because of the
complex linkage between biological and social aspects
of sex. Granted the difficulties, we will, nevertheless,
employ the distinction in this essay. We use the term
"gender-sensitive perspective" precisely because we
believe that not just biological differences between the
sexes are relevant to the development of physical education programs. We do not wish to beg any questions
about the nature or causal explanation of gender differences. We are interested in the implications we think
they should have for educational practice. Hence, we
invoke the concept of gender, but we use it solely as
a descriptive term. For an insightful discussion of the
difficulties with the distinction between sex and gender
see Margrit Eichler, The Double Standard: A Feminist Critique of Feminist Social Science (London:
Croom Helm, 1980), pp. 10-19.

9. A good general introduction to the problem of the interpretation of the ideal of sex equality may be found in
Jane English, ed., Sex Equality (Englewood Cliffs,
N.J.: Prentice-Hall, 1977), Section II. For a discussion of whether this ideal requires the abolition of
sex roles see: Alison Jagger, "On Sexual Equality"
in that volume.

10. An interesting discussion of this controversy and its implications for sports activities is set out in two papers:
Richard Wasserstrom, "Racism, Sexism, and Preferential Treatment: An Approach to the Topics,"
U.C.L.A. Law Review (February 1977), pp. 581-615;
and Bernard Boxill, "Sexual Blindness and Sexual
Equality," Social Theory and Practice, 6 (Fall 1980),
281-299.

11. The philosophical discussion of this point occurs in the context of debate about the morality of affirmative action programs. See: S. Bishop and M. Weinzweig, eds., Philosophy and Women (Belmont, Calif.: Wadsworth, 1979), chapter 7; C. Gould and M. Wartofsky, eds., Women and Philosophy (New York: G. P. Putnam's Sons, 1976), Section IV; Barry Gross, ed., Reverse Discrimination (Buffalo, N.Y.: Prometheus Books, 1977).

12. The prima facie case against sex-segregated sports is summed up by Mary Anne Warren in "Justice and Gender in School Sports," Chapter 1 in this volume. The same case holds against sex-segregated physical education classes.

13. For a chronicle of the limited participation permitted women in the Olympic games see: Ellen Gerber, Jan Felshin, Pearl Berlin, and Waneen Wyrick, The American Woman in Sport (Reading, Mass.: Addison-Wesley, 1974), chapter four.

14. This experiment is reported in Jean Cochrane, Abby Hoffman, Pat Kincaid, Women in Canadian Sports (Toronto: Fitzhenry and Whiteside, 1977), p. 81. See also Jack Wilmore, They Told You You Couldn't Compete with Men (Toronto: University of Toronto Press, 1969). It is doubtful that one can overestimate the powerful impact early sex role socialization has on a child's sense of her own physical abilities. From the moment of birth we are subject to biased judgments and expectations of our physical abilities. One study, for example, reports that as early as twenty-four hours after birth parents have different expectations for infants based on sex alone. Among infants who did not differ on any physical or health measures, fathers judged sons as "firmer, larger featured, better coordinated, more alert, stronger and hardier"; daughters were judged as "softer, finer featured, more awkward, more inattentive, weaker, and more delicate" (emphasis ours). J. Rubin, F. Provenzano, Z. Luria, "The Eye of the Beholder: Parents' Views on Sex of Newborns," in A. Kaplan and J. Bean, Beyond Sex Role Stereotypes (Boston: Little, Brown, 1976), p. 183.

15. Reported in Jackie Hudson, "Physical Parameters Used for Female Exclusion from Law Enforcement and Athletics," in Women and Sport, ed. by C. Oglesby, p. 52. See this article for scientific refutation of many myths about women's natural inferiority in sports. In

addition to the tremendous increase in women's performances in conventional Olympic events, Hudson reports on women's world records in endurance events
such as long distance running and swimming.

16. Jean Cochrane, et al., Women in Canadian Sports, p.
80.

17. Mary Domb Mikkelson, "Co-ed Gym--It's a Whole New
Ballgame," Journal of Physical Education and Recreation (November/December 1979), p. 63. Something
akin to this sentiment was expressed long ago by Elizabeth Cady Stanton. She recalled her own experience
in an all girls school: "The thought of a school without boys, who had been to me such a stimulus both in
study and play, seemed to my imagination dreary and
profitless." Quoted in Roberta J. Park, "'Embodied
Selves': The Rise and Development of Concern for
Physical Education, Active Games and Recreation for
American Women, 1776-1865," Journal of Sport History, p. 39.

18. For a discussion of the literature on sex bias in teacher
expectations in physical education see Patricia Scott
Griffin, "Developing a Systematic Observation Instrument to Identify Sex Role Dependent and Sex Role
Independent Behavior Among Physical Education Teachers," Doctoral Dissertation, University of Massachusetts, 1980 (University Microfilms International No.
8101326). See also R. Allard, "Teacher Behavior
Directed Toward Individual Students in Physical Education Classes: The Influence of Student Gender and
Class Participation," unpublished doctoral dissertation,
University of Massachusetts, 1979.

19. A recent report, "The Classroom Climate: A Chilly
One for Women," issued by the Project on the Status
and Education of Women, Association of American
Colleges, 1982, documents this sort of male domination in coeducational settings. For a recent review
of the literature on the role of social power in coeducation and on the differential effects of single-sex education and coeducational settings on the educational attainments of girls and boys see: J. Finn, J. Reis,
and L. Dulberg, "Sex Differences in Educational Attainment: The Process," Comparative Education Review, 24, no. 2, part 2 (June 1980), s33-s52.

20. Griffin, p. 10.

21. For a concise exploration of the ambivalence some women
coaches have about women adopting so-called male attitudes towards competition see: Joanna Rohrbaugh,

Women: Psychology's Puzzle (New York: Basic Books, 1979), chapter 17.

22. This argument is put forth by both women and men physical educators and it appears in its sophisticated form in Boxill, "Sexual Blindness and Sexual Equality." Interestingly, those male and female physical educators who argue against coeducation do so on the same grounds, but their interpretation of the reasons differ. Both contend that it will mean a loss of opportunity and a change in the valuation of the activities. However, women contend it will mean a loss of opportunity for all but the very best girls; men contend that it will mean a loss of opportunity for the better male athletes. Women worry that girls will pick up what they consider to be morally questionable male attitudes towards competition; men worry that the girls' participation will trivialize or devalue the activities or increase the risk of male humiliation in defeat. It should, of course, be noted that the sex differences in those attitudes are not clear cut. There are many men who defend coeducation in this area and deplore the dominant combative model for sports. There are also women who argue that girls should not infringe on male sports territory. A good discussion of these general attitudes can be found in Jan Felshin's chapter, "The Social View," in Ellen Gerber, et al., The American Woman in Sport.

23. Jane Roland Martin, "The Ideal of the Education Person," Presidential Address, Philosophy of Education Society Proceedings (1981), forthcoming.

24. For an extended discussion of the different conceptions of physical education that have influence in contemporary education see Daryl Siedentop, Physical Education: Introductory Analysis (Dubuque, Iowa: W. C. Brown, 1972). For a less systematic, but fairly representative sampling of contemporary influences see R. Cobb and P. Lepley, eds., Contemporary Philosophies of Physical Education and Athletics (Columbus, Ohio: Merrill, 1973).

25. Alix Kates Shulman, Memoirs of an Ex-Prom Queen. Copyright © 1969, 1971, 1972 by Alix Kates Shulman. Reprinted by permission of Alfred A. Knopf, Inc. and Granada Publishing Limited. The passage quoted is from pages 18-21.

26. The sexist hidden curriculum of schools is fully documented in Frazier and Sadker, Sexism in School and Society (New York: Harper & Row, 1973); Judith Stacey, et al. (eds.), And Jill Came Tumbling After:

Sexism in American Education (New York: Dell, 1974);
and Bonnie Cook Freeman, "Female Education in Patriarchal Power Systems," in P. Altbach and G. Kelly,
Education and Colonialism (New York: Longman, 1978),
pp. 207-242. See also a special issue, two parts, on
Women and Education, Harvard Educational Review,
49, no. 4 (November 1979) and vol. 50, no. 1 (February 1980). A good general introduction to what we
call the sexist hidden curricula for women in non-
school settings can be found in V. Gornick and B.
Moran, eds., Woman in Sexist Society: Studies in
Power and Powerlessness (New York: Basic Books,
1971). The best general introduction to a systematic
explication of sexism in society can be found in Sexual
Politics in the chapter "Theory of Sexual Politics,"
Kate Millett, Sexual Politics (Garden City, N.Y.:
Doubleday, 1970).

27. Our usage of the term "hidden curriculum" follows
closely that employed by Jane Roland Martin in her
paper "What Should We Do with a Hidden Curriculum
When We Find One?" Curriculum Inquiry, 6, no. 2
(1976), 135-151. To our knowledge Martin is the first
to draw a distinction between the hidden curriculum of
a setting and the hidden curriculum for a learner. For
a further discussion of the hidden curriculum see Elizabeth Vallance, "Hiding the Hidden Curriculum," Curriculum Theory and Network, 4, no. 1 (1973-1974).

28. Enactment of the proposed Family Protection Act could,
in effect, force the deliberate curriculum into even
greater alignment with sexist conventions in the larger
society. The Act, if passed, would prohibit the use
of federal funds for educational materials that "do not
reflect a balance between the status role of men and
women, do not reflect different ways in which women
and men live, and do not contribute to the American
way of life as it has been historically understood."
Ann Pelham, "Family Protection Act: Dear to New
Right, but Unlikely to Get Out of Committees." Con-
gressional Quarterly Weekly Report, 39 (Oct. 3, 1981),
p. 1916. This Bill (S1378, HR3955) has been referred
to five different Senate and House Committees.

29. Jane Roland Martin, "What Should We Do with a Hidden
Curriculum When We Find One?" p. 149.

30. Wilma Scott Heide, "Feminism for a Sporting Future,"
in Women and Sport, ed. by Carole Oglesby, p. 197.

31. Jane English, "Sex Equality in Sports," Philosophy &
Public Affairs, 7, no. 3 (Spring 1978), 269-277.

32. Griffin, pp. 137-38.
33. Griffin, p. 136.
34. Projects funded by the Women's Educational Equity Act
    Program (WEEAP) have developed materials to aid
    teachers in addressing sexism in education. A com-
    plete listing of these can be found in the catalog of
    materials published by WEEAP.
35. Linda L. Blair, "Implementing Title IX: Concerns of
    Undergraduate Physical Education Majors," Journal of
    Physical Education and Recreation (November/Decem-
    ber 1979), p. 77.
36. Griffin, p. 139.
37. Nancy Henley, Body Politics (Englewood Cliffs, N.J.:
    Prentice-Hall, 1977), p. 38. The quotation is origi-
    nally from Marge Piercy, Small Changes (New York:
    Doubleday, 1973), p. 438.
38. Iris Young, "Throwing Like a Girl: A Phenomenology
    of Feminine Body Comportment Motility and Spatiality."
    Human Studies, 3 (1980), p. 143.
39. Adrienne Rich eloquently reminds us of this: "Women
    and men do not receive an equal education because
    outside the classroom women are perceived not as
    sovereign beings but as prey. The growing incidence
    of rape on and off campus ... is certainly occurring
    in a context of widespread images of sexual violence
    against women, on billboards and in so-called high
    art. More subtle, more daily than rape is the verbal
    abuse experienced by the woman student on many cam-
    puses.... The undermining of self, of a woman's
    sense of her right to occupy space and walk freely in
    the world, is deeply relevant to education. The capa-
    city to think independently, to take intellectual risks,
    to assert ourselves mentally, is inseparable from our
    physical way of being in the world, our feelings of
    personal integrity." Adrienne Rich, On Lies, Secrets,
    and Silences (New York: W. W. Norton, 1979), pp.
    241-242.
40. There is an enormous literature on sex role socializa-
    tion. Some frequently cited books include these:
    Shirley Weitz, Sex Roles (New York: Oxford Univer-
    sity Press, 1977); Lenore J. Weitzman, Sex Role So-
    cialization (Palo Alto, Calif.: Mayfield, 1979); A.
    Kaplan and J. Bean, eds., Beyond Sex Role Stereo-
    types: Readings Towards a Psychology of Androgyny
    (Boston: Little, Brown, 1976); and Irene Frieze, et
    al., Women and Sex Roles (New York: W. W. Nor-
    ton, 1978). A short summary of the literature may

be found in Lenore J. Weitzman, "Sex Role Socialization" in Jo Freeman, ed., Women: A Feminist Perspective (Palo Alto, Calif.: Mayfield, 1979), pp. 153-216. Much research and writing on sex differences and sex role socialization is fraught with bias. A good explication of some of the difficulties plaguing the literature can be found in Margrit Eichler, The Double Standard: A Feminist Critique of Feminist Social Science (London: Croom Helm, 1980).

41. John Money and Anke Ehrhardt, Man & Woman Boy & Girl (Baltimore: Johns Hopkins University Press, 1972), p. 19.

42. E. Maccoby, "Sex Differences in Intellectual Functioning," in E. Maccoby, ed., The Development of Sex Differences (Stanford, Calif.: Stanford University Press, 1966), pp. 25-55.

SUGGESTIONS FOR FURTHER READING

In addition to the works cited in the notes, the following are suggested for further reading:

Diana Nyad and Candace Lyle Hogan. Basic Training for Women. New York: Hogan and Hilltown Press, 1981. Especially chapter 1, "The Mind."

Margrit Eichler. The Double Standard: A Feminist Critique of Feminist Social Sciences. London: Croom Helm, 1980.

Carol Gilligan. In a Different Voice: Psychological Theory and Women's Development. Cambridge, Mass.: Harvard University Press, 1982.

M. Ann Hall. "Sport, Sex Roles and Sex Identity," The CRIAW Papers. Ottawa, Canada: CRIAW, 1981.

Kathryn Morgan. "Androgyny: A Conceptual Analysis," Social Theory and Practice (forthcoming).

Dale Spender. "Education: The Patriarchal Paradigm and the Response to Feminism," in Dale Spender, ed., Men's Studies Modified. New York: Pergamon Press, 1981.

QUESTIONS

(1) a) In your opinion, which is the strongest of the arguments in support of sex-integrated physical education, and which is the strongest of the arguments against sex-integrated physical education? (In each case you may choose either an argument presented by Diller and Houston, or one which you thought of yourself, or one which was suggested to you by another author or some other source.)

b) If both the arguments that you have just identified had all true premises, then which of them would be stronger? (If necessary, review the section entitled "Background on Arguments" in the General Introduction.)

c) Explain why you agree or disagree with each of the premises of each of the two arguments which you have been considering.

(2) a) What does the term "hidden curriculum" mean?

b) Identify part of the hidden curriculum of a school or a non-school physical education program with which you are familiar. Give an example which illustrates the part of the hidden curriculum which you have identified.

c) Diller and Houston sketch six alternative responses which an educator can make to hidden curricula. In your opinion, which of these six responses would be best for dealing with that part of the hidden curriculum which you have identified in your answer to part (b) above? Why? Do you think Diller and Houston would agree? Why or why not?

(3) a) In the authors' view, what is the moral responsibility of a physical educator with regard to sexist hidden curricula in each of the three cases (a)-(c) which they discuss in section V.2. of their essay?

b) Present the strongest objection you can to some aspect of the authors' view which you have just presented.

c) What is the best reply that can be made to your objection?

d) Is this reply to your objection satisfactory? Why or why not?

(4) a) Give an example of a gender-differentiated physical norm in our society (e.g., physical behavior that is thought unladylike but not ungentlemanly).

b) In your view, should physical educators study our society's gender-differentiated physical norms to identify the ways in which these norms can interfere with physical self-determination on a basic level? Why or why not?

(5) In your view, how important is it to learn about the sexism that has been associated with the history of women's physical education in order to make a wise decision about what a program of physical education should be today? Why?

(6) What else would you like to discuss from Diller and Houston's essay?

15. THE ETHICS OF GENDER DISCRIMINATION:
A Response to Ann Diller and Barbara Houston's
"Women's Physical Education:
A Gender-Sensitive Perspective"

Linda J. Nicholson

Ann Diller and Barbara Houston are absolutely correct in emphasizing that any adequate approach to women's physical education must be "gender-sensitive." Because I believe that the concept of "gender-sensitivity" is both important and complex, I would like to carry on their task of elaborating its meaning and its implications for women's physical education.

One point which is fundamental in clarifying this concept is that discrimination is not necessarily evil. Discrimination is a necessary component of being human. We make discriminations all the time and it would be difficult to envisage a world in which this were not so. The association with evil that has attended the concept of discrimination is a consequence of the fact that discriminations have frequently been made in the service of bad ends. Moreover, there are certain specific criteria of discrimination which historically have been most notorious in this regard, particularly the criteria of skin color, ethnic background, religious faith, and sex. However, as there is nothing inherently evil in the act of discrimination, so also is there nothing inherently evil in discriminations based on any of these criteria. That these criteria have often been used in the service of bad ends does not preclude the possibility that all such criteria could be employed in the service of worthy ends. Thus, if it has been empirically shown that people of a certain skin color or a certain ethnic background tend to develop a certain disease, then making discriminations amongst school children on the basis of such criteria for the purpose of giving vaccinations may be ethically sound.

The question that must always be asked in reference to discrimination in general and in reference to these criteria in particular is what is the end for which the discrimination is being made? Historically, discriminations in reference to sex have often been made for the purpose of constituting and reinforcing further distinctions between two sets of attitudes and behaviors known respectively as "masculinity" and "femininity." Since the onset of feminism, many have come to recognize that this latter distinction, a distinction of gender linked to but not the same as sex, is neither necessary nor necessarily beneficial to women or to men. Many have argued that this latter distinction encourages the adoption of attitudes and behaviors that limit rather than expand human flexibility and diversity and are often detrimental in their own right. Thus, encouraging young boys to become "masculine" has often meant a restriction on the range of responses available to them and a general overemphasis on the adoption of certain undesirable traits, such as aggressiveness and insensitivity to others' feelings. Similarly, the socialization of young girls into becoming "feminine" has frequently entailed a suppression of the development of certain physical, intellectual, and emotional capabilities.

We must ask, however, whether the fact that distinctions based on gender have often been used in the service of questionable ends entails that such criteria ought to be rejected altogether. Even if we are committed to the position that such distinctions are more harmful than not and an androgynous world is the preferred ideal, is the best means to that end an elimination of such criteria? The message that we might take from women's studies is that the answer to this latter question is no. As scholars in many disciplines have pointed out, without a heightened sensitivity to gender, the existing gender bias of the disciplines would go on unabated. Killing a tiger often requires more than ignoring it. As Diller and Houston point out, we need a women's studies component of physical education that is a means for becoming self-conscious about the very phenomena we might wish to eliminate.

It is not only women's studies which attest to the need for sometimes employing the very criteria we might wish to eliminate. It is a lesson which can be learned from many political struggles of the twentieth century. For example, many black people in the United States in the 1960s became aware that unless black people were to take pride in the very criteria for which they were often denounced--skin color and the culture historically linked with it--they would never over-come the feelings of inferiority which had been generated by past use of such criteria. As both blacks in the 1960s and women in the 1970s also came to recognize, there may be times when it is necessary for members of a certain group to use the very criteria of their past involuntary exclusion as grounds for voluntary separation. Thus, many have noted that without separate caucuses and political organizations for blacks and women, the just demands of either group might never be heard. Similarly, both groups have pointed to the possible positive benefits of schools limited to members of such groups. As Jean Paul Sartre long ago pointed out in his essay "Anti-Semite and Jew" and as Adrienne Rich has noted in many of her poems and essays, the demand for inte-gration or for an unqualified humanism may not be the most appropriate position for an oppressed group to adopt. While integration or humanism may be our end goal, its attempted adoption at too soon a point in the struggle to achieve it might itself negate that very end.

To reiterate the point: the question is not whether or not we introduce criteria of gender, but rather, what are the purposes for which such criteria are being introduced? Be-cause the elimination of gender bias often does require em-ploying criteria of gender, I fully endorse Diller and Hous-ton's position on the need for a "gender-sensitive perspec-tive." Indeed, I would claim that creating an equitable and desirable physical education curriculum requires extremely deep attention to issues of gender. For example, one point which we need to consider is whether our present physical education programs are gender-biased, not only in their em-phasis on certain sports rather than others, but more seri-ously in their emphasis on sports at all. In other words, does an emphasis on sports as a means of physical develop-ment itself reflect a gender bias, perhaps harmful to women and undesirable in itself?

It has been widely recognized that women, more often than men, tend to dislike and stay away from competitive ac-tivities. Thus forms of physical activity that involve compe-tition, such as most sports, would understandably tend less frequently to attract young women than young men on the grounds of competitive nature alone. If our goal in phys-ical education is physical development and not development in becoming competitive, it would appear that a physical educa-tion program that emphasizes sports, rather than other forms of physical activities, discriminates against women.

The question of competition in sports is a large and important issue and rightfully a whole section of this book is devoted to it. Even it, however, does not exhaust the problem of how sport itself, rather than certain particular sports, might be biased against women. To clarify this last point, I would like to turn to the work of such theorists as Carol Gilligan and Nancy Chodorow. Gilligan draws attention to studies by Janet Lever which note certain interesting differences between games played by little girls and games played by little boys. The games of the boys, rather than being disrupted by conflict, tended to thrive on it. Rules were often created to solve the conflict. Conflict, on the other hand, tended to end the games played by little girls. As Gilligan remarks on this, "Rather than elaborating a system of rules for resolving disputes, girls subordinated the continuation of the game to the continuation of relationships."[1]

There are obvious implications of these studies for the difficulties women might have with sports which involve conflict. Less obvious, though perhaps more basic, are the difficulties women might have with physical activities in general that involve rules, which include most sports. Certainly many of the games engaged in by little girls, such as playing house or doctor or school, are games that involve recreating life situations rather than following prescribed rules. Gilligan notes this further implication of these studies and finds further grounding for it in certain observations of Piaget. Piaget, she remarks, "finds boys becoming through childhood increasingly fascinated with the legal elaboration of rules and the development of fair procedures for adjudicating conflicts, a fascination that, he notes, does not hold for girls.... Girls are more tolerant in their attitudes toward rules, more willing to make exceptions, and more easily reconciled to innovation."[2]

These differences in boys' and girls' games accord well with the differences in skills needed by men and women in their traditional roles. Thus, from the games that boys play they "learn both the independence and the organization skills necessary for coordinating the activities of large and diverse groups of people."[3] A typical girls' game on the other hand, taking place often in smaller, more intimate groups and being less concerned with rules, "fosters the development of the empathy and sensitivity necessary for taking the role of 'the particular other' and points toward knowing the other as different from the self."[4]

These remarks by Gilligan extend the type of theoretical analysis found in the work of Nancy Chodorow. Chodorow claims that male gender development, because carried out in the context of frequently absent fathers or male models, tends to involve learning abstract rules and roles on what it means to be a man. Female gender development, since carried out in the context of an ongoing relationship with a present mother, tends rather to involve the adoption of a more specific, concrete model. Female gender identity is also tied to affective relationships with others; whereas male gender identity is based more on separation or connectedness through abstract rules:

> Externally, as internally, women grow up and remain more connected to others. Not only are the roles which girls learn more interpersonal, particularistic, and affective than those which boys learn. Processes of identification and role learning for girls also tend to be particularistic and affective-- embedded in an interpersonal relationship with their mothers. For boys, identification processes and masculine role learning are not likely to be embedded in relationships with their fathers or men but rather to involve the denial of affective relationship to their mothers. These processes tend to be more role-defined and cultural, to consist in abstract or categorical role learning rather than in personal identification. 5

Chodorow's work, I believe, is most helpful for informing us about gender development in those cultures like our own which make sharp separations between a domestic sphere associated with women and children and a public sphere, highly rule-governed and dominated by men. In a previous paper I have argued that this kind of separation between a domestic and public sphere in modern industrial societies helps explain both the development and nature of public schools in such societies. 6 I claimed that a primary function of a school system in such societies is to serve as a type of bridge, socializing young people into the values and forms of behavior appropriate to the public world which are not those of the home. Increasingly within this past century this function of public schools has been directed to young girls as well as to young boys. Because, however, the values and forms of behavior associated with the public world are also those which have been traditionally associated with masculinity, girls, to succeed in the public world and the

higher levels of schooling which make it possible, must often
undergo a "characterological sex-change operation." In short,
for young women to succeed in school is to become like men.

The most obvious response to this type of argument
would be, "Yes--but so what?" It would be claimed that it
is good that our schools now are teaching girls as well as
boys how to become men. After all, it is only through ac-
quiring the proper attitudes, skills, and behavior traditionally
expected by men in the public sphere that women will be able
to operate in that sphere, enjoying its rights and privileges.
Is it not therefore appropriate that women learn in physical
education classes as well as other types of classes the prerequisites for success in that sphere?

This question raises an issue which has been key in
the contemporary American women's movement: what is the
goal of feminism? On this issue one might range American
feminists along a continuum. On one side of this continuum
stand those who believe that the goal of feminism is for women
to be able to occupy the same positions of power and responsibility as those traditionally limited to men. On the other
side of the continuum stand those who question the desirability of those positions of power and responsibility for men as
well as for women. Many feminists, of course, combine
some mixture of both positions. The idea of the continuum,
however, is helpful in reminding us that at least from the
perspective of one point on it, the answer to the question
posed in the previous paragraph is "No, it is not appropriate that women learn in physical education classes or in other
classes the prerequisites for success in the public sphere."

This answer follows if one believes that there are aspects of our public world, which are expressed in sports,
that are undesirable in themselves. For example, one might
criticize our modern public sphere on the grounds of its being a very segmented sphere where physical activities are
limited to certain occupations or clearly delineated "recreational time." This aspect of our public sphere might be contrasted with cultures such as many in Africa, where physical
movement in the form of dance is integrated within many life
activities. Indeed, the highly rule-governed nature of sport
might directly follow from its isolation from other ongoing
life concerns. This interpretation is also suggested by one
of the meanings of "sport," that it is not a "serious" activity
but one separate from that which in life really matters. In
so far as we celebrate sport as a means of physical develop-

ment, we might also, therefore, be celebrating the fragmentation and specialization of modern life, expressed in divisions between mental and physical activities and amongst different types of physical activities.

There are other features of sport that replicate features of our public world which could also be criticized from the perspective of physical well being. The aggressive and competitive nature of many sports have their physical liabilities. For example, it has widely been remarked that games such as football are often detrimental to one's health. Sports that induce a great deal of stress could also be classified within this category.

Thus one could say that although sports may serve as a good introduction for a woman to a "man's world," success in this world may not be what feminism is all about. Certainly, there are aspects of both sports and this world that are positive in themselves; aspects that women need to incorporate within their lives. The ideal of excellence in body movement is one positive component of sports that has occupied too small a role in women's development. The much touted rewards of learning how to work on a team or of becoming a "team-player" may also have some valuable components. However, while recognizing that sports may have some positive aspects that women need more of, we also need to consider what sports leave out. We need to think more about what aspects of women's lives can also contribute to an ideal of physical well-being. In sum, one might say that a gender-sensitive perspective (that is, a perspective which is sensitive to the ways in which gender has affected our models of physical development) must be aware of the positive and negative components of both masculinity and femininity if it is to create an ideal worthy of surpassing both.[7]

NOTES

1. Carol Gilligan. In a Different Voice: Psychological Theory and Women's Development (Cambridge, Mass.: Harvard University Press, 1982), p. 10.
2. Ibid.
3. Ibid.
4. Ibid., p. 11.
5. Nancy Chodorow. The Reproduction of Mothering: Psychoanalysis and the Sociology of Gender (Berkeley: University of California Press, 1978), p. 177.

6. Linda J. Nicholson. "Women and Schooling," Educational Theory, vol. 30, no. 3 (Summer 1980), pp. 21-26.

7. I would like to thank Susan Franzosa, Jane Martin, Jennifer Radden, Janet Farrell Smith, as well as Ann Diller and Barbara Houston, for their contributions to a discussion of Diller and Houston's paper at a meeting of the study group "Phaedra." That discussion greatly aided me in this response.

SUGGESTIONS FOR FURTHER READING

Ellen W. Gerber and William J. Morgan, eds. Sport and the Body: A Philosophical Symposium. Philadelphia: Lea and Febiger, 1972.

Jane English. "Sex Equality in Sports," Philosophy and Public Affairs, vol. 7, no. 3 (1978), pp. 269-277.

Iris Young. "Throwing Like a Girl: A Phenomenology of Feminine Body Comportment Motility and Spatiality," Human Studies, 3, 137-156 (1980).

Iris Marion Young. "The Exclusion of Women from Sport: Conceptual and Existential Dimensions," Philosophy in Context, vol. 9 (1979), Cleveland State University.

QUESTIONS

(1) a) List all the reasons you can think of against taking gender into account in a program of physical education.

b) For each reason which you have just listed, answer the following: How would Nicholson challenge that reason? Do you agree with Nicholson in this case? Why or why not?

(2) a) Why might someone think that physical education in general (or physical education of females) ought to emphasize activities which involve rules?

b) Why might someone think that physical education in general (or physical education of females) ought to de-emphasize activities which involve rules?

c) What is your own position on this question? Why?

(3) Nicholson explains why some people may accept the following statement: "In so far as we celebrate sport as a

means of physical development, we are celebrating the fragmentation and specialization of modern life...."

a) In your own words, explain what the quoted statement means, and the reasons for believing it.

b) Do you agree with the quoted statement? Why or why not?

c) What sort of physical education program could discourage the "fragmentation ... of modern life"? (Joan Hundley's essay as Chapter 11 of this volume is relevant here.)

(4) What else would you like to discuss from Nicholson's essay?

16. PUTTING AWAY THE POM-POMS: AN EDUCATIONAL PSYCHOLOGIST'S VIEW OF FEMALES AND SPORTS

Linda Nielsen

Traditionally, educational psychologists have chosen to devote their attention to improving Caucasian boys' academic skills. The vast majority of the research in adolescent and educational psychology has been based on and designed for white males, and has been applied more to academics than to athletic goals.[1,2,3] Yet a growing body of research in educational psychology is relevant to the contemporary American female's participation in physical exercise and in organized sports. This research can help us answer several questions for physical education teachers and for individuals who are committed to the physical welfare of American girls and women. This chapter addresses several of those questions: What are some of the psychological, social, and academic benefits for girls who participate in sports or who engage in regular physical exercise? What discourages America's females from engaging in more physical exercise and organized sports? How can we encourage more girls and women to develop and to profit from their athletic potential and physical exercise?

The Benefits of Physical Exercise

Most of the publicity promoting physical exercise and sports focuses on the obvious biological payoffs for being physically fit. But most American girls are seemingly unaware of the academic benefits that often accrue as a consequence of participation in sports. In high schools and colleges, coaches often provide counseling and academic tutoring services for athletes that nonathlete students do not receive. In one survey of 270 high school male basketball players, the coach

287

was also named as the third most influential person in determining the adolescent's educational and vocational future.[4] Another coach helped to improve the reading skills of male students in his physical education classes by supplying books on sports that the students could borrow.[5] This coach worked in conjunction with the school's reading teacher and librarian so he knew which books to recommend to each boy on the basis of the student's reading deficits. There is even some evidence that participating in certain sports improves a student's mathematical skills. In her book, Overcoming Math Anxiety, Sheila Tobias states that female athletes consistently outperform nonathletic males on tests of spatial skills. These spatial skills contribute to mathematical problem solving, leading Tobias to suggest that girls' poor performance in math may be linked to their lack of athletic experience.[6] Recent data from a national longitudinal survey of black and white adolescents confirm earlier conclusions that athletic participation usually enhances academic achievement.[7]

In addition to academic benefits, girls who are athletic often gain skills that enrich their vocational and personal lives. From their study of successful business women, several researchers agree that competing in sports teaches girls the verbal and emotional assertiveness and self-confidence to survive in male-dominated professions as adults.[8,9] Hennig and Harragan concur that girls are deprived of valuable lessons that boys usually master through sports: how to accept criticism without being emotionally upset, how to achieve personal goals while still serving the group's needs, how to relate to authorities like coaches and referees, and how to sacrifice individual glory for a group's goals. The sense of mastery and competence that young girls derive from sports could also teach them to take more risks, to cooperate with other people, to compete without reservations and guilt, to test their physical and mental limits, and to develop self-discipline. Sports have the potential to teach participants independence and assertiveness that serve them well as adults in their vocations. In their book on coaching girls and women, Neal and Tutko appeal to coaches to create ambition, independence, and tough-mindedness in females.[10] These characteristics are often those necessary for financial survival in the adult world.

Some critics may contend that becoming assertive is not beneficial to girls and that this aspect of sports is detrimental to a female's development. Many adolescent and educational psychologists, however, disagree that assertiveness is an unhealthy human trait.[11-16] Schools should be places where we encourage students to express their opinions and to ask questions, especially in the presence of authorities. Yet many girls and women are too frightened or passive to assert themselves in class or in social situations. Consequently, these shy females often remain confused about academic material and remain unknown to teachers who might later have helped them with recommendations or vocational guidance. Being unassertive and inhibited also contributes to physical and psychological stress. On their "Self Expression Scale," Galassi and Galassi help people identify the specific situations in which their unassertive behavior is nonproductive or stressful.[17] Girls who do not learn to assert their opinions, state their needs, and ask questions may even become aggressive and hostile, rather than expressing themselves in a calm, rational, and assertive manner. For these reasons females who learn to assert themselves through their experiences with sports are developing a skill that can serve them well in nonathletic domains where assertion is necessary for self-preservation or psychological well-being.

There is also evidence that physical exercise can decrease a person's feelings of depression and anxiety. Girls who participate in sports generally have high self-concept scores, more feelings of well-being, and better grades than nonathletic girls.[18,19] Though we could assume that these girls were already self-confident achievers who therefore chose to participate in sports, research indicates that exercise creates optimism and self-esteem in females who are initially anxious and depressed before their exercise program begins. Kaplan reports that lethargic, depressed girls become mentally and physically more energetic and less anxious when they engage in regular physical exercise.[20] She believes this physical exertion can be more effective than chemical tranquilizers in altering depression. Other researchers report that both males and females become more optimistic and more confident as a consequence of physical exertion.[21,22] In one experiment anxious college students were subjected to various degrees of physical exercise and several traditional counseling techniques. The most successful method for reducing their anxiety was jogging.[23] In another college study students improved their self-concept scores and felt more relaxed after one semester's participation in a jogging group that included some of their professors.[24] These studies are only a few of many that testify to the potential of rigorous exercise to alleviate depression and tension. Some superb athletes even report euphoric and religious feelings in the midst of strenuous exercise.[25]

Skeptics initially scoffed at reports that exercise reduced depression and produced self-confidence, but the physiological bases for these psychological changes are being seriously researched. [26-28] Chemicals called endorphins are released in the bloodstream after vigorous exercise. These endorphins act like opiates, causing relaxation and perhaps even euphoria. Although the exact impact of endorphins on human emotions remains unknown, they may be the primary chemicals accounting for the psychological benefits of exercise. Amines are also being considered as possible causes of the antidepressant effects of exercise. But whether caused by actual chemicals or by the sense of satisfaction that accompanies physical fitness and exercise, many females do overcome their lack of self-confidence in areas other than athletics through physical exercise. For this reason some counselors advocate physical exercise as an integral part of any female's psychological counseling. [29] The proponents of physical exercise as therapy believe that a female's feelings about her body undeniably affect her mental confidence and moods. This suggestion assumes special significance when we realize that many American women and girls resort to alcohol, hallucinogens, and tranquilizers to cope with their depressions and lack of self-esteem. [30] Although physical exercise is by no means a panacea for every frustrating or depressing situation, men long ago realized the vital role that sports can play in alleviating stress and creating self-esteem.

Educational psychologists have also begun to admit that food and air have an impact on academic achievement. For example, there is evidence that stale air inside areas like schools and office buildings contains toxic pollutants and an imbalance of ions (electrically charged particles that are in the air). The chemical composition of the air can make people sleepy, lethargic, headachy, and forgetful. [31, 32] Girls who are athletic will avoid some of these debilitating effects of indoor air through their daily exercise. Because girls who are physically active are likely to eat well, get out of doors, and be attuned to their bodies' signals of stress, sports can serve as a boost to mental energy as well as to physical health. Physically fit girls and women are also likely to be receiving sound advice from coaches or health directors regarding proper diets. Correcting iron deficiencies and eliminating excessive sugar, for example, can cause many females to feel more energetic, less nervous, more mentally alert, less aggressive, and more peaceful. [33] One program even improved delinquent girls' behavior by eliminating jelly, bread, canned meats, and sugared tea from their diets.[34] Teachers and coaches are also likely to discourage athletic girls from smoking, thereby reducing nicotine in the blood. This usually results in more oxygen reaching the lungs and brain, thereby improving mental and physical energy.[35] Many nonathletic girls and women resort to sugar as a stimulant during mid-morning slumps or late afternoon drowsy spells. The result is often the "sugar blues"--an immediate surge that is soon followed by a rapid decrease in power and increase in irritability.[36] Females who exercise, however, discover that physical energy and mental concentration improve after exercising. The research on nutrition and fresh air has given educational psychologists an empirical basis from which to advocate that people care well for their physical selves in order to maintain or create intellectual acumen.

Others are gathering evidence that athletics can enhance a female's feelings of personal power and control over her life. Psychologists refer to a person's attitudes about power over life's events as "locus of control."[37] People with an external locus of control believe that both failure and success in life are primarily determined by sources beyond their own control such as luck, task difficulty, other people's actions, or God's will. Sports participants with an external locus of control would blame outcomes on factors beyond their control such as poor coaching, unfair referees, or not playing on the home court. But individuals with an internal locus of control attitude believe that outcomes depend essentially on their own actions, such as not exerting enough effort, choosing friends unwisely, not eating properly, or staying up too late before the game. Most studies show that compared to males, American females have a more external locus of control when accounting for their successes and a more internal locus of control when accounting for their failures.[38-40] Females are less likely than males to take credit for their own accomplishments and are more likely to give others credit: "My boyfriend and parents were so supportive, and that's why I won." In general, girls have less confidence in their own mental and physical abilities, lower expectations for success, and more inclination to blame failure on their own lack of abilities than boys.[41]

Female students also tend to be more sensitive than males to feedback from adults and to care more about approval from authorities than about their own accomplishments.[42] Females then tend to behave as though they are helpless and powerless--a phenomenon known as "learned helplessness."[43] One example of the difference in males' and females' locus of control attitudes is a study in which female athletes felt more ashamed of themselves than males when their team lost.[44] The males tended to feel ashamed of the whole team than personally blaming themselves. Another study showed that male basketball players were more likely than female ones to blame their losses on other players and on external factors like unfair referees.[45] This research suggests that female athletes may need special training not to blame themselves unnecessarily for outcomes which are not within their personal control.

Despite these differences in male and female athletes, athletic girls are nevertheless more likely to develop a healthy balance between external and internal locus of control attitudes than their nonathletic peers. Sports can help females feel more personally responsible and powerful in nonathletic situations.[46-48] Through physical exercise and team sports, players learn that many outcomes are controllable, but that other outcomes are unavoidable. Through physical activity girls and women can learn to distinguish between situations in which an external locus of control attitude is appropriate and those in which this attitude is absurd. Athletic confidence (internal locus of control) affects other domains of the player's life: "If I have been able to build my body in this manner, then I'll bet I can also exert control over my grades." Females who participate in physical exercise or sports have opportunities to learn that they are not powerless physically and that this sense of personal power can extend beyond playing fields and courts.

Discouraging the Physical Skills of Females

If physical exercise and organized sports have the potential to benefit participants academically, psychologically, and vocationally, then why don't more women and girls abandon their cheerleading pom-poms and don their track shoes or tennis gear? Since federal legislation now mandates that females must receive a closer to equal share of a school's money for sports, why are many American girls still physically unfit and unwilling to engage in sports?

The most apparent reasons why American girls and women are not more physically active lie behind us in the pages of history. American females are still influenced by the message repeated throughout the centuries: girls sit and watch while boys play and compete. Stephanie Twin highlights the historical background underlying contemporary attitudes toward females and physical exercise.[49] Greek women were not allowed to watch or to participate in the Olympics. But the girls of Sparta were trained in running, jumping, and javelin throwing because Spartans believed this would make women healthier breeders. Sports were a way to increase a woman's physical endurance and emotional stamina for giving birth to Sparta's future warriors and statesmen. Sparta, however, was one of the few patriarchal societies to associate childbirth with a woman's physical fitness through sports. By 1850 American girls were encouraged to conserve their energy and ward off illness by avoiding any physical exercise. In the early 1900s sports gained increasing popularity with American boys and psychologists began proclaiming the virtues of male sports: building a young man's character, diminishing crime and sexual misconduct by channeling excessive physical energy into games, and overcoming a boy's "feminine" characteristics. During this period women's sports also grew, but for different reasons. Sports were touted as leisure activities for rich women to while away their time, not as activities to build character or to develop physical fitness. The consensus was stated in 1907 by sociologist William Thomas, who asserted that although girls did need some mild physical exercise, they should not participate in any sport. Thomas went on to state, "woman resembles the child and the lower races"; she was not capable of being athletic.[50] Researchers continued adding to these myths. Many educators and psychologists joined the civic leaders who protested against the few women who participated in the 1928 Olympics. In 1939 renowned psychologist Lewis Terman concluded that athletic girls had more masculine personalities than their nonathletic peers. And in 1969 philosopher Paul Weiss voiced his opinions that women were "truncated males" who were only capable of playing "foreshortened versions" of males' sports.[51] Weiss went on to add that a girl's body "naturally matured" into a graceful and functional entity, whereas boys needed to train their bodies through sports. Weiss stated that a girl's mind would automatically function in behalf of her body's interests and that she was not subjected to body relationship tensions as a boy was.

It would be comforting to believe that statements from psychologists and researchers such as these from the "good old days" are no longer influencing Americans' attitudes about girls and their athletic skills. Unfortunately, attitudes almost

as archaic as those from the 1920s still survive. For example, in 1976 Michener wrote in Sports in America that pre-
adolescent girls and boys should not play sports together because a boy's defeat "might be interpreted as a failure of
manliness."[52] Old attitudes about sports also influence ordinary citizens. In 1975 a Little League coach who was opposed to the federal legislation on athletic equity forced the
only girl on the team to wear an athletic supporter because
the regulations called for each player to wear one.[53] The
National Collegiate Athletic Association also opposed Title IX
legislation by spending as much money lobbying against Title
IX as the Association for Intercollegiate Athletics for Women
spent on seventeen national championship tournaments for
women.[54] The fact remains that attitudes from the past
still have a grasp on our contemporary conduct towards girls
and sports. Inequities continue in athletic facilities, coaching, scholarships, housing and dining privileges, publicity,
academic tutoring, uniforms, medical services, travel ar-
rangements, and schedules.[55, 56]

Psychologists and educators have yet to correct many
girls' misperceptions about their physical abilities, which de-
ter them from being more physically active. For example,
many females believe that rigorous exercise builds large
muscles, but in reality large muscles are a consequence of
the male hormone testosterone. Likewise, the myth that
menstruation interferes with athletic excellence is contradicted
by numerous Olympic medalists and other female athletes who
know that exercise decreases menstrual distress. The physiological differences between boys and girls have been well
documented by many researchers with results that should inspire girls and women to be more athletic.[57-59] But this
research is not being disseminated to enough young women,
given the popularity of many myths about females' physical
potential.

Just as educational and social psychologists have found
that sex role stereotypes detract from females' academic and
vocational development, we have evidence that a major deter-
rent to a girl's athletic participation or physical activity is
her concept of "femininity." Women have been told throughout history that vigorous exercise, sweating, developing the
muscles of the human body, and competing seriously against
others (especially men) are "unfeminine." The emphasis has
been on a woman's physical beauty, not on her physical fitness.[60] Although young girls often enjoy their bodies' movements and exhausting exercise, this joyful activity generally

diminishes at the onset of puberty when being a "tomboy" is taboo. [61, 62] Even some female athletes try to reduce others' anxieties about their "femininity" by wearing frilly athletic uniforms and jewelry and by announcing beliefs in traditional femininity off the playing courts and fields. [63, 64] Athletic girls are still subjected to charges of lesbianism; and outstanding female athletes are still ridiculed if they behave too assertively or in an "unladylike" fashion. [65] In some surveys both males and females agree that sports like track and basketball detract from a female's "femininity," but that gymnastics and tennis are acceptable. [66] Sports that are not considered "feminine" are those that require the lifting or manipulation of heavy objects (weight lifting and discus throwing), projecting the body through space over long distances (pole vaulting), or making body contact with other players (football, basketball). Gymnastics, tennis, skating, and ballet do not violate these sex role stereotypes. In one study males and females stated that female athletes who succeeded in a "masculine" sport would be sadder, uglier, more aggressive and less popular than girls who competed in "feminine" sports. [67] Most girls are socialized to be dependent on other people rather than to act assertively or competitively. [68] Consequently they avoid most sports because the games require independence, assertion, and competition. The physical activities that require less direct assertion or competition against opponents, like golf and tennis, are the most popular with girls. [69] The traditional definitions of "femininity" still detract from many girls' commitment to and enjoyment of physical exercise or organized sports.

Psychologists have been investigating another phenomenon called the "Pygmalion Effect." The term comes from George Bernard Shaw's play Pygmalion, in which Professor Higgins transforms an uneducated flower girl into a fair lady, thereby confirming Higgins' philosophy that "the difference between a lady and a flower girl is not how she behaves but how she's treated." Since their controversial research was popularized in the 1960s, Jacobsen and Rosenthall have contended that people often create a "prophecy" for other individuals based on first impressions or incorrect data and that we respond to each other in ways that force these prophecies to come true. [70] In subsequent research, psychologists observed that acting on unconscious prophecies, we do often respond to others so that the initial expectation is fulfilled, hence the term "self-fulfilling prophecy." [71, 72] For example, the race or sex of a student conjures up a set of expectations in the teacher's mind: "This student is Mexican American, therefore, she is going to be less talented than my other students." "This player is a girl, therefore, I can't expect her to run as well as any of the boys." Although psychologists disagree on the extent to which our expectations or prophecies can alter another person's performance or personality, there is no dispute that our prophecies do influence our own conduct towards other people. As a result of our expectations, we may unintentionally overlook certain evidence about or the behavior of the person when that information contradicts our initial beliefs. For instance, if coaches expect females to perform poorly in sports, then they will treat these students as though they were weak, incompetent, uncoordinated or whatever else is in the prophecy. The girl herself will eventually pick up these verbal and nonverbal messages and will begin to believe that she is not athletic. After years of receiving covert and overt messages from coaches, parents, and friends, this girl will probably fulfill their prophecy by avoiding sports because she has no athletic self-confidence and no physical skills.

The self-fulfilling prophecy, of course, is not limited to females, nor does it always have a negative impact on the individual. For instance, coaches and parents can act in accord with a very positive expectation for a child. If Leroy's parents and coaches believe that he will become a talented gymnast, then their conduct toward and messages to Leroy will be very supportive and inspirational. Most girls, however, do not receive a positive self-fulfilling prophecy about their athletic abilities.

Encouraging Females' Athletic Activities

What then can we do to help American girls and women overcome the discouraging forces that undermine their participation in sports and their commitment to physical exercise? Probably the single most influential step is for parents and teachers to provide girls with role models of athletes and of other women who enjoy exercising their bodies. Research shows that women who enjoy physical activity were encouraged to be athletic during their childhood by their parents.[73] For adolescents the most influential people are usually friends and teachers. But as girls approach adulthood, female role models become especially important. This means that the school's curriculum, parents' comments, and teachers' advice could be inspiring more girls to enjoy themselves and reap the benefits of physical exercise and organized sports. Unfortunately, most schools, especially at the high school and college level, still place more emphasis on males' sports and physical fitness than on females'. As long as beauty contests, cheerleading try-outs, prom committees, and dates continue to be touted as the primary ways to achieve personal fulfillment and popularity, few girls will use their leisure time to develop or to enjoy their own bodies through sports and physical movement. School personnel and parents must be willing to debunk the myths about "femininity" and to popularize the benefits of exercise before more girls will feel comfortable jogging a few miles with their friends instead of practicing on the cheerleading squad in support of someone else's physical fitness.

The psychologists Patsy Neal and Thomas Tutko offer numerous ideas for coaching girls and women. [74] To insure that girls enjoy vigorous exercise, coaches must inform them about their bodies' abilities and give them appropriate training techniques. Merely applying the methods traditionally used for males to the training of physically active females is not appropriate. Males and females are physiologically different and these differences must be taken into account in preparing individuals for physical exercise. Likewise coaches and physical education teachers cannot ignore sex role stereotypes and the sexist attitudes that society has instilled in most young women about their athletic abilities. Adults must understand that society has trained girls to be less assertive, less competitive, and less physically self-confident than boys. This sex role socialization does undermine girls' participation in and enjoyment of physical activity. Coaches and teachers, therefore, need to discuss sexism and sex roles with females in an effort to help exorcise the messages about "femininity" that undermine the joy of physical activity. Tutko and Neal also advise us to be especially aware of the sex role ideas that religious girls often need to overcome in order to become athletic. Coaches and teachers may even have to intervene on a girl's behalf with her parents if they oppose her development through physical exercise. Using Neal and Tutko's book as a guideline, adults can help girls transform their passivity into the kind of assertiveness, self-confidence, and independence that is necessary for physical activity.

A school's curriculum could also motivate girls to develop their physical selves by providing accurate information about physiology and sports from elementary school through college. This means giving girls information that contradicts many of the myths about women's bodies and athletic potential.

Girls' athletic participation might also be enhanced by coeducational cheerleading squads, equal athletic facilities, equivalent attention to girls' athletics in school and community newspapers, trophy cases and awards banquets, and physical education teachers who are knowledgeable about the unique athletic needs of girls and women. School personnel and parents also need to insure that girls' first athletic experiences are joyful ones. If a girl's first contact with exercise is exclusively with a group of people whose athletic abilities far surpass her own or if others automatically assume that she has had the same previous training as boys her age, then the outcomes are more likely to be humiliation and self-blame than joy and motivation. Girls who are decked out in skimpy sandals, skirts, tight clothing or cumbersome jewelry are also more likely to discover the pains of sprained ankles and awkward movements than the exhilaration of jumping, running, and swinging without restraint. Females who are not informed about warm-up exercises, for instance, will not be inspired to return to the track for another run when their shin splints and pulled Achilles tendons ache. The kind of information that most males accumulate through informal channels like television and older boys in the neighborhood will usually have to be conveyed to girls in a more organized, pre-planned fashion by adults. Girls are less likely to pick up athletic advice than boys without the conscious efforts of adults to assist them.

Psychologists have also known for some time that segregating students into different classes on the basis of their intellectual differences is not motivating to slower students.[75] In the same way, segregating the least talented people from the more talented athletes is a poor strategy for helping those who have many new skills yet to learn. Males and females who receive their athletic training together can share their talents with one another and learn from those whose abilities surpass their own by modeling after them.

In 1975 Title IX legislation stated, "no person in the United States shall on the basis of sex, be excluded from participation in, be denied the benefits of, or be subjected to discrimination under any education program or activity receiving federal financial assistance." Yet the National Federation of State High School Associations says that girls' participation in sports declined after the passage of this federal act.[76] Only in 1981 did the federation report a 6 percent increase since 1979 in the number of female high school athletes.[77] If physical exercise and participation in organized

sports were only a matter of physical fitness, the plight of
American girls and women would be less worrisome. But
as the research demonstrates, physical exercise and sports
have psychological, academic, and vocational benefits that
nonathletic girls and women cannot enjoy. Many of us have
embraced the view that the intellect, the spirit, and the physical self are three distinct and unrelated entities. Yet there
is empirical evidence that these three dimensions are intri-
cately related in each of us. Psychologists and practitioners
are realizing that physical exercise and sports can contribute
to females' intellectual and personal well-being. Some sports
enthusiasts even contend that we are entering the most ex-
citing period in the history of athletics because we are dis-
covering the connection between the physical self and our
mental powers. By inspiring young girls and women to put
away their cheerleading pom-poms and to participate in athletic activities, we are restating the wisdom of a few faint
voices from our own past: "I earnestly wish to point out in
what true dignity and human happiness consists. I wish to
persuade women to endeavor to acquire strength, both of mind
and body" (Mary Wollstonecraft, 1792).

NOTES

1. Joseph Adelson, Handbook of Adolescent Psychology (New
   York: Wiley Interscience, 1981), preface.
2. Linda Nielsen, How to Motivate Adolescents (Englewood
   Cliffs, N.J.: Prentice-Hall, 1982), ch. 6.
3. Max Sugar, Female Adolescent Development (New York:
   Brunner Mazel, 1979), preface.
4. E. Snyder, "Athletes and Their Coaches," Sociology of
   Education, 1972, 45, 313-25.
5. E. Thomas, Improving Reading in Every Class (Boston:
   Allyn and Bacon, 1977), 403-9.
6. Sheila Tobias, Overcoming Math Anxiety (New York:
   Norton, 1978).
7. J. Braddock, "Race, Athletics and Educational Attainment," Youth and Society, March 1981, 335-50.
8. Betty Harragan, Games Mother Never Taught You (New
   York: Warner Books, 1978).
9. Margaret Hennig, The Managerial Women (New York:
   Simon and Schuster, 1977).
10. Patsy Neal and Thomas Tutko, Coaching Girls and
    Women: Psychological Perspectives (Boston: Allyn
    and Bacon, 1976).
11. R. Alberti and M. Emmons, Your Perfect Right: Guide

to Assertive Behavior (San Luis Obispo, Calif: Impact Press, 1974).

12. Lynn Bloom, The New Assertive Woman (New York: Dell, 1976).

13. L. Nielsen, "The Meek Shall Inherit Nothing, " Tennessee Education, 1977, 7, 10-22.

14. J. Galassi and M. Galassi, "The Self Expression Scale," Behavior Therapy, 1974, 5, 165-71.

15. Manvel Smith, When I Say No, I Feel Guilty (New York: Dial Press, 1975).

16. Alberti and Emmons, 1974.

17. Galassi and Galassi, 1974.

18. E. Snyder and J. Kivlin, "Women Athletes and Aspects of Psychological Well-being, " Research Quarterly AAHPER, May 1975, 191-3.

19. F. Harper, "Outcomes of Jogging: Implications for Counseling, " Personnel and Guidance Journal, October 1978, 74-78.

20. Janice Kaplan, Women and Sports (New York: Viking, 1979).

21. R. Driscoll, "Exertion Therapy, " Behavior Today, 1975, 6, 10-16.

22. Walter McQuade and Ann Aikman, Stress (New York: Dutton, 1974).

23. Driscoll, 1975.

24. Harper, 1978.

25. T. Kostrubala, The Joy of Running (Philadelphia: Lippincott, 1976).

26. W. Bortz, "The Runners High, " Runners World, April 1982, 58.

27. R. Markoff and others, "Endorphins and Mood Changes in Long Distance Runners, " Medicine and Science in Sports and Exercise, 14, 1, 1982, p. 11-15.

28. C. Ransforth, "A Role for Amines in the Antidepressant Effect of Exercise, " Medicine and Science in Sports and Exercise, 14, 1, 1982, 1-10.

29. L. Harmon, "And Soma, " in Lynn Harmon, Counseling Women (Monterey, Calif.: Brooks Cole, 1978), pp. 123-26.

30. Maggie Scarf, Depression and Women (New York: Doubleday, 1981).

31. M. Diamond, "Uppers and Downers in the Air, " Psychology Today, June 1980, 128.

32. J. Brody, "Now It's Perilous to Breathe Indoors, " Herald Tribune, February 5, 1981, p. 1.

33. Saul Miller and Joanne Miller, Food for Thought (Englewood Cliffs, N.J.: Prentice-Hall, 1979).

34. R. Williams, Nutrition Against Disease (New York: Bantam Books, 1973), p. 43.
35. Miller and Miller, 1979.
36. William Duffy, The Sugar Blues (New York: Warner Books, 1975).
37. B. Weiner, "A Theory of Motivation for Some Class-room Experiences," Journal of Educational Psychology, 71, 1979, 3-25.
38. J. Taynor and K. Deaux, "When Women Are More De-serving Than Men," Journal of Personality and Social Psychology, 1973, 28, 360-7.
39. N. Feather and J. Simon, "Reaction to Male and Fe-male Success and Failure," Journal of Personality and Social Psychology, 1975, 31, 20-31.
40. J. Nichols, "Causal Attribution and Other Achievement Related Cognitions," Journal of Personality and Social Psychology, 1975, 31, 379-89.
41. I. Frieze and others, "Attributions of the Causes of Success and Failure as Barriers to Achievement in Women," in Julia Sherman (ed.), Psychology of Women (New York: Psychological Dimensions, 1978).
42. Nielsen, 1982, ch. 6.
43. C. Dweck and others, "Sex Differences in Learned Help-lessness," Developmental Psychology, 1978, 14, 268-76.
44. A. Zander and others, "Attributed Pride or Shame in Group or Self," Journal of Personality and Social Psy-chology, 23, 1972, 346.
45. M. McHugh and others, "Beliefs About Success and Failure: Attribution and the Female Athlete," in Carole A. Oglesby (ed.), Women and Sport (Phila-delphia: Lea and Febiger, 1979), pp. 173-91.
46. E. Burke and others, "Psycho-social Parameters in Young Female Long Distance Runners," Canadian Psycho-Motor Learning and Sport Psychology Sym-posium, Quebec, 1975.
47. McHugh, 1979.
48. S. Birrell, "Achievement-Related Motives and the Woman Athlete," in Oglesby's Women and Sport, 164.
49. Stephanie Twin, Out of the Bleachers: Writings on Women and Sport (New York: McGraw-Hill, 1980).
50. William Thomas, Sex and Society (Chicago: University of Chicago Press, 1907), ch. 1.
51. Paul Weiss, Sport: A Philosophical Inquiry (Carbondale: Southern Illinois University Press, 1971, p. 215.
52. James Michener, Sports in America (New York: Ran-dom House, 1976), p. 126.

53. Twin, 1980, p. xxvii.
54. Bonnie Parkhouse and Jackie Lapin, Women Who Win: Exercising Your Rights in Sports (Englewood Cliffs, N.J.: Prentice-Hall, 1980).
55. Ibid.
56. M. Dunkle, Competitive Athletics: In Search of Equal Opportunity (Washington, D.C.: H.E.W., 1976).
57. Twin, 1980.
58. John Marshall, The Sports Doctor's Fitness Book for Women (New York: Delacorte, 1981).
59. Kaplan, 1979.
60. Neal and Tutko, 1976.
61. Oglesby, 1979.
62. Ellen Gerber and others, The American Woman in Sport (Reading, Mass.: Addison-Wesley, 1974).
63. Ibid.
64. Oglesby, 1979.
65. Kaplan, 1979.
66. J. Rohrbaugh, "Femininity on the Line," Psychology Today, August 1979, 30-42.
67. E. Methany, "The Feminine Image in Sports," in George Sage's Sport and American Society (Reading, Mass.: Addison-Wesley, 1974), 289-301.
68. Nielsen, 1982, ch. 6.
69. Birrell, 1979, p. 158.
70. Robert Rosenthal and Lenore Jacobson, Pygmalion in the Classroom (New York: Holt, Rinehart, 1968).
71. Thomas Brophy and Jere Good, Teacher Student Relationships (New York: Holt, Rinehart, 1974).
72. Pat Insel and Lenore Jacobsen, eds., What Do You Expect: An Inquiry into Self Fulfilling Prophecies (Menlo Park, Calif.: Cummings Press, 1975).
73. Susan Greendorfer, Female Sport Involvement (Atlantic City, N.J.: National Convention of Health, Physical Education and Recreation, March, 1975).
74. Neal and Tutko, 1976.
75. Nielsen, 1982.
76. Parkhouse and Lapin, 1980.
77. "Girls Boost Numbers of School Athletes," Education, December 1981, p. 4.

QUESTIONS

(1) a) List the benefits of physical activity discussed by Nielsen.

   b) For each of the benefits of physical activity discussed

by Nielsen, answer the following: Is this benefit a significant aid to the student's education? Why or why not?

(2) a) List the one or two most interesting recommendations for reforming physical education which are considered in each of the essays by Klein, Atherton, Diller and Houston, and Nicholson.

b) For each of the recommendations which you have just listed, answer the following: Does Nielsen's essay give reason to think that this recommendation would have desirable or undesirable consequences for female students? Explain.

(3) a) Of Nielsen's suggestions for encouraging females to participate in athletic activities, list the three which would be the most helpful in your opinion.

b) For each of the three suggestions which you have just listed, answer the following: Is this suggestion compatible with the ideal of modified pluralism advocated by Klein? Why or why not? Is it compatible with the assimilationist ideal advocated by Atherton? Why or why not?

(4) For each of Nielsen's suggestions which you listed for question 3(a) above, answer the following: Would Diller and Houston say that physical educators at your school had a moral responsibility to act on this suggestion? Why or why not? Do you agree with Diller and Houston about this? Why or why not?

(5) What else would you like to discuss from Nielsen's essay?

NOTES ON CONTRIBUTORS

KATHRYN PYNE ADDELSON is a member of the Philosophy Department and the Project on Women and Social Change at Smith College. She is currently writing a book on the social organization of morality, using abortion as a case study. Addelson also writes on topics in the philosophy of science and has previously published under the name Kathryn Pyne Parsons.

MARGARET ATHERTON is Assistant Professor of Philosophy at the University of Wisconsin--Milwaukee. She has previously published papers on education in Proceedings of the Philosophy of Education Society and Educational Theory. Most of Atherton's present research is in the history of philosophy, with particular attention to problems in the philosophy of mind.

RAYMOND A. BELLIOTTI has taught philosophy at Virginia Commonwealth University and is currently an attorney with Barrett, Smith, Schapiro, Simon and Armstrong in New York City. His research interests are in the fields of ethics, political philosophy, and philosophy of law.

ANN DILLER is Associate Professor of Philosophy of Education at the University of New Hampshire. Her professional articles and research interests focus on ethical issues in education. Diller's current work is on connections between the ethics of child-rearing, conceptions of parental rights and responsibilities, and related considerations for educational and social policy.

RUTH B. HEIZER is Associate Professor and Chairman of Philosophy at Georgetown College (Kentucky), where she has served as Chairman of the Faculty Athletic Committee and as Faculty Athletic Representative. Practical ethical issues are her primary research interest, as evidenced by some of her publication titles: "Is Reverse Discrimination in Hiring Ethically Defensible?"; "Hare on Theory, Intuition, and Abortion"; and "Euthanasia and the Defective Newborn." In her contribution to this volume Heizer combines this interest with her concern for athletics. Her Ph. D. is from Indiana University.

BARBARA HOUSTON is Assistant Professor in the Faculty of Education at the University of Western Ontario (Canada). She has been actively involved in the women's movement in Canada and in the development of women's studies at her university. She teaches courses on ethics, philosophical issues in feminism, and sexism in education. Houston's current research interests are feminist ethics, gender identity, and the relation of women's conceptions of self to their morality.

JOAN HUNDLEY is a former athlete and a former coach. At the present she is a doctoral student in physical education at the University of Tennessee. Her area of emphasis is philosophy of sport. Hundley's research interests are sport's influence on culture and women in sport.

DREW A. HYLAND is a Charles A. Dana Professor of Philosophy at Trinity College, Hartford, Connecticut. He is married to ceramic artist Anne Hyland. In addition to helping raise two children, he has published two books, The Origins of Philosophy and The Virtue of Philosophy: An Interpretation of Plato's Charmides. Hyland has published numerous articles on the philosophy of sport and is presently working on a book on the significance of play for human beings.

J. THEODORE KLEIN, who has a Ph. D. in Philosophy from Boston University, is presently Professor of Philosophy at Urbana College in Urbana, Ohio. He has published articles in a variety of philosophical areas, including ethics, social and political philosophy, philosophy of mind, and philosophy of education. Among the topics on which Klein is now doing research and writing are cultural pluralism, moral education, respect for persons, androgyny, and sexual equality.

RAMON M. LEMOS is Professor of Philosophy and Chairman of the department at the University of Miami. He has published over two dozen articles and three books: Experience, Mind, and Value: Philosophical Essays (1969), Rousseau's Political Philosophy: An Exposition and Interpretation (1977),

and Hobbes and Locke: Power and Consent (1978). Lemos
has recently completed work on a fourth book, on morality
and politics, and is presently working on a book on meta-
physics.

JANICE MOULTON plays soccer and does research in feminism, linguistics, and philosophical methodology. She teaches
philosophy at Smith College. She has written The Guidebook
for Publishing Philosophy and, with G. M. Robinson, The
Organization of Language. Moulton began running at 33,
learned to play softball at 35, and fell in love with soccer
at 39.

LINDA J. NICHOLSON is currently Associate Professor in
the Department of Educational and Social Thought, and Ad-
junct Associate Professor in Women's Studies at the State
University of New York at Albany. She is currently at work
on a book which explores the challenges that contemporary
feminism makes to political philosophy.

LINDA NIELSEN is co-author of Understanding Sex Roles and
Moving Beyond and author of Motivating Adolescents: Applications of Adolescent and Educational Psychology. She has
also written numerous journal articles on motivation and sexism and two handbooks for teachers of learning disabled and
suspended adolescents. She won the 1980 author's award for
women scholars from the U.S. Office of Education, and in
1981 she won a postdoctoral fellowship from the American
Association of University Women. Dr. Nielsen holds a master's degree in Counseling and a doctorate in Educational Psychology. She teaches in the Department of Education at Wake
Forest University.

BETSY POSTOW, the editor of this book, teaches philosophy
at the University of Tennessee. She has been working for
some time in several areas relevant to the concerns of this
book: ethics, philosophy of feminism, social and political
philosophy, and philosophy of sport. She has published articles in all these areas. Her next major project is an elementary textbook on the philosophical foundations of ethics.

MARY VETTERLING-BRAGGIN received her doctorate in philosophy from Boston University. She is currently General
Editor of Women's Studies Books for Littlefield, Adams and
Co. of Totowa, N.J. She coedited Feminism and Philosophy,
and edited Sexist Language as well as "Femininity," "Masculinity," and "Androgyny," all of which are available from
Littlefield, Adams.

MARY ANNE WARREN received her Ph.D. from the University of California, Berkeley, in 1975, and currently teaches philosophy at San Francisco State University. Her areas of interest include feminist philosophy, medical ethics, and other areas of applied moral philosophy. She has published articles on the moral issues of abortion, affirmative action, population policy, the moral status of nonhuman animals, and the concept of androgyny. Warren has also published an encyclopedia of feminist and antifeminist thought, The Nature of Woman (Edgepress, 1980).